Rebellious Laughter

Rebellious Laughter

PEOPLE'S HUMOR IN AMERICAN CULTURE

Joseph Boskin

SYRACUSE UNIVERSITY PRESS

First Edition 1997
97 98 99 00 01 02   6 5 4 3 2 1

The paper used in this publication meets the minimum requirements of
American National Standard for Information Sciences—Permanence of
Paper for Printed Library Materials, ANSI Z39.48-1984. ∞™

Library of Congress Cataloging-in-Publication Data
Boskin, Joseph.
   Rebellious laughter : people's humor in American culture / Joseph
Boskin.
     p.   cm.
   Includes index.
   ISBN 0-8156-2747-5 (cloth : alk. paper). — ISBN 0-8156-2748-3
(pbk. : alk. paper)
    1. Popular culture—United States—History—20th century.
2. American wit and humor—History and criticism.   3. Ethnic wit and
humor—United States—History and criticism.   4. United States—
Social conditions—1945–   I. Title.
E169.02.B64   1997
306.4'0973—DC21   97-11092

Manufactured in the United States of America

We walked briskly, reconnecting the dangling thoughts of our dinner. I told him more about the quirks I kept encountering in writing about this subject. He wryly suggested I offer the book as testament to a quirky life. Without thinking, I blurted out that some time ago I had decided on a dedication, then quickly tried to retrieve the statement. He looked at me questioningly. I hesitated—and thought, Why the hell not? "Well, it's actually dedicated to you." He was totally unprepared and went silent. Then he turned to me and exclaimed, "Hey, why aren't you home writing?"

FOR MARK

Humour is not resigned; it is rebellious. It signifies the triumph not only of the ego, but also of the pleasure principle, which is strong enough to assert itself here in the face of the adverse real circumstances.

—Sigmund Freud,
Collected Papers, V

Joseph Boskin is a professor of history and director of the Urban Studies and Public Policy Program at Boston University. He is the author of *Into Slavery: Racial Decisions in the Virginia Colony* and *Sambo: The Rise & Demise of an American Jester*. He is also editor of *Urban Racial Violence in the Twentieth Century* and co-editor of *Seasons of Rebellion: Protest and Radicalism in Recent America*.

Contents

Acknowledgments

A book may be the work of one, but many by their illuminating guidance and joyous presence have enabled the process of completion.

Special gratitude goes to those trusted friends, and outsiders, who in one way or another scrutinized the manuscript and proffered valuable and often pivotal counsel: Robert Erwin, Helen MacLam, S. M. Miller, Sam Bass Warner, Jr., William M. Tuttle, Jr., and John T. Harney.

Vigorous friends furnished primary materials: Larry Roth, Matthew Boskin, Vic Walter, David Kunzle, Trevor Kaye, and David Broome. Special colleagues scattered across the country barraged with spirited jives: Murray Levin, Sarah Blacher Cohen, Joel Tarr, Joe Nyomarkay, Herbert Hill, Lenny Quart, Harvey Mindess, Joe Dorinson, Richard Weiss, William F. Fry, Jr., and Merle Goldman.

Seminal writing on the subject, in particular Alan Dundes's voluminous oeuvre and John Lahr's commanding insight into American popular culture, always produced excitement and directed attention to significant interedisciplinary relationships.

An array of keen friendships provided solace and vital perspective at problematic moments: Ruth Chad, Michael Benari, Allen Jay Friedman, Erica Harth and David Gallant, Rita and Max Lawrence, Sheldon Benjamin, Nancy and Herb Bernhard, Damon and Marian Lawrence, Jason Finkle, Aaron M. Roth, Kathy and Sharon G. Roth, Arnold Shapiro, Mitch Geffen, Louise and Sidney Peck, Dennis Thomson and Betsy Broadman, Majorie Kunzle, Marlene Hoy Flower, and M. J. Lunine. The formative Brighton Beach years have been wonderfully sustained by the oldest of ties, Selma Fine Goldfield and Sy Ross.

The creative impulses of Erwin Palmer of SUNY, Oswego, have always moved me.

By their distinctive presence was time spent on the work immeasurably eased: Peter Mavrikis, Michael Mavrikis, Amy Collins, Richard and Dorothy Pemstein, Neal Roberts, Johanna Madden, Robert Barry, Rahla Hall, Larry Devore, Paul Witty, Roseann McGrath, and Lester Conrad.

Especially beneficial was Donald Altschiller's bibliographical expertise at Mugar Library. Administrative support came from Jim Dutton and Al Sargis in the Department of History.

Finally, family members warmly and gently nudged the project along: Julie, Gary, and Alyssa Scott; Lori and Deborah Boskin; Herbert Boskin and Carolyn Webb.

Throughout, the embrace of Dorothy Kaufmann has sustained the connection one covets yet so rarely achieves in life.

Rebellious Laughter

1

Introduction

This book is about people's humor. All too frequently this behavior is expressed as "jokes." Jokes, though, circumscribe what people do; rather, there is *joking,* omnipresent and inventive, as people in their daily routines cope with changes, grapple with issues, and endeavor to attain perspective. In contrast with the practitioners of humor, people's joking is spontaneous and anonymous.

This work is further about the interaction of time and place in people's joking. Explored is how issues and events have triggered humorous response and how the comedic responses by their very presence have defined and defused the historic situation. The time frame here is the second half of the twentieth century, selected because the tumultuous social, political, and technological episodes produced several vigorous and unusual expressions of humor in people's repertoire: the joke cycles and joke wars.

The term "people" is not meant monolithically. Humor in the United States reflects an idiosyncratic array of ethnic and gender groups, social interests, and political concerns. But at the same time there is a high degree of coherence in the comedic narrative that arises from the bottom rungs of society and eventually surfaces in the larger public arena. There are, in short, common reference points in the humor that enable people of differing stripes and classes to plug into the scene and to derive meaning from it.

Other forms of humor emanating from institutional arrangements—stand-up performers, radio and television sitcoms, cartoons and comic strips, and filmic comedy—clearly illuminate attitudes and enlarge people's repertoire. For my purposes, however, such forms are utilized minimally and brought into the larger picture only when they serve as backdrop or amplify the pattern of joking.

The folk humor offered in this work originates from a broad swath of the populace: whites, blacks, and Hispanics; university students; professionals; women; gays and lesbians; conservatives and liberals; skilled and semiskilled workers; the power brokers and the powerless. Taken together, the joking is indirect and in-your-face; vibrant and nuanced; elevating and demeaning; and devious and instructive. It offers a burnished mirror in which to view the complex processes of joking, of the different ways in which people have humorously grappled with the prosaic and profound over the past half-century.

At the same time, it should immediately be noted that the many forms and patterns explored in this work are not exclusive to this culture. Humor's texts, in at least several instances, often transcend national boundaries. Joke scripts, for example, can be found outside the United States, as can jokes involving gallows humor and ethnicity. Parallels with other societies clearly exist. Nonetheless, insofar as humor's meaning and import largely reflect an indigeneous cultural code, I have opted to limit this work to the ways people's humor functions in the United States.

Joking is a finely tuned form of people's language, honed in large part on the overall role that humor has played throughout the course of American history. I claim considerable cultural power for humor as a social fulcrum in this culture, one that acts as a divisive as well as a coalescing agent. My assertion, moreover, is not more than that which Constance Rourke offered over sixty years ago in her seminal work, *American Humor: A Study of the National Character* (1931): "Humor has been a fashioning instrument in America, cleaving its way through the national life, holding tenaciously to the spread elements of that life." Rourke contended that an unconscious objective of such humor has been the creation of "fresh bonds, a new unity, the semblance of a society and a rounded completion of an American type" where none had previously existed.[1]

Recognition of humor's magnitude, in fact, has produced a series of treatises from expected as well as unusual quarters. Ex-Marxist Max Eastman, for example, in *Enjoyment of Laughter* (1936), grandly wrote that the "comic imagination, then, or what I prefer to call poetic humor, would stand out not only at the beginning, but also close to the center of my brief history of America's imaginative culture."[2]

Indeed, the dynamics of humor's presence led essayist E. B. White to savvily pinpoint an exclusive American pitch: "Whatever else an American believes or disbelieves about himself, he is absolutely sure he has a sense of humor."[3] Anthropologist Mahadev L. Apte carried this thought further, noting humor as a dominant cultural value: "People in all walks of life are either encouraged to acquire a sense of humor or are praised for having it. . . . Societal consensus in America seems to be that a personality with a sense of humor is more sociable, easier to get along and to work with, innovative, and capable of facing adversities and overcoming them, and is therefore more desirable than one without."[4]

Not surprisingly, therefore, anxiety over humor's lapse, its suspension, or far worse, its retrogress, has been an attendant concern. Its being undermined by political repression, or exhausting itself in triviality, or being overwhelmed by cataclysmic events, or just running out of creative steam—all these have piqued trepidation. Writers, scholars, and practitioners of humor, including Walt Kelly, James Thurber, Jesse Bier, Jules Feiffer, Clifton Fadiman, even the editors of *Time*, have at one time or another questioned humor's future, both the people's and the media's. In the context of this work, at least twice within the past fifty years the bells of distress have sounded, the first time in the 1950s and 1960s. Citing the "dark" and "sick" jokes of the 1960s as a clear indication of downfall, Jesse Bier in his literary history *The Rise and Fall of American Humor* (1968) rued "the loss of the comic instinct."[5] Responding to McCarthyite repression, the Beat poet Kenneth Rexroth expounded on "The Decline of American Humor." Not long thereafter came the theater critic Robert Hatch's comment to the effect that "humor, in fact, has become a tough business."[6] And at the end of the century, critics from opposing ends of the social and political spectrum blamed "political correctness" for humor's withering constriction: "Something has happened to us, whether it's degenerative bone disease or what," lamented Henry Beard, a founding editor of the *National Lampoon* and coauthor of *The Official Politically Correct Dictionary and Handbook*. A 1990s headline in the *Boston Globe* on the controversy surrounding the politically correct issue summed it up: "Losing Our Sense of Humor Is No Laughing Matter."[7]

Yet, not only did humor survive, its scope and language actually were vastly expanded in the popular culture over the past fifty years. And its presence was ongoing in hundreds of films, innumerable sitcoms, talk shows, and television specials that offered Jewish, African-American, and women's comedy. On television alone a preponderant number of long-running revues, comedies, and sitcoms filled prime-time slots: *Your Show of Shows, I Love Lucy, You Bet Your Life!, Sanford and Son, The Jack Benny Show, The George Burns and Gracie Allen Show, Laugh-In, The Phil Silvers Show, All in the Family, The Mary Tyler Moore Show, M*A*S*H, Maude, Cheers, The Bill Cosby Show, Roseanne, Seinfeld,* and the most barbed, *Saturday Night Live.* The other motif vying and coexisting with comedic fare in the media during these same decades was violence.

The electronic scene was augmented by the rise of comedy clubs in hundreds of cities and towns from the late 1970s through the mid-1990s. More than three hundred full-time night spots in one hundred cities of thirty-four states, including eight national chains, presented the routines of a thousand to twenty-five hundred stand-up comics. Exclaimed the owner of New York's Catch a Rising Star at the height of the comedy club's popularity: "Comedy is the rock 'n' roll of the '80s."[8]

At the visible apex of comedy's place came a new type of performer, the comic shaman. Like shamans in ancient cultures, who applied forms of magic in order to divine hidden forces, heal the sick, and balm social schisms, particular comedians honed humor as a way of confronting social issues and taboos. In so doing, they broadened the social ground for shared beliefs. Mark Twain had preceded them, but it was Will Rogers as the Everyman stand-up performer who early in the twentieth century carved out the role of social and political critic.

In the period following the Second World War came Lenny Bruce, whose iconoclastic social and ethnic streetwise commentary wholly rearranged the comic boundaries of language and subject matter. Others had supporting roles—Tom Lehrer, Mort Sahl, Elaine May and Mike Nichols, Shelley Berman, Dick Gregory, and Godfrey Cambridge—but it was Bruce who dragged the various furtive stereotypes and social hypocrisies into public view.

After Bruce's unexpected death in 1966, the counterculture swiftly obliterated the remaining taboos constricting public comedy. Issues and vocabulary expanded, and the performers are now more likely to be women and minorities. Once the domain of Jewish males with a smattering of Irish and others—African-Americans played almost exclusively in segregated clubs, and women had been collectively stigmatized as not even possessing the rudiments of humor—the entertainment industry was pried open. By the 1980s matters of race, religion, and sexual behavior saturated comedy-club routines and television sitcoms.

The comedian as shaman—the major figures include Lily Tomlin, Bill Cosby, Garrison Keillor, Robin Williams, George Carlin, Richard Pryor, Whoopi Goldberg, Roseanne Barr, Eric Bogosian, Paul Rodriguez, and Woody Allen—was a phenomenon resulting from the fusion of people's humor with public comedy. In anthropologist Stephanie Koziski's view, the comedian had become a type of cultural overseer: "They pattern their comic material close to everyday reality, making obvious behavioral patterns explicit and tacit operating knowledge and other insights about American society objects of conscious reflection."[9]

Humor's aura and its import were further magnified during the decades by several presidents whose adroit use of wit, the deft joke, and the clever turn of phrase extended their popularity, and consequently their maneuverability. Even though politics has always had its joking component, public image has become political destiny with humor in a notably enlarged role. John F. Kennedy's quick wit and Ronald Reagan's time-honored jokes and stories deflected criticisms and enlarged their human image.

The increasing usage of humor went far beyond politics and entertainment. Launched by Norman Cousins's *Anatomy of an Illness* (1979), a book written by the editor of a prestigious literary journal who had apparently overcome a degenerative spinal disease by a quixotic mixture of vitamin and humor—massive doses of vitamin C, the Marx Brothers, and Allen Funt's *Candid Camera*—a movement emerged centering on the healing art of health through laughter. A multitude of workshops and organizations generated The First International Congress on Humor in Psychotherapy (Stanford University) and the *Journal of Therapeutic Humor* (New York), and it was not long before the concept filtered down. Humor as a therapeutic device for wayward traffic violators was instituted in various cities, wherein the guilty could choose among traditional remedial sessions, the AAA Comic Relief Traffic School, and the Improv Traffic School. Conferences in the religious community delved into the "interface between humor and spirituality," and an unusual perspective on cosmology appeared as science writer Chet Raymo recalled an ancient Mediterranean creation story in which God ordered the universe with a hearty laugh: "Fifteen billion years ago there was nothing. Then God laughed. Energy sprang into being from nothingness and flowed instantly into matter. . . . God's first *Hha* was no snicker, but a roaring belly-laugh."[10]

The time of this work covers the period when the nation became scripted in a rebellious humor that informed every social, racial, and political condition. A comedic surge so contoured the culture that the raucous laughter appeared to be thoroughly natural, as if it had always been so. In fervent response to disruptive social forces and political schisms—a terrifying episode of political repression; generational upheaval; ethnic, racial, and gender clashes; technological disasters; and a gnawing anxiety about socioeconomic expectations—there was invoked a comedy on a scale unequaled in American history.

Only popular music surpassed humor as a cultural force in daily life; only violence superseded as a media theme—and humor was often infused to offset its impact. Never before had there been so much creating and so many offerings of humor, involving so many differing forms. "Whether in print, the spoken word, or on-screen," wrote Tony Hendra of the *National Lampoon*, "humor of all kinds—high, low, witty or witless, satire, parody, lampoon, pastiche, slapstick, pure shtick, sitcom, ethnic, beatnik, precious or presidential—has been inflicted on the American people with a frequency unmatched in its history."[11]

Intersecting and undergirding these different levels was a complex construct of people's joking articulating the flows of societal change and conflict. From the simplest conundrum to the most intricate joke, institutional forms reflected as well as borrowed from the populace. "We must believe," maintained Maurice Charney, that "high and low comedy fertilize each other, rather than being set apart in antithetical social worlds."[12] Laughter to an astonishing degree filled people's daily lives as they literally spoke to one another via faxed jokes, on bathroom walls, on the telephone and the Internet, via automobile bumper stickers and hexagonal signs, T-shirts, office graphics, and in all their intimate habitats.

In the global village created by mass communications, moreover, a joke of one person instantly became a joke of many. Folklorist Alan Dundes observed that "those unfamiliar with modern twentieth-century folklore and its often truly remarkable speed of transmission, thanks to various innovations in communications technology, never cease to be astonished by the rapidity with which a particular joke or series of jokes spreads." What was surprising, Dundes noted, was that the subject of a joke—a major disaster, for example—may have occurred just the day before. "Oral transmission remains one of the most quick and efficient means of disseminating information."[13]

This book delves into several major patterns of people's humor in the global village, primarily the joke scripts and joke wars, with focus on the social and political. These forms not only serve as a cultural barometer of issues and changes that have confronted people, they also highlight the role of humor as resistance and reconciliation—an ameliorating factor in healing fractures in society. Constantly energizing the laughter were palpable incongruities arising from the gap between the democratic expectations and realities, an ongoing condition that has produced, in Louis D. Rubin, Jr.'s apt phrase, the "great American joke."[14]

An illuminating place to begin this journey into the connection of time, place, and humor is a public bathroom stall. The space is the men's room in the Student Union at Dartmouth College, specifically the right wall in the left stall. The time is the afternoon of May 5, 1982. Among the various scribbling on the painted wood, the majority nonsensical or sexual, was this play on the traditional romantic rhyme:

> Roses are red,
> Violets are blue,
>   I'm schizophrenic,
> And so am I![15]

It was a humorous comment—clever and complex.

How is this verse to be interpreted? Did it convey more than just a statement made by a single male about his personal life? Did it reflect an overall student mood at the college? Or could it possibly be extrapolated as reflecting the psychological confusions of the post-counterculture generation, their response to the Reagan counter-revolution?

Initially, I was buoyed by its fresh originality. Later, though, a university student reported having seen the verse in a bathroom at a Cambridge coffeehouse, and a faculty friend at a neighboring institution remembered reading it in an editor's comment in a small magazine. Was it possible that the verse appeared in many bathrooms in college communities across the country at approximately the same time? Who penned it first?

Can we ever know? The question is crucial because interpretation often depends on antecedents, as historians and folklorists know. Then there is the compounded problem of distinguishing the personal from the communal. By way of the surface it is sometimes possible to separate idiosyncratic and group. In a bathroom cubicle in the terminal for the Martha's Vineyard ferry, for example, one male shakily wrote:

> All things are relative
> All relatives are things
> My relatives took all my things.[16]

I hesitate to identify this as the exclusive retaliatory railing of one individual. Retaliatory humor has lengthy roots in this immigrant society and even today is a powerful thread woven into the fabric of ethnicity. Indeed, to be an American is often an act of retaliation itself, against a personal past or a previous culture. Regardless, relatives are often us.

The origin of such joking invokes the perennial query about the social group most responsible for its continuous flow. At one time or another different clusters have been singled out, invariably male: prisoners with nothing but time on their hands; investment brokers with little time but furious computer hands; locker room athletes; glad-handing salesmen; and bar patrons.

But the nub of the matter is that every segment contributes to the cornucopia of comedy. Humor is an integral part of the garden of human communication and springs from deep cultural roots. And from the many streams comes a communal coda. The question is not which group creates humor for the rest of society but, rather, which jokes and tales achieve social signification—which, in short, form the basis of meaning for the majority of folks.

And therein lies the problem of unraveling humor's social complexities. Paul Weiss has observed that "the historian never arrives at certainty; he rarely ends with more than a not altogether sifted totality of plausible, hypothetical guessed-at and imagined formulations of what had been." This incompleteness convinced Weiss that "history is not given but won."[17]

Clearly an element in historical interpretation demanding unraveling is the intent and content of people's laughter—the jokes, quips, sallies, tales, conundrums, anecdotes, graffiti, and tricks—as a measuring instrument of cultural change. Easily identifiable as oral and written communication anonymously conveyed, joking is more often spontaneously conceived and delivered but also borders on the perishable. Related briskly, it is almost as quickly forgotten or repressed, and frequently obliterated. Initial jokes, quips, asides, and tales are forgotten or give way to updated versions; bathroom graffiti are washed out and painted over; and the graphic flyers are discarded in wastebaskets.

As much as contemporaneous humor fades, it nonetheless reappears, in some new form or other, in response to a recurrent demanding or fresh situation. Humor's grapevine constantly bears fruit, ensuring a coded vernacular message over time. Seemingly ephemeral as people's humor is, its specifics are often recorded. Storytellers and folksingers preserve comedic tales and stories. A substantial portion appears in print—in the past, in farmer's almanacs, political pamphlets, joke books, church bulletins, and newspapers; and in the present it finds its way into office graphics, magazine digests, news magazines, commercial collections, and onto the Internet. In addition, stand-up comics, whose early routines derived from the neighborhood, rearrange and repeat them as their own, thus providing a humor that reflects community language and folkways. Last, by their painstaking tracing of specific texts, offering in effect a unique source of information, folklorists provide a base from which to delve into people's humor. I am not, moreover, unaware that virtually every text presented in this work has its own history and, in many instances, scholarship.

Over the past half-century, overlapping and intersecting joke cycles and racial, ethnic, and gender sallies have instructed the comedic zeitgeist. The joke cycles—sick or cruel, Polish, elephant, light bulb, Helen Keller, Jewish American princess, WASP, disaster, dumb blonde, and so on—were in response to powerful socioeconomic changes and technological catastrophes. Although they flowed over the years, constantly being recounted and extended, the cycles made their appearance in each of the decades from the post–World War II period to century's end. I do not argue that they fall precisely within a ten-year stricture but, rather, are defined by its orientation. The subversive humor of the 1950s grappled with the repressive tactics of the McCarthyites, followed swiftly by the guerrilla humor of the counterculture. And the interplay of oppression and resistance, backlash and retaliation, between the majority and minorities produced a major joke war.

Of these various byplays, the joke cycle is the most intriguing, without doubt the mode that contains and reveals people's feelings and attitudes about the times in which they live. Seemingly inconsequential and unrelated, joke cycles have nonetheless recurred in virtually every period—six major scripts surfacing within the past fifty years—and serve as a popular fad in joking. Many a cycle has appeared in paperbacks, has been offered up by talk show hosts, and has been rapped by schoolchildren. Although this study concentrates on the past fifty years, humor's content, style, and language have been shaped by forces operating throughout the century. The American Dream, the urban milieu, and the multicultural have influenced the entire course of people's humor. For this reason, these catalysts are analyzed prior to exploring the cycles and wars.

What end does all this joking serve? The content, thrust, and energy of such behavior more than strongly suggest that humor possesses transformative qualities. Humor is the working out of uncertainty and confusion, not only providing psychological release but also enabling perspective. Sigmund Freud emphatically noted, "Humour has in it a *liberating* element. But it has also something fine and elevating, which is lacking in the other ways of deriving pleasure from intellectual activity. It refuses to be hurt by the arrows of reality or to be compelled to suffer."[18] Joking, in short, enables people to take unto themselves aspects of shamanism.

Humor does not always, of course, provide such balming or psychological value. Derogatory joking is a seasoned American ploy. Especially in the competitive atmosphere of American culture has a considerable portion of humor been used to inflict psychological harm, to humiliate through stereotyping. Onslaughts of derisive joking have been directed toward the new immigrant, the powerless minority, the physically disadvantaged, the sexual "deviant," the economically downtrodden. At the same time, however, humor's extraordinary qualities enable acts of retaliation, leading in effect to an ongoing cultural conflict between groups. While much of humor emanates from aggressive intent, its overall thrust, as Freud noted, liberates.

It is folly to ignore the sociocultural and historical dimensions of folk or people's humor. Jokes form a unique record, one that is underutilized in historical analysis. To slight such expression limits the historical chronicle, reinforces the false notion of humor's irrelevance, and undermines a significant scholarly tool. At the very least, this work offers a social record of people's humor in operation while at the same time highlighting the extent to which humor was at the center of social change and conflict. During this period a rebellious humor reaffirmed communal identities and empowerment while enlarging personal and national perspective.

PART ONE

Twentieth-Century Accents

2

American Dream/American Laugh

From the very beginning, American humor and the American Dream have been symbiotically entwined. Optimism and despair, tolerance and abuse, refinement and tastelessness, faith and skepticism—these polarities have defined thinking and laughter.

The cumulative effect of such swings has given rise, in Louis D. Rubin, Jr.'s estimation, to the "great American joke." The great joke on and by Americans is fueled by a vast incongruity, by the discrepancy "between the cultural ideal and the everyday fact, with the ideal shown to be somewhat hollow and hypocritical, and the fact crude and disgusting."[1] Thus every aspect of the time-honored prerequisites for attaining the good life in America—progress, individualism, competition, hard work, opportunity, entrepreneurship, and family loyalty—has been subjected to ironic play. And irony, as Paul Fussell has astutely noted, is occasioned when people perceive "some great gulf, half-comic, half-tragic, between what one expects and what one finds."[2] American humor has consistently paid homage to the ideals of the Dream while slyly bad-mouthing its underside, occasionally succumbing to gallows asides.

Its most inventive form has been the good news/bad news joke that juxtaposes dreams and expectations against disasters and reality:

General George Washington at Valley Forge to his troops: "The good news is that you're going to get a change of underwear. The bad news is that you have to change it with the man next to you."

After an examination the doctor says to his patient,
    "I've got some good news and some bad news."
    "Tell me the good news first," says the patient.

15

> "The good news is that your penis is going to be two inches
> longer and an inch wider."
> "That's fantastic!" responds the patient. "What's the bad news?"
> "It's malignant," replies the doctor.[3]

A cheerily bleaker version has taken hold in recent decades:

> A doctor calls his patient to give him the results of recent tests.
> "I have some bad news and some worse news. The *bad* news is
> that you have only 24 hours to live."
> "Good God," exclaims the man, "what could be worse?"
> "I've been trying to reach you since yesterday."[4]

So, too, has it been regarding the gospel of individual striving
and success. Moses Rischin in *The American Gospel of Success* (1965)
pointed out that "the magnetism of individual success" has been
more potent than any other inspiration in America. "Indeed, perhaps
nowhere else in the world has a seemingly materialistic cult been so
uninhibitedly transformed into a transcendent idea, indeed into a veritable gospel that has been called a dream."[5] Individualist heroes
range from nineteenth-century robber baron industrialists to twentieth-century macho actors. The individualist's symbolism has been
the ballad "My Way" (1969), popularized by Frank Sinatra, deemed
by many to be America's true national anthem.

The vision of "making it" in America must be seen as constantly
being played out on a stage with success and failure linked. The
Dream's fancy of fame with fortune, critic John Lahr remarked, is
"America's Faustian bargain: a passport to the good life that belittles
endeavor while seeming to epitomize it."[6] An extreme situation, to be
sure, but excess has easily frolicked in the theater of American popular culture. Analysts have long noted the American penchant for
treating history and events in hyperbolic terms.

Although the rougher side has often been downplayed, people's
experience has led them to a clear perception of the Dream's two-
sidedness. Most know, despite their indifference to the past, that opportunity is often been thwarted by the reality of scarcity; that the
individual can be subverted by the power of the organization; and
that reliance on technological prowess has led to personal and environmental disaster. A Janus-faced myth, in other words, the Dream
holds out the expectation of the golden ring but conceals the pains.

"When we think of America, and her huge success," D. H. Lawrence observed, "we never realize how many failures have gone, and still go, to build up that success. It is not till you live in America, and go a little under the surface, that you begin to see how terrible and brutal is the mass of failure that nourishes the root of the gigantic tree of dollars."[7]

Without question, the Dream calls for attaining singularity, of making a name for oneself. To make your name—meaning, in the twentieth century, to see your name in lights—heralds the romance of individualism because "fame is democracy's vindictive triumph over equality: the name illuminated, the name rewarded, the name tyrannical," John Lahr discerningly noted.[8] For this reason, pop artist Andy Warhol's caustic observation, "everyone will be world-famous for fifteen minutes," has become a contemporary aphorism. Even prior to this pithy phrase was the popular saying, "I don't care what they say about me, just as long as they spell my name right!"

Thus, how to sustain a visible presence within the vast, technological organization—a problem analyzed in depth by *Fortune* editor William H. Whyte, Jr., in *The Organization Man* (1956) and wryly examined by Herb Gardner in his play *A Thousand Clowns* (1962)—has been a profound issue, and one that remains largely unresolved. The inherent contradiction between the values of individualist striving and the objectives of the organization is one that constantly wrenches. A collection of office graffiti, *Work Hard and You Shall Be Rewarded: Urban Folklore from the Paperwork Empire* (1975), by Alan Dundes and Carl R. Pagter, offers the rebellious response of middle-level white-collar workers to their impersonal existence within the company.[9] Anonymous flyers circulating in offices across the country portray corporate America as hypocritical: on the one hand extolling the Dream while on the other callously thwarting it. It is not individualism or hard work that is rewarded—though the latter can accrue particular advantages at times—but selfless identification with the organization itself. Nonconformist behavior invites ostracism, or worse: "No good deed goes unpunished at this university," declared historian Sam Bass Warner, Jr., describing the administration's response to actions deemed outside the traditional mode.[10]

Paeans hang like fruit from the tree of the work ethic. Poets, novelists, politicians, workers, professors, minorities all honor its profitability. Work begat acquisition, and acquisition became the cherished goal, the test of worthiness, the bellow of the powerful. Nonetheless, a sophisticated populace has long complained about the hypocrisy extant in the corporate world. Among the numerous items in the Dundes-Pagter graffiti collection is one featured on its title page but found throughout the book. It is a figure of a forlorn, middle-aged white-collar worker with a large screw twisted through his midsection, bearing the caption: "Be A Hard Worker/Be Loyal and True/Be Kind and Good Natured/You'll Always Get Your Just Reward!"[11] Frustration engendered by the organization can be seen in a graffito memorandum of biblical proportions that circulated in the 1980s:

The Twenty-Third Format

THE SYSTEM is my shepherd, i shall not err;

IT maketh me to put holes in green cards;

IT restoreth my purpose for being;

IT leadeth me through loops for its own sake.

Yea, though i tremble in the face of truth, i shall fear no evil;

For THOU art with me, Thy speed and Thy accuracy, they comfort me.

THOU cleanseth my mind of value, my tears show my gratitude.

Surely binaries and octals shall follow me all the days of my life;

And i shall dwell in the House of THE SYSTEM forever.

(Translated from the original cards found in a cave near the Dead Sea)[12]

A scene at the University of California at Berkeley in 1964, during the first major student uprising of the period, is another illustration. Repeatedly taught in school and by the popular culture that the individual is the capstone of society, university students were more than chagrined when they read Chancellor Clark Kerr's thoughts on the function of the contemporary "multiversity." Kerr advanced the proposition that the individual within the structure of higher education was subservient to the requirements of a technological society. In the first several days of the Free Speech strike, a group of students held aloft the symbol of the new organizational order, a large IBM card with dark letters printed across the bottom—DO NOT FOLD, MUTI-LATE, OR BEND—and marched through the campus folding, muti-lating, and bending IBM cards and tossing them to the ground.

Even the goal of a place in the American sun has been peppered with put-downs: "Nothing sucks like success" and "Remember, even if you win the rat race—you're still a rat." A response to failure: "If at first you don't succeed, redefine success." Few have failed to escape the economic fallout involved in the frenetic quest for success. All have the right to compete, but not all will succeed; everyone may dream, but for some it will turn out a nightmare. Pursuit of the goal has resulted in an acknowledged national pecking order, the "num-skull" jokes being its most epigrammatic consequence.

Avoidance of failure, of winding up on the lower rungs of society's ladder, comes with the acceptance of competition as the driving force in the state of nature. In the late nineteenth century, the application of Charles Darwin's evolutionary concepts to the social sphere provided the rationalization for competitive behavior, and also established the image of society as a human jungle. A 1930s joke featuring Tarzan and Jane, a couple popular in comic strips and films, made its point:

> Tarzan returns from work and demands of his dutiful companion, "Jane, me want a martini."
> Jane is startled. "A martini?"
> Tarzan raises his voice, "Jane, me want a double martini."
> Again Jane expresses surprise and asks, "Tarzan, why do you want a double martini?"
> Tarzan looks intently at her and shouts, "Jane, it's a jungle out there."[13]

Graffiti declarations, while less humorous, have proved equally instructive. Wrote one male on a bathroom stall at Logan International Airport in Boston during the Yuppie epoch:

> The world is a shit sandwich!
> The more bread you have
> The less shit you have to take![14]

Transmission of such values occurs in many ways, and in a popular 1892 ballad, "Daisy Bell," a marriage proposal by a suitor of limited means was sweetened by the allure of a tandem bicycle:

Daisy, Daisy, give me your answer true.
I'm half crazy, all for the love of you!
It won't be a stylish marriage,
I can't afford a carriage,
But you'll look sweet upon the seat
Of a bicycle built for two!

But in the early decades of the twentieth century, urban teenagers had reworked the song along "jungle" lines. Their version was an unsentimentalized poke:

Harry, Harry, here is my answer true.
I'm not crazy over the love of you!
If you can't afford a carriage,
There won't be any marriage,
'Cause I'll be damned
If I'll be crammed
On a bicycle built for two![15]

Pronouncements by political and sports figures highlighting, if not actually extolling, the "jungle" spirit have become the bumper stickers of the American mind. Even if indifferent students know nothing about history, many know of President Theodore Roosevelt's foreign policy dictum, "Speak softly and carry a big stick." Many more can identify baseball manager Leo Durocher's warning, slightly twisted from the original, of how players should comport themselves in *the* American game: "Nice guys finish last." Football coach Vince Lombardi's proclamation, "Winning isn't everything, it's the only thing"; President Jimmy Carter's "Show me a good loser and I'll show you a loser"; and pitcher Satchel Paige's whimsical caution, "Don't look back. Something may be gaining on you," are familiar references in American folklore. "Losing is like dying" and "When the going gets tough, the tough get going" are contemporary epigrams. These and other goads are meant to provide direction for surviving in society's jungle.

Acceptance of the jungle motif, moreover, has legitimized aggression and belligerence in behavior. Not that this was difficult to do in a country formed by the converging experiences of a frontier, a militant foreign policy, and a Calvinist point of view. Shaped by these elements, American humor largely corroborates Freud's interpretation of the relation between wit and aggression. Freud and others, including ethologist Konrad Lorenz, have expounded on the aggressive ends that humor serves. Hostility, Freud stated, takes the form of "tendentious humor," a veiled attack satisfying an aggressive motive, and in certain instances, "the triumph of narcissism, the ego's victorious assertion of its own invulnerability."[16]

Making it in the society's jungle requires acquiring one's own territory. Recognition of property's value was commented on by outsiders early on. In *Democracy in America* (1830s), Alexis de Tocqueville emphasized that "In no country in the world is the love of property more active and more anxious than in the United States; nowhere does the majority display less inclination for those principles which threaten to alter, in whatever manner, the laws of property."[17] Proverbs warn of financial pitfalls: "A fool and his money are soon parted" and "Money doesn't grow on trees."[18] Even the literary folk have delivered guidance on money's place. On his ninetieth birthday, when asked to give advice to young writers and poets, the prolific anthologist Louis Untermeyer wryly responded, "Write out of love, write out of instinct, write out of reason. But always for money."[19]

Joking about money has been one way the culture has grappled with its greedy tendencies. "At our worst," the critic Louis Kronenberger expounded, "we have made our humor the handle of our acquisitiveness, a trick way of getting our foot in the door."[20] And in keeping it there. For this reason, Jack Benny's heralded extended pause and exasperated answer on his radio show in 1938 is one of the culture's classic rejoinders. To the thief who posed the gallows choice "Your money or your life!" Benny remained silent, then, "I'm thinking! I'm thinking!"

The fear of being stigmatized a loser in the competitive struggle—in effect *named* a bum, tramp, shirker, or welfare chiseler—has worked as a vital prod to the Dream. A broadside from the post-Eisenhower years flayed shirker and government alike for sapping the moral fiber of the nation—a major theme on the conservative agenda that formed the rhetoric of President Ronald Reagan's policy of "getting the government off our backs" and his tales of "welfare queens."

Washington: The 1960 census states that the population of the United States is 160 million. 62 million are over 60 years of age.

This leaves 98 million to do the work.
54 million are under 21.
This leaves 44 million to do the work.
21 million are government employees.
This leaves 23 million to do the work.
6 million are in the armed forces.
This leaves 17 million to do the work.
14 million are in state, county and city offices.
This leaves 3 million to do the work.
2,500,000 are in hospitals, asylums, etc.
This leaves 500,000 workers.
450,000 are bums or others who will not work.
This leaves 50,000 to do the work.

It may interest you to know that there are 49,998 people in jails and prisons. That leaves just two people to do all the work, brother— that's *you* and *me* and *I'm* getting sick and tired of doing all the work by myself, so let's get with it.[21]

But initiative, hard work, and pluck have their limits and they account for just so much. An unstated yet clearly understood part of the Dream's manifesto is shrewdness or, as relayed to Charles Dickens countless times in his travels throughout the country, "smart dealing." In *American Notes* (1843), Dickens observed that wily action "gilds over many a swindle and gross breach of trust; many a defalcation, public and private; and enables many a knave to hold his head up with the best, who well deserves a halter." He recounted a typical dialogue with a townsman that focused on the character of the area's wealthiest individual:

"Is it not a very disgraceful circumstance that such man as So-and-So should be acquiring a large property by the most infamous and odious means, and notwithstanding all the crimes of which he has been guilty, should be tolerated and abetted by your Citizens? He is a public nuisance, is he not?"
    "Yes, Sir."
    "A convicted liar?"
    "Yes, Sir."
    "He has been kicked, and cuffed, and caned?"
    "Yes, Sir."
    "And he is utterly dishonourable, debased, and profligate?"

"Yes, Sir."
"In the name of wonder, then, what is his merit?"
"Well, Sir, he is a smart man."[22]

A half-century later a New York Tammany Hall district captain, George Washington Plunkett, added his street experience to the folklore of "smart dealing." Plunkett hinted at how an ordinary man in a middling position could achieve millionaire status. With tongue in cheek as he distinguished honest from dishonest graft, Plunkett unabashedly declared: "If my worst enemy was given the job of writing my epitaph when I'm gone, he couldn't do more than write: 'George Washington Plunkett. He seen his opportunities and he took 'em.'"

Opportunity, in business as well as in politics—the twin pathways to wealth and power—has produced its share of mocking jokes. A story of the early 1960s involved three of the nation's very powerful politicians: President John Kennedy, Attorney General Robert Kennedy, and Chicago's Mayor Richard Daley were in a rowboat that suddenly sprang a leak. One person would survive, but only if the other two occupants jumped overboard.

> The President stood up and said, "I'm the leader of the Free World. If I go under, the Free World is imperiled."
> The Attorney General stood up and said, "As Attorney General, I represent law and order. If I go under, law and order are imperiled."
> The Mayor stood up and said, "As Mayor, I represent the diversity of people. If I go under, diversity is imperiled."
> They decided to put the matter to vote. Mayor Daley won, 5–2.[23]

What is it, then, that has kept the American Dream so alluring and compelling? Until the closing decade of the nineteenth century, as Robert L. Heilbroner noted in *The Future as History* (1959), Americans tended "to conceive our traditional optimism as a *personal* philosophy" that rests on "a judgment about our historical capacities."[24] Historical capacities have been tested many times: by economic depressions, turbulent social change, organizational demands, technological disasters, among other changes that undermine allegiance to the creed. And in each instance an incongruous humor informs the circumstance and reaffirms the Dream's magic. A national comic vigil has constantly highlighted the optimistic.

Reflecting the future unbounded was a story that Ronald Reagan as president—a foremost keeper of the faith—retold many times while in office:

> A couple went to a psychiatrist about their twins. "What seems to the problem?" he asked.
>
> The parents explained that their two children were identical physically but opposites psychologically. "One is a pessimist, the other an optimist. We don't know what to do about it."
>
> The psychiatrist said that before he could properly diagnose the problem, he would have to see how it manifested itself. He separated the twins and placed them in different rooms. The pessimist was put into a room well lit, cheerful, and filled to the brim with toys and games. The optimist went into a room that was dark, dank, and filled with manure. The psychiatrist closed the doors and returned after fifteen minutes.
>
> The pessimist was full of complaints. "Oh, you closed the door and left me alone. The head of one of the toys came off. The clouds came and shut out the sun. I couldn't understand the directions of some of the games." The psychiatrist left and went to the optimist's room.
>
> He opened the door and saw the child furiously shoveling manure from one pile to another. "What are you doing?" the psychiatrist inquired after a few minutes. "With all this manure," the boy exclaimed, still shoveling, "there's got to be a pony somewhere underneath here."[25]

Thus has humor served as a custodian and faciliator of the American Dream. By challenging its basic tenets and lampooning its effects, a tone of ironic razzing persists. In this way, comic castigations balance the Dream's vulnerabilities.

Nonetheless, at century's close, as this history demonstrates, people's laughter turned exceedingly sour with the erosion of national consensus, exacerbated by major socioeconomic problems and technological disasters. This was not the first time in the century that people's humor was so rancorous, taunting, and acidic, but its profundity signified deep-rooted national anxieties. The American Dream was being tested again, and in ways that were unusually problematic.

3

The Urban Fulcrum

To paraphrase a memorable observation by the historian Richard Hofstadter, American humor was born in the country and moved to the city in the twentieth century.[1] The sounds of national laughter that once reverberated throughout the rural landscape, though not quite silent, are certainly muted. Particular elements of its original focus and style remain, scattered regionally, but mainstream humor expresses little of its initial form or flavor. When the humor of preindustrial America is evoked, it is frequently nostalgic or derisive.

It is the urban milieu that refracts people's laughter, reflecting and adapting its style and structure, scope and language, and embracing its diversity and friction. The city has supplied more than enough raw material for a vibrant people's comedy. The "urban frontier," Samuel Lubell's noted phrase in *The Future of American Politics* (1952), with its distinctive mixture of first-generation ethnics and farm migrants, dramatically reshaped the caliber and clamor of humor that once echoed the style and rhythm of preindustrial rural and small-town life.

Yet there appears, on occasion, a reminder of the type of humor that earlier generated native laughter. Garrison Keillor's *A Prairie Home Companion*, on National Public Radio and in print from the mid-1970s to the 1990s, rekindled the comedic embers of rural life. One scholar has argued that Keillor's format was an "urban parody of a rural form, a post-modern setup of the surface appearance of rural humor"[2]—but to regard it as parody seriously undercuts its homage to the past.

Here was a fictional umbilical connection to small-town life that presented insight into a tightly knit kinship system, a preindustrial sense of time, a play of double-entendre language, and was immersed in story line. Initially broadcast from St. Paul, Minnesota, for over a decade the program provided an ongoing relationship with the past that was much more than a nostalgic nod to a bygone time.

Keillor's Lake Wobegon—"that time forgot, that the decades cannot improve, where all the women are strong, all the men are good-looking and all the children are above average"—was mystically rooted in a universe possessing different rules of engagement. The show's small town and rural forebears were the twentieth-century works of Sinclair Lewis, Edgar Lee Masters, Sherwood Anderson, and Thornton Wilder's classic drama *Our Town*. Lake Wobegon was not without its conflicts centering on religious disputes, family bickering, generational distance, inadvertent misunderstandings, the lack of privacy, and other squabbles. It was, however, a place secure in its own sense of community and time frame.

Keillor's identity lies with storytelling. In preindustrial society it was the tale that mattered in creating a format for laughter. Joke was subtly entwined in plot, leaving to the listener the task of uncovering the narrator's intent. Mark Twain once instructed that "the humorous story is told gravely; the teller does his best to conceal the fact that he even dimly suspects that there is anything funny about it."[3] His own response to the news report of his demise remains a classic illustration of this feint:

> This reminds me—nine years ago when we were living in Tedworth Square, London, a report was cabled to the American journals that I was dying. I was not the one. It was another Clemens, a cousin of mine, who was due to die but presently escaped by some chicanery or other characteristic of the tribe of Clemenses. The London representatives of the American papers began to flock in with American Cables in their hands, to inquire into my condition. There was nothing the matter with me and each in his turn was astonished, and not gratified, to find me reading and smoking in my study and worth next to nothing as a text for transatlantic news. One of these men was a gentle and kindly and grave and sympathetic Irishman, who hid his disappointment the best he could and tried to look glad and told me that his paper, the *Evening Sun*, had cabled him that it was reported in New York that I was dead. What should he cable in reply? I said, "Say the report is exaggerated."
>
> He never smiled, but went solemnly away and sent the cable in

those exact words. The remark hit the world pleasantly and to this day it keeps turning up, now and then, in the newspapers when people have occasion to discount exaggeration.

The next man was also an Irishman. He had his New York cablegram in his hand—from the New York *World*—and he was so evidently trying to get around that cable with invented softness and palliations that my curiosity was aroused and I wanted to see what the cable really did say. So when occasion offered I slipped it out of his hand. It said "If Mark Twain dying send five hundred words. If dead send a thousand!"[4]

The full-length story was not the only comic mode in preindustrial society. Sketches, playlets, monologues, lectures, the "pitch," and other variations were stock theatrical forms offering humorous scenarios. A considerable amount of narrative humor appeared in poems, epigrams, and epitaphs. Comedy, not quite as oblique as Mark Twain would have us believe, generally strove to provide a wider context. A late-eighteenth-century story:

A blind man having contracted a violent passion for a certain female married her contrary to the advice of all his friends, who told him that she was exceedingly ugly. A celebrated Physician, at length, undertook to restore him to sight. The Blind Man, however, despised his assistance. "I should be deprived of the love I bear my wife; a love which renders me happy."

"Man of God!" replied the Physician, "tell me which is of most consequence to a Rational Being, the attainment of *Happiness,* or the attainment of *Truth?*"[5]

From the same period, a spoof directed at lawyers, perhaps the professional group most ridiculed down through the centuries:

A counsel, not long since, in cross-examining a witness, asked him, among other questions—Where he was on a particular day:—to which he replied, he was in company with two friends—"Friends!" exclaimed the counsel, "two thieves I suppose you mean."—"They may be so," replied the witness, "for they are both lawyers."[6]

Poetry in particular was a popular staple of rural humor. Newspapers, journals, almanacs, and broadsides regularly offered a large number of items covering a multitude of subjects. At the turn of the century, a feminist twist:

He and She

When I am dead you'll find it hard,
    Said he,
To ever find another man
    Like me.

What makes you think, as I suppose
    You do,
I'd ever want another man
    Like you?

                    Ironquill

And a rejoinder to the Calvinist work ethic:

Nothin' Done

Winter is too cold fer work;
Freezin' weather make me shirk.

Spring comes on an' finds me wishin'
I could end my days a-fishin'.

Then in summer, when it's hot,
I say work kin go to pot.

Autumn days, so calm an' hazy,
Sorter make me kinder lazy.

That's the way the seasons run.
Seems I can't git nothin' done.[7]

                  Sam S. Stinson

However, somewhere between the opening of the first textile mill in Massachusetts in the 1830s and Henry Ford's automobile assembly line in Michigan in the 1910s, storytelling gradually faded from the national scene. So much so that an attempt to reenergize its form in the later decades of the twentieth century—storytelling societies and festivals dotted the countryside along with 150 children's programs on radio and local television—went largely unnoticed. The public's lack of response to the preindustrial format was painful to the performers. "Storyteller is a funny word in our culture," rued Jay O'Callahan, a widely known dramatic teller. "People don't know what it means. The very word suggests a kids' show. One guy running a theater I was doing a production for called it a cursed word."[8]

Nonetheless, it cannot be said that contemporary urban comedy is totally devoid of narrative. Robust elements of storytelling persist. Fusion humorists blend narrative and the one-line joke into social and gender commentaries: Bill Cosby extrapolating his personal experiences in coping with a strong father, moaning in the dentist's chair, accusing adults of wanting to kill children with the modern playground; Woody Allen, the vulnerable, neurotic male, constantly beset by emotional relationships, posing cosmic questions of life and death; Richard Pryor, mired in highly personal terrain conversing with his heart attack, cocaine inflammation, a growling German shepherd, his sex organs; Lily Tomlin, pouring herself into the experiences of diverse characters and situations—a bag lady, middle-class aerobics, singles—all of whom interconnect; Eric Bogosian, corrosively character-sketching sex and rock culture; Spalding Gray, deftly peering into life's travails; and Robin Williams, the ultimate comic bopster, rapping maniacally about every subject in his and everyone else's head.

These are the latter-day storytellers who instruct in the ongoing relationship with narrative. And they are fueled by street storytelling. As folklorists Gary Alan Fine, Sanford Pinsker, and Jan Harold Brunvand have convincingly demonstrated in the city-as-folklore studies, city streets abound in people's anecdotes, stories, and legends, the stuff of narrative.

Nonetheless, Keillor and the performers are the exceptions rather than the rule of stand-up comedy, and people's humor is more often than not laconic. What for centuries in American culture the small-town and pastoral ways of life were to humor, the massive metropolis has been in the twentieth century. In place of the storyteller is the stand-up, and in place of the story is the one-line joke. Rural stories presented an organic relationship to an environment that evolved slowly, in recognizable ways, and to groups within a traditional community, reflecting the pace of seasonal change. Urban jokes present the ongoing struggle within a fragmented world, constantly in flux, its pace hip-hopping to a city bounce. The figurative milieu, then, is the city's ceaseless surprises, raucous environment, and brisk movements.

Symbolic figures in the terrain of American joking pinpoint the distance people's humor has traveled from its rural origins to its urban place. Throughout the late eighteenth and the nineteenth centuries the city slicker, always befuddled, invariably lost, and hungering for the farmer's innocent, nubile daughter, was a staple of comedy among farmers and small-town folk. When the city assumed preeminence, the tables were turned and the joke focused on the innocent farm boy seduced by the woman of the streets, or the hayseed sold the Brooklyn Bridge. Sensing this change, Will Rogers, the lariat-twirling, Oklahoma-drawling storyteller of the 1920s *Ziegfeld Follies*, whose routines combined frontier dialect with city phrasing, retaliated: "I would rather be the man who bought the Brooklyn Bridge than the man who sold it."[9]

Small-town America was a put-down routine of Lenny Bruce. A hip, New York boy whose enfant terrible scenarios of the 1950s and 1960s transformed the content and language of comedy, Bruce was, figuratively, lost in America's hinterlands. In one particular routine he sardonically described his ordeal at being sent by his agency to a foreign country west of the Hudson River, to "a nice place called Lima, Ohio."

> When you travel in these towns, there's nothing to do during the day. They're very boring. All right, the first day you go through the five-and-ten. That's one day shot. Right?! The next day you go see the cannon, and that's it. Forget it. Then the lending library and the drugstore. There's two Fanny Hurst novels. And a Pearl Buck. Yeah, it doesn't make it.
>
> Just completely depressing. At night, a city like this, I can go to hear a jazz group, the Jazz Workshop, but in these towns you step out of the club and you don't see anything but stars. Stars. Beautiful stars, and a Socony station, you know. And these guys that work at night just don't swing. "OK, Fred, let me see the rack again!" And they always give you matches.[10]

The city wrought a humor embodying itself: expansive, eruptive, hard-driving, and bursting with dialects. Even the urban tall tale reverberated to "the faster, hipper rhythms of city life," as Sanford Pinsker aptly noted.[11] Common in the city were the snappy quip, the rapid-fire joke, the sarcastic rejoinder, the bopping sally. The laconic works best in an urban environment. "Its essence lies in its brevity," observed critic Stephen Leacock in 1936, "it must be as short as possible and then a little shorter still."[12] Its fractured style makes it easy to tell on the run, and its pace adjusts to the sudden turns of city existence. Surprises in daily life are met with comic immediacy. The city as event becomes, in effect, the joke as event.[13]

Seen from the bottom up, the shift away from narrative was striking. Even Mark Twain was cognizant of this transformation when he critically differentiated between "story" and "comic" telling: "The teller of the comic story tells you beforehand that it is one of the funniest things he has ever heard, then tells it with eager delight, and is the first person to laugh when he gets through. And sometimes, if he has good success, he is so glad and happy that he will repeat the 'nub' of it and glance around from face to face, collecting applause, and then repeat it again. It is a pathetic thing to see."[14]

Although separated by light-years, the disparate Mark Twain and Henny Youngman are emblematic of the change in humor. Twain, who lectured around the turn of the century, is the epitome of the storytelling humorist; Youngman, whose appearance in show business dates from the 1930s, is the master of the one-liner. Twain's plots revolved around social relationships, satirical and ironic; Youngman's nonplot routines refract the city lifestyle, its human relationships disconnected, besieged, and bewildering. Youngman's nonstop monologues represent what Pinsker described as "power, pure and simple—the power of language, of words heaped and piled and sprawling one atop the other."[15] When in the mid-1960s the New York Telephone Company added Dial-A-Joke to its series of one-minute recordings, whose topics included prayer and poetry, Youngman was chosen as its leadoff comic. Intriguingly, at exactly the same time New Yorkers were dialing Youngman for a sixty-second lift, a two-hour production of Mark Twain's writing and performances starring Hal Holbrook was touring the country to capacity audiences.

Youngman's approach, like the acts of the majority of stand-up comics, was in stark contrast to the motif and pace of preindustrial humorists. Comedians over the last half-century have striven to deliver as many jokes as possible within a prescribed time frame. Subjects tumble forth without regard to plot, routines bop to a frenetic beat, and the tempo of one-liners creates a *Bolero* flourish. Holding a violin as an inanimate sidekick, Youngman would rattle off dozens of quick bits:

> Fellow walked up to me and said: "You see a cop around here?"
>   I said, "No."
>   He said, "Stick 'em up!"

> Drunk puts a dime in a parking meter. The arrow goes to 60. Drunk says: "Gee, I lost a hundred pounds!"

> I said to my mother-in-law, "My house is your house." Last week she sold it!

> Doctor, examining patient, says: "You will live to be seventy."
>   Patient says: "I am seventy."
>   Doc: "What did I tell you?"

And his most oft-quoted line, first delivered in the 1930s: "Take my wife—please."[16]

In the era of jokester comedy, stand-up acts and talk-show hosts— jumping from one subject to another in staccato fashion—mirror the swift and agitated movements of city existence. Steven Wright's dead- pan absurdist view of contemporary existence was the apotheosis of the urban one-liner approach:

> I have a microwave fireplace. I lay down in front of the fire for the evening in eight minutes.

> I had trouble going home from there 'cause I had parked my car in a tow-away zone and when I got back, the entire area was gone.

> I used to work for the factory that made hydrants, but you couldn't park anywhere near them.

> Well, you can't have everything. Where would you put it?[17]

Time and form interact in humor, and city life has altered time as well as form. In an agrarian culture, time was bound up in seasonal rhythms. With no preconceived timetable, storytelling was a form without an end except insofar as the teller wished to limit it. "Our grandfathers," wrote Stephen Leacock, "loved prolixity. They wanted a thing told at full length, like a ghost story told around the fire-place of an inn. They didn't want the sudden electrocution of a good thing by ending it up with a short snappy point."[18]

Time in industrial societies is inextricably bound to the clock. As Lewis Mumford has instructed, the clock is "the key-machine of the modern industrial age. For every phase of its development the clock is both the outstanding fact and the typical symbol of the machine: even today no other machine is so ubiquitous."[19] When Frederick Winslow Taylor applied the stopwatch to the factory system and business organizations at the turn of the century, the intrusion of time on all levels of work was virtually ensured. Taylor loftily termed his system Scientific Management—his followers grandly labeled it the American Plan—but regardless of terminology, it signaled the triumph of production over workmanship.

In his trenchant analysis of work and society in industrializing America, Herbert G. Gutman cited a garment worker's harsh poem to the clock's insistent demands:

> The Clock in the workshop,—it rests not a moment;
> It points on, and ticks on: eternity—time;
> Once someone told me the clock had a meaning,—
> In pointing and ticking had reason and rhyme. . . .
> At times, when I listen, I hear the clock plainly;—
> The reason of old—the old meaning—is gone!
> The maddening pendulum urges me forward
> To labor and still labor on.[20]

The clock informs work *and* play in contemporary culture—and humor is bonded to both. As efficiency became the byword in the production of goods at the turn of the century, so, too, in the production of humor. Early-twentieth-century theater, burlesque, and vaudeville, and the comedy of the silent films as well, adhered to the new order. Motion-picture images speeded up the comedic actions of Charlie Chaplin, Harold Lloyd, and Buster Keaton, who inventively speeded up the pace. Slapstick comedy, the mainstay of the silents, mirrored the harsh strictures of the factory system and the demands of daily urban existence.

Virtually all popular entertainment has been controlled by time in the twentieth century. Humor came under the domination of the stopwatch: its pacing more precise, its play more formulaic. In this setting the complex narrative gave way to the succinct: the photographic print, quick joke, sharp repartee, canned laughter track.

Early in the century, pulp joke and jest books were a feature of public humor, one of the most widespread being *Joe Miller's Joke Book*. Originating in England in 1739 as the "jest" book, the cheap, small, easy-to-read-and-repeat format sold millions of copies in the United States, disseminating witticisms, puns, and ripostes and providing a recognizable form of the modern joke. The American edition, first published in 1865, in time came to include more than 1,200 items.

Advances in electronic communication have added immeasurably to this folklore. Joke repetition has been ensured by the Internet, E-mail, and a system of fax machines, all of which instantaneously transmit jokes from any person plugged into the network. An underground fed by hundreds, if not thousands, of anonymous operators pours jokes and quips into the system, reviving old cycles, such as the 1970s light bulb jokes, and constantly adding new material to existing cycles, such as the dumb blonde script of the early 1990s.

Posed as a riddle, the cycle joke conforms to the structure of the one-liner. The crux here is a dramatic shift—an issue or event—that makes a sudden, disturbing, and incongruous appearance. All are phenomena of an urban landscape, a vast response to happenings small and large.

The development of burlesque in the second half of the nineteenth century and the rise of its upscale cousin, vaudeville, at the turn of the century further reveal the changes from a rural to urban venue. In his analysis of the emergence of modern city culture, Gunther Barth in *City People* (1980) noted that "the precision of acts, the split-second timing essential to the success of the routines, and the air of punctuality at curtain time impressed the spectators strongly."[21] Like the factory system and urban sports, working-class theater played within the strictures of the clock.

As with all commercial ventures, working- and middle-class theater responded to a constantly shifting, heterogeneous population, the stage routines reflecting the kaleidoscopic energies of city life. With diverse ethnic and racial groups swelling the population at an astonishing rate, burlesque and vaudeville reworked the comic language of the past. In the preindustrial period the woven story laced together strengths and foibles, engendering an ambience of communalism. Urban comedy, by enumerating a variety of experiences, made capital of dissimilarities. Barth observed that "the frequently brutal humor of vaudeville departed from the traditional American approach of language *with* people."[22] Urban comedy became one that more frequently than not laughed *at* others.

At the same time, burlesque and vaudeville also introduced strangers to one another. Popular theater offered not a melting pot but a salad bowl, and more often than not its comedy was routinized portraiture. Each ethnic group had "its stock prototype on the stage, usually portrayed at the level of the lowest common dominator":[23] the drunken Irishman, greedy Jewish merchant, chicken-stealing black farmer, numskull Slav, greasy Italian, rural rube. Yet these portrayals— "whether in song, comedy or sketches—could be mined for more complex and humane meanings than appeared on the surface. And representations of ethnics were bound to be problematic at a time when the stresses of immigration and acculturation left many in a state of upheaval."[24] Consequently, in a curious, almost contradictory way, such humor tended "to dispel animosity by bringing cultures together, using shared human failings as a common denominator."[25]

For the tens of millions of European immigrants and American agrarian workers—whites and blacks driven by massive depressions and the industrialization of farm life—burlesque and vaudeville provided both an escape from and a confrontation with circumstances. Urban dwellers grappled with an expanding machine culture from packed trolleys and subway trains to assembly lines, all movements organized around a clock that dictated schedules and production. Everyday existence was compounded by a density of bodies crammed into small apartments and spilling out onto crowded streets. Inevitably, the modern city exacted a grievous toll in twisted and abusive family relationships.

The brand of comedy offered by burlesque and vaudeville illuminated the timbre and character of the physical setting. Is it any wonder that the routines, many of which became features in silent films, were physically rattling, verbally vituperative, particularly slapstick? Vaudeville expressed "the terror and the magnificence, the pity and the cruelty" of the city's newest residents. The result was a humor of extreme distortion. "Mad comedy, noisy satire, and the physical ordeal of the fall guy slapped across the stage by the elegantly dressed brute reduced to a zany act the story of the underprivileged that most spectators knew by heart."[26]

Hence many of the acts in burlesque included the pie in the face, the female chase, problems of money, gold-digging wives and harping mothers-in-law, the salacious/unobtainable woman, and the defiance of authority. Within immigrant culture there existed all kinds of suspicion, especially a residual carryover from the old country regarding politicians and government. One locale of burlesque comedy was the august courtroom, but with prisoners and lawyers squirting water at each other from seltzer bottles, the judge wielding a wooden potato masher and demanding order in the court.

Replaced were the traditional figures of the frontier and agrarian past, the larger-than-life swaggering, confident John Henrys and Mike Finks. The twentieth-century metaphorical figures have been the comedic representatives of the underdog: Charlie Chaplin's Tramp, Robert Benchley's Little Man, James Thurber's Walter Mitty, Lily Tomlin's Trudy, Woody Allen's Neurotic Everyman, who have struggled against enormous social forces and survived—hardly the overpowering figures of the world's most powerful nation.

Theater and silent film comedies refracted the urban setting. A sense of victimization most certainly permeated the comedic scene, yet the performers *and* viewers still managed to wrest a degree of control; as Larry Mintz noted, they were "vulnerable fools," but they achieved "ironic victories and expressed many of the social proclivities of their audiences, as well as a more realistic if not more admirable view of their worlds."[27] By way of the small elements of dominion in this comedic environment, the theater provided one of the few places where a smidgen of mastery over one's own circumstances could be imagined.

The complex processes of assimilation, and the particular function of humor in social dynamics, played out throughout the century. "The history of assimilation of immigrant groups into the American mainstream can be seen to a certain extent in joke patterns: closely following the waves of immigrants came waves of immigrant jokes; in part, these jokes functioned as a socializing mechanism, pointing out what one could and could not do, what the immigrant did, and how the American would react."[28] As a consequence, humor served a doubly useful social function. Because "jokes can be shaped and reshaped to fit any potentially dangerous intergroup situation," laughter mediated conflicts between groups and dispelled animosity "by bringing cultures together, using shared human feelings as a common denominator."[29] In constantly seeking the most efficacious and dignified pathways to mainstream society, minorities eventually redefined the social landscape—but always against a backdrop of defying society's comedic strictures.

Twentieth-century humor, then, mirrored and echoed urban existence, a mixture of ethnic and racial groups who responded to their circumstances by speeding up humor's pace and expanding its repertoire and language. Informed and transformed by the city, what started as outsider humor eventually became mainstream.

4

Outsiders/Insiders

Humor's peculiarity lies in its elastic polarity: it can operate for or against, deny or affirm, oppress or liberate. On the one hand, it reinforces pejorative images; on the other, it facilitates the inversion of such stereotypes. Just as it has been utilized as a weapon of insult and persecution, so, too, has humor been implemented as a device of subversion and protest. In the absence of cosmological affirmation, humor fills a void. "When no other strategy is to be found to avoid the pitfalls of life," wrote Daniel Royot, "humor is the ultimate substitute for faith."[1] Yet it cannot be a faith in itself.

Nowhere in American humor has this duality, this refractory set of opposites, been more sharply delineated than in the experience of minority groups. America's outsiders—Jews, African-Americans, women, Hispanics, gays and lesbians—represent this paradigm. Their marginal presence, highlighted against the backdrop of the American Dream, has, as much as any factor, reshaped the configurations of American humor.

"The comic spirit," wrote critic Eric Bentley in *The Life of the Drama*, "tries to cope with the daily, hourly, inescapable difficulty of being. For if everyday life has an undercurrent or cross-current of the tragic, the main current is material for comedy."[2] Struggling on the knife edge of urban environments, their jokes and routines offering an ongoing summons, minorities have recast the language, character, and tempo of national humor. Nineteenth-century Irish immigrants, later joined by incoming Jews, migrant African-Americans, and women and other groups after the 1950s, forged a style and practice of comedy that was subversively wicked and sly, prodding and absurdist, indirect and undercutting. A mélange of masks—the trickster, the con man, the affable rogue, the role-reversing jokester—emerged as minorities coped with discriminatory practices and stereotypes, turning negative features into virtues.[3]

Protest and resistance have constantly fueled outsider comedy. Concomitantly sustaining morale while resisting encroachment, minorities have woven their way through society's obstacles with raillery. Indeed, long before the rise of multiculturalist politics, there was already in place a well-honed pluralistic comedy. Offering a social commentary that comically displayed the harshness of industrial life, on occasion employing slapstick and satire that plunged into anarchy, the outsiders frequently accomplished the "corrective laugh."[4] By the latter decades of the century, the corrective laugh had finally forced native American culture to take stock of its oppressive policies.

It was a combination of the Irish and Eastern European Jews that first pried open the boundaries of entertainment humor. Because the nascent entertainment industry—burlesque and vaudeville, nickelodeons and films—was held in such low esteem, minority performers and producers gravitated to its ranks. Jewish comics and entrepreneurs quickly rose in eminence and command. Isaac Deutscher astutely observed that Jews, having "dwelt on the borderlines" of various civilizations, took refuge in the nooks and crannies of society. "Each of them was in society, yet not in it, of it yet not of it. It was this that enabled them to rise in thought above their societies, above their nations, above their times and generations, and to strike out mentally into wide new horizons and far into the future."[5]

A stockpile of folk humor tangling and combining with urban experiences created a new comedic vitality. "The earthiness of their wit, the tautness of their one-liners—uttered as if in preparation for flight—the extravagance of their routines, and the brio and agility of their deliveries constituted a new comic style—comic modernism—that simply outpaced the droll and folksy humor associated with the likes of Mark Twain and Will Rogers, and in more recent times, Garrison Keillor of *A Prairie Home Companion*."[6] So dominant were Jewish entertainers in vaudeville, radio, theater, television, and the nightclub circuit before the 1970s, that though they constituted less than 3 percent of the population, Jews made up about 80 percent of all professional comedians. That percentage would drop considerably in the following decades as African-Americans, women, Hispanics, Asian-Americans, and some Native Americans poured into the profession of comedy. Even then, the preponderance of Jewish writers and producers in the centers of entertainment remained high by century's end.

Segregated in the "Chitlin Circuit," by contrast, black humor and its performers were little known. There were white jazz musicians, folklorists, and the members on the cultural left who were privy to the tales, jokes, witticisms, and skits of black culture, who on occasion had witnessed a routine, but they were few in number or had no power. Black humor flowed into society in the performances and writings of whites, in the guise of Joel Chandler Harris's *Uncle Remus*, the blackfaced songs of Al Jolson, and the radio comedy *Amos 'n' Andy*. While offering idiomatic nuances, these presentations were distanced from the original.

Authentic black humor, however, did make its way into the mainstream from the segregated black minstrel shows, musicals, songs, stage routines, and more widely read short stories and novels—though it was rarely acknowledged or recognized as such. Then in 1960, at a Playboy Club in Chicago, the first black comic finally made it onstage before a largely white audience. Dick Gregory's arrival and brilliant, provocative performances signaled one of the most consequential changes in entertainment history, comparable in effect with Jackie Robinson's appearance in a Brooklyn Dodgers uniform at Ebbets Field in 1947. (The thirteen years separating these two events signified the power of ridicule: segregation walls came tumbling down much faster in sports than in humor. By the 1980s black humor, like black music, had become a considerable part of mainstream American culture.)[7]

Like other oppressed groups, African-Americans quickly learned the lesson of laughing out of earshot of their detractors. A Southern black man in the late 1960s recalled a special "box" in his childhood town: "In my hometown there was a laughing box. Any time a Negro wanted to laugh, he had to run to the box, stick his head into it, laugh, and proceed home. If you lived too far from the box, you could put the laugh into an envelope and mail it, or put it into a bag and take it to the box."[8] More often than not, "the laughter was dark and removed."[9]

When Stokely Carmichael uttered his thunderous phrase during the Meredith March in 1966—"We Want Black Power! We Want Black

Power!"—whites were already being publicly mauled and subjected to revengeful jokes and satirical jibes. Trotting his heavyset frame onto stages, a puffing Godfrey Cambridge would exclaim to the largely white audiences, "I hope you noticed how I rushed up here. No more shuffle after the Revolution. We gotta be agile." A chorus of militant humorous acts greeted whites as legal and psychological barriers came down. Dick Gregory playfully threatened to picket the Weather Bureau until it named a hurricane "Beulah," which in fact it eventually did. Dr. Martin Luther King, Jr., ended his "I Have a Dream" speech at the March on Washington in 1963 with an old slave witticism: "We ain't what we ought to be and we ain't what we're going to be, but thank God we ain't what we was." Amiri Baraka and several friends in the 1960s mocked the watermelon stereotype by sitting and eating and melons on a busy Washington, D.C., thoroughfare during rush hour. At the height of the Watts Revolt in 1965, blacks placed two white mannequins in an obscene position in the middle of a street.

Comics on the nightclub and concert circuits kept up the assault, and though many of their routines reflected idiosyncratic styles, portions derived from a vast body of folk experience. "The remarkable thing about this gift of ours," wrote Jessie Fauset about black laughter in the 1920s, "is that it has its rise, I am convinced, in the very woes which beset us. . . . It is our emotional salvation."[10] The emergence of old-style comedians—"Moms" Mabley, "Pigmeat" Markham, Redd Foxx, Nipsey Russell—together with the rise of a younger generation of performers—Gregory, Cambridge, Bill Cosby, Flip Wilson, Richard Pryor, and Eddie Murphy—reflected the insistent challenge to the social structure.

By the later decades of the century, major elements of Jewish and black cultures' comedic styles and content had worked their way into the national lexicon. Stand-up comedy, novels, films, and jokes refracted their diverse genres and approach. In the wake of their gallows humor, for example, came the novel *Catch-22*, the film *Dr. Strangelove*, good news/bad news jokes, and the sick and disaster cycles to some extent.

Perched on the edge of personal destruction, gallows humor confronts a seemingly hopeless situation. It is an unmistakable index of group morale, an élan of resistance; its absence reveals either resigned indifference or a breakdown of the will to resist.

Psychiatrist Victor E. Frankl, incarcerated for three years at Auschwitz and other Nazi concentration camps, remarked that a stranger would be surprised to find art in the concentration camp barracks and "even more astonished to hear that one could find a sense of humor there as well—[if] only the faint trace of one," and "then only for a few seconds or minutes." Gallows humor, in short, has its limitations. Nonetheless, Frankl described humor as a "soul weapon" in the struggle for self-preservation: "It is well known that humor, more than anything else in the human makeup, can afford an aloofness and an ability to rise above any situation, even if only for a few seconds."[11]

Outsider tales invariably evoked expiration. "Well, what's new today?" asked Simon of a friend during the Nazi period. "At last," replied Nathan, "I do have something new. I have just heard a brand new Nazi joke. What do I get for telling it?" "Don't you know by this time?" Simon quickly fired back. "Six months in a concentration camp." A similar African-American version of what the critic Touré called "making light of personal horror": "Can you tell me where the Negroes hang out in this town?" a black man asked a policeman shortly after his arrival in a Southern town in the 1930s. "Yes," said the officer. "Do you see that tall tree over there?"[12]

A whimsical fatalism coursed through both cultures. A Jewish version:

Three men lay dying in a hospital ward. Their doctor, making the rounds, went up to the first and asked him his last wish. The patient was a Catholic. "My last wish," he murmured, "is to see a priest and make confession." The doctor assured him he would arrange it, and moved on.

The second patient was a Protestant. When asked his last wish, he replied, "My last wish is to see my family and say goodbye." The doctor promised he would have them brought, and moved on.

The third patient was, of course, a Jew. "And what is your last wish?" the doctor asked.

"My last wish," came the feeble, hoarse reply, "is to see another doctor."[13]

A comparable black rendering:

Two black men were visited by a fairy who told them she would grant them their fondest wish. The first man turned to his friend and exclaimed, "I'm going to buy me a white suit, white shirt, white shoes, white Cadillac, and drive to Miami Beach and lay in the white sand."

He then asked his friend what wish he desired most. His friend quickly replied, "I'm going to buy me a black suit, black shoes, black Cadillac, and drive to Miami Beach and watch them hang your black ass."[14]

In dealing with their oppressors, both groups worked language as a weapon to offset suspicion of improper thought and hostile action. The ironic curse, an intent concealed by a statement meaning the opposite, pervades Jewish folklore; the double entendre and triple entendre function in African-American communities. Jews sarcastically refer to their detractor's welfare: "My enemy, he should live so long" or "He should live and be well!"; alluding to his illness, "It couldn't happen to a nicer person!" To blacks, all whites are the heavy, *The Man.* "The Man has it all" is its summation.

Viewed with contemptible amusement was the ineptitude, if not downright stupidity, of their oppressors. A *goyishe mind* is the ultimate Jewish put-down; for blacks, it is *dumb.* Nicknames and insults are crucial ploys. Before the acronym WASP came into extensive usage in the 1970s and 1980s, the word *goy* encompassed the Christian majority. Far more inventive have been black terms: Ofay, Mr. Charlie, Miss Ann, honky, splib, vanilla, dude, pig.

Each group in its own way assailed social and economic restrictions. For Jews the assault was directed against representations of authority, as expressed in Groucho Marx's classic refusal to join a club that would have him as a member. Assaulting the system was this black joke:

"Good morning, ladies and gentlemen," announced the first black pilot of a major commercial airline company. "Welcome aboard Flight #606, bound for New York. We will be taking off in a few minutes, after we receive the go-ahead from the tower. Our flight plan is to fly at an altitude of 38,000 feet. Right now the weather across the country looks good and we anticipate no major turbulence. I will point out interesting sights long the way. Should you need anything, our stewardesses will be more than happy to make your trip as comfortable as possible. Now, if you will please fasten your seatbelts and observe the 'no smoking' sign, I'll see if I can get this motherfucker off the ground."[15]

Maneuvering against stereotypes, both Jews and African-Americans developed a high degree of self-mockery. It was poet Marianne Moore who observed that one's sense of humor is "a clue to the most serious part of one's nature."[16] And the most serious part of one's nature, argued Spanish philosopher Miguel de Unamuno, involves coping with ridicule. "The greatest height of heroism to which an individual, like a people, can attain is to know how to face ridicule; better still, to know how to make oneself ridiculous and not shrink from the ridicule."[17]

Throughout the centuries Jews have deployed subtle forms of self-derision as a means of deflecting criticism and inverting ridicule. Several versions from the 1970s and 1980s:

How do you say 'fuck you' in Yiddish?
  Trust me.

How many New Yorkers does it take to screw in a lightbulb?
  None of your goddamn business.

How can you prove Jesus Christ was Jewish?
  He lived at home until he was thirty.
  His mother thought he was a god.
  He went into his father's business.
  He thought his mother was a virgin.[18]

One of the most potent black jokes played off the African past with American urban existence. Sitting on a curb after an exhausting day of seeking work, an unemployed black man winds up in a conversation with God:

"Tell me, Lord, how come I'm so black?"
  "YOU'RE BLACK SO YOU COULD WITHSTAND THE HOT RAYS OF THE SUN IN AFRICA."
"Tell me, Lord, how come my hair is so nappy?"
  "YOUR HAIR IS NAPPY SO THAT YOU WOULD NOT SWEAT UNDER THE HOT RAYS OF THE SUN IN AFRICA."

"Tell me, Lord, how come my legs are so long?"
"YOUR LEGS ARE LONG SO THAT YOU COULD ESCAPE FROM THE WILD BEASTS IN AFRICA."
"Then tell me, Lord, what the hell am I doing in Chicago?"[19]

Just as black humor swept into the national consciousness, so did women's. If Jews and blacks can be said to have been historically entwined, so, too, in a curious way were blacks and women. Without question, no other group in American society has been so stigmatized for so long as natural buffoons. Only a handful of social clusters have been so depicted as being comical without intent. For women there existed an even more insidious perception, one that centered on creating and articulating humor itself. As Germaine Greer asserted in *The Female Eunuch* (1970), "Her expression must betray no hint of humor, curiosity or intelligence."[20]

Ann Beatts, one of the very few women who wrote for the comedy trade in the 1970s, dissected the rationale undergirding this notion. "Humor is aggression [and] aggression is 'hard.' Women have always been supposed to be nice to men." Beatts caustically noted that "it is more than a myth; it is a rule to live by: women have no sense of humor—though [men] might prefer to phrase it, 'Chicks just ain't funny.'"[21]

The belief that women lacked a sense of humor made them particularly open to ridicule. Images in print and electronic media, cartoons and comic strips, invariably displayed females as silly, verbose, intellectually lacking, and mechanically dependent. Paradoxically, the situation was ludicrous because women were also required to provide an appreciative audience for male joking: How could they possibly know when to laugh if they lacked comic facility?

Psychologically sentenced to humorlessness, largely denied access as writers and performers, in effect comedically invisible, women thus played largely to themselves. Dorothy Parker, Mae West, Lucille Ball, and Erma Bombeck were the exceptions to the rule and had a measurable influence on mass media.

In *A Very Serious Thing: Women's Humor and American Culture* (1988), a pioneering work on the subject, Nancy A. Walker wrote that in initiating a scholarly study she "ventured into uncharted territory. Studies of American humor abounded, but, as is the case in so much traditional scholarship, the women were left out or relegated to footnotes." Naturally curious about such an egregious exclusion, Walker noted that it came down to the stereotypical canard: "Women aren't supposed to have a sense of humor. Time and again, in sources from the mid-nineteenth century to very recently, I encountered writers (male) commenting—and sometimes lamenting—that women were incapable of humor, and other writers (female) explaining that they knew women weren't *supposed* to have a sense of humor and then proceeding to be very funny indeed."[22]

Excluded from the mainstream of political and economic power, women's humor took its cue from the domestic realm, from immersion in the homestead that involved children and community, and from male-female relationships. It was a humor concertedly more inwardly rebellious than retaliatory.[23] Being removed from power did not mean that women shied from exploring humor's impact on themselves or others. Rather, women's critique of American society was indirectly couched, "with authors and *personae* adopting a less confrontational and frequently an apparently self-deprecatory stance more in keeping with women's traditional status."[24]

By the late 1970s, however, the focus dramatically shifted away from the self-deprecatory. Like blacks, women regaled themselves with hostile and aggressive joking, intent on making men squirm. "Do you know how sex and a snowstorm are alike? *You never know how long it's going to last or how many inches you're going to get.*" Females chuckled as men squirmed.[25]

In a special issue in 1979 devoted to women's laughter, the editors of the radical journal *Cultural Correspondence* wrote that "the precise forms of the new women's humor are still in the process of creation."[26] Within a decade, however, women had redefined the script. Deriding patriarchal institutions, ridiculing male sexual behavior, plunging into taboos such as menstruation, lesbianism, and abortion, they vastly extended the humor landscape.[27] Explicit retorts and jokes excoriating males crisscrossed the country, highlighting the differences between the sexes.

> Stanley was on his knees, entreating his love to marry him. "Be my wife," he beseeched her, "and for you I will climb mountains and swim the tortuous seas."
>
> Shaking her head, she said, "I don't think you'll do. I want a husband who'll stay home and carry out the garbage."[28]

Dependence on men was particularly scorned. A popular graffito made the rounds: "A Woman Without a Man Is Like a Fish Without a Bicycle." And a story jiving male weakness:

> Vernon's wife died. At her burial he wept and wailed. He was beside himself with grief. After the funeral, a friend said to him, "Vernon, I know how attached you were to your wife. I can understand your grief. But you are still young. Wounds heal. You'll meet another woman and in due time you will marry again."
>
> Tears streaming down his face, Vernon blubbered, "Yes, I know. I know. But what am I supposed to do for a wife until then?"[29]

Not all humor was confined to rebellion and revelation. Ideology called into question the social basis of humor itself. Positing the difference between "female" and "feminist" humor, Gloria Kaufman in *Pulling Our Own Strings: Feminist Humor and Satire* (1980) struck a responsive chord when she noted that woman "are ridiculing a social system that can be, that must be changed. *Female* humor may ridicule a person or a system from an accepting point of view ('that's life'), while the *nonacceptance* of oppression characterizes feminist humor and satire."[30]

Feminist humor confronted, as did female humor, but it sought major transformation. It demanded an end to stereotypical formulas in the popular culture along with the creation of a distinct consciousness and sense of empowerment. A graffito exchange symbolizing the message appeared in a college bathroom in the 1980s:

> Initial Statement: "I don't know what to do. I'm married to Benjy. But I'm in love with Mike. I'll die if I can't have Mike."
>
> First Response: "Run way with Mike. Love conquers all."
>
> Second Response: "Have an affair with a third guy and you'll love Benjy again. It worked for me."
>
> Final Response: "Don't die for love. Live for love. Have an affair with a woman."[31]

By the 1990s, confrontation with traditional male values and the hierarchal structure became commonplace: "We are all equal in the eyes of the Goddess."[32] Viewing this challenge as a substantial threat to their status, men counterattacked by accusing feminists of "lacking a sense of humor" and promptly launched a revival of the "dumb blonde" jokes in the 1990s. The tactic failed as women retaliated with "dumb male" jokes, totally silencing the opposition.

"An essential purpose of humor is to call the norm into question," wrote Nancy Walker in 1988.[33] By challenging traditional cultural values and seeking empowerment within the institutions of entertainment, the early outsiders provided founts of humor. Although early in the century each group had its own agenda, each nonetheless countermanded entrapping stereotypes and outsider status, and their routines and jokes paved the way for the emergence of others—Hispanics, Native Americans, Asian-Americans, gays and lesbians—who further enlarged the multicultural perspective.

PART TWO

Time Frame

5

The Child and the Giant

Writing at the close of the 1950s, his head turned in partial derision, a deep sigh passing his lips, the historian Eric Goldman composed an epitaph: "Goodbye to the fifties—and good riddance." Articulating a theme echoed by virtually all observers throughout the decade, ironically including politicians—a theme encapsulated in *Time* magazine's cryptic phrase the "Silent Generation"—Goldman excoriated the age for its absence of national humor. It was, he declared, "a heavy, humorless, sanctimonious atmosphere, singularly lacking in the self-mockery that is self-criticism. Probably the climate of the late Fifties was the dullest and dreariest in all of history." Peering around, Goldman wondered, "Where are the guffaws in this country, the purifying wit and humor, the catharsis of caricature, the outcries against all this nonsense? Sometimes I think we are just boring ourselves to death."[1]

Other joined the chorus fearing the demise of American humor. Early in the decade the country's premier humorist, James Thurber, gave "humor and comedy five years to live." A few years later, however, he concluded that this harsh sentence had been a trifle inaccurate, diagnosing instead that humor "just went crazy." Walt Kelly, the creator of the satiric comic strip *Pogo,* stated what many had fearfully come to believe, namely, that political freedom and the corresponding access to ridicule and wit were on the wane: "Our most recent laughter has been somewhat nervous. We have been trying to keep an eye on all sides before we laugh but the true humorist has found it nigh impossible to laugh . . . while peering back over his shoulder." Likewise, the Beat poet and commentator Kenneth Rexroth angrily railed against "the decline of American humor." From his perch as theater critic, Robert Hatch lamented that "the Eisenhower Administration was easily as laughable as Hoover's but by then we had so lost a sense of destiny that attempts to lampoon Ike and his entourage turned rancid." The result was that "humor, in fact, has become a tough business." Jules Feiffer, whose cartoons reflected the period with sardonic luminescence, likened the remaining humorists in the nation to "members of an underground."[2]

Playwright Thornton Wilder saw things in a different and, in view of succeeding events, prophetic light. Dissecting the phrase "silent generation," Wilder incisively argued that it was essential to test *Time's* declarations that the 1950s generation "do not issue manifestos, make speeches, or carry posters . . . want a good secure job . . . [and] either through fear, passivity, or conviction, they are ready to conform . . . are looking for a faith." Wilder proffered that the young were responding in a creative and thoughtful manner to a unique set of circumstances. This generation was silent because the vast changes occurring in the post–World War II period called "not for argument but for rumination. . . . These young people are setting new patterns for the relation of the individual to the society about him. The condition of being unimpressed by authorities and elders has thrown them back more resolutely on themselves. They are simply unimpressed by time-honored conventions."[3]

Wilder's assessment was a partial corrective to the pronouncements of malaise. Essentially, it insisted that the postwar period be viewed as a transition from one set of circumstances to another and far more perplexing one. Contrary to the widely held assertion that the silent generation was indulging in irrelevancies, it was, in fact, subjecting society's basic assumptions to humorous scrutiny. It was, to be sure, a scrutiny coded in such a way as to confuse even the most sensitive observers. Nonetheless, rather than silence, there was restrained laughter; rather than acquiescence, there was doubt; rather than closed possibilities, there was receptivity for unusual forms.

What was certain was that political humor, a presumed mainstay of the nation's repertoire, had been largely beaten into submission. But the new forms that humor took, the patterns that suddenly emerged during the 1950s and early 1960s, were so divergent, so incomprehensibly jolting that many failed to grasp what these forms were communicating.

The decades' popular humor—labeled "cruel" and "sick"—and the two major joke cycles of that period—the child and the elephant—illustrate the complex ways in which people's humor responded to the swift and unsettling changes of the postwar years. The child-oriented cycle that suddenly made its appearance in the later years of the 1950s and early 1960s reflected the deep-seated anxieties of young adults to the vast socioeconomic changes that were occurring, transformations that not only affirmed their behavior as upwardly mobile consumers but were perpetuated by their adherence to bourgeois values as well. The elephant riddles expressed those ambivalent concerns about the nation as a superstate, specifically, the triumph of consumerism and the policy of Pax Americana.

The dynamic rush of national and international events in the postwar period was the catalyst for unique types of humor. Following its global victory in 1945, the United States embarked on fulfilling the consumer expectations that had been suddenly and brutally cut short first by the Great Depression and then by the demands of the global war. Once there was freedom from the deprivations of both circumstances, there ensued a frenzied rush to attain the American Dream: an ensured middle-class status buttressed by material goods and entitled services. Fueled by the needs of a war-torn world and undeterred by competing national economies, the surging prosperity indeed elevated a substantial majority into the hallowed middle classes. The suburban house and two-car garage became the symbol of family enterprise, the achievement of the Calvinist work ethic and capitalist faith.

The triumph of American technology transcended the continent. Never truly isolated, and assuredly no longer merely a leveraged player in the international scene, the United States assumed a global hegemony. The result was the rise of the state as a superpower, the nation as a colossus capable of directly influencing the internal policies of countries throughout the world. Acquisition of the atomic and hydrogen bombs and the development of a B-52 force patrolling the skies every minute, every day, every year further fueled and expanded this sense of power.

The child and the state moved to assert their new riches and military might. While the nuclear family sought to achieve economic status in a fiercely competitive society, the superstate sought dominance in a savagely contested ideological world. The efforts to achieve these goals were enormous; the cost to ordinary existence, monumental. The family was immediately racked by conflict between the generations and increasingly frayed by divorce; the superstate was feared as the potential destroyer of civility and civilization.

Within the reaches of the American psyche there arose a powerful need to cope with, and rail at, events that were unalterably rearranging familial and international configurations. It was a need imperative enough to invoke a humorous assessment of events, because humor serves to reduce tension and, at the same time, to reorder meaning arising from social and political upheavals.

Preceding Allen Ginsberg's immense poem *Howl* (1956), which cut through modern American culture like a scythe, a howling humor emerged. The family, because of its unbridled consumerism, and the superstate, because of its unchecked power, became the essential targets of the new laughter in the postwar decades. This change did not take hold without first obliterating certain hallowed boundaries. The sanctified nature of the family and government made it necessary to pare away the cultural restrictions on humorous topics. This surgery occurred in swift order as the first generation of postwar humorists and stand-up comics began poking fun at areas hitherto regarded as off-limits, if not downright taboo.

Directed by those who grew up in the years of deprivation and political and social realignments—led by Lenny Bruce, Mort Sahl, Shelley Berman, Jules Feiffer, Second City Review in Chicago, the Committee in San Francisco, and Compass Players in New York—a major assault on the changing character of American life emerged in the mid-1950s. Encompassing both a literary and a popular dimension, the new humor was quickly disseminated by the mass media.

Establishment culture was totally unprepared for the irreverent onslaught on the character and direction of American society. While the baby boomers embraced these new wave comics, many of their elders were horror-stricken by the satirical criticism of their universe. Weaned on the consensual comedy of radio comedians Bob Hope, Jack Benny, Burns and Allen, Fibber McGee and Molly, later replicated by televison's Milton Berle, Lucille Ball, Phil Silvers, Donna Reed, and others, the older generation regarded the new humor as downright subversive. It would be but the first of several rifts that would occur between the generations over the next decades.

Routines and jokes skewering the political and social landscape were immediately lumped together as "gruesome" or "sick," as if such derogations would demean their import or drive them away.

Reinforcing this impression was the sudden appearance in 1952 of Harvey Kurtzman's *MAD* magazine. Instantly embraced by the 1950s generation, its title alone produced consternation, and its contents were indeed maddening. Parodying other comic books, it delighted in criticizing social customs and cultural models. It was, as Adam Gopnik correctly noted, "a riot of manic detail and overflowed with indignation at the absurdities of the adult world."[4] Venerable symbols were skewed: "G.I. Joe" became "G.I. Shmoe"; Mickey Mouse was "Rickey Rodent"; "Prince Valiant" was "Prince Violent."

Nothing appeared sacred any longer as "sick" humor broadly canvassed a spectrum of taboo subjects—intolerance and racism, religion, abundance and malnutrition, thermonuclear bombs and devastation, sex and venereal disease. In coffeehouses, small nightclubs, and neighborhood theaters, embryonic comics confronted the old bourgeoisie and the emerging garrison state. At best, the content of their humor was highly critical of particular socioeconomic change and political direction; at worst, it assumed catastrophe in the short run.

The roots of such dark humor lie deep in American cultural soil. Mark Twain was not the only writer to whimsically portray societal values in a cynical light, against the backdrop of a gilded age populated by robber barons. Shattering economic depressions of the 1890s and 1930s had also produced a bountiful harvest of grim jokes, quips, and songs. Moreover, as folklorist Alan Dundes has pointed out, earlier joke cycles revealed similar versions of "sick" humor: the "Little Willie" quatrains from the early 1900s to the 1930s, followed by the "Little Audrey" cycle.[5] But the travails of these decades certainly warranted such biting humor. By contrast, "sick" humor curiously arose after the triumphant global war, a time of bursting economic and material expansion accompanied by an extraordinary sense of optimism regarding the fulfillment of the American century. The contradiction between the good economic times and the younger generation's dark humor was bewildering. Desperately trying to stem its tide, the media excoriated the humor in harsh terms. It was variously labeled "sick," "cruel," "meanie," "Bloody Mary," "hate," or "gruesome," and its upholders were castigated as "sickniks."[6] Hence the generation got it both ways: first they were "silent" on the issues; then, when they offered their humor, it was termed "nauseating."

Vacillating between endorsement and befuddlement, writers and intellectuals were split on the new humor. James Thurber thought the comedy "crazy" for identifying itself with the very tension and terror it was trying to alleviate: "The line is thinly drawn between American comedy and American insanity." Novelist Kingsley Amis mused that "perhaps laughing at sick jokes is the liberal's way of misbehaving: he's tired of being on his best behaviour all the time about racial questions, but he still musn't laugh at them, so he laughs about something else that's 'unmentionable' but far more remote." Literary editor and book columnist Kenneth Allsop was furious because these "proselytizers of irreverence and underminers of public confidence . . . traduce the American Good Life and lampoon such status fetishes as the self-lubricating auto, the backyard swimming pool, Brooks Brothers clothes, martinis on the patio, and the fundamental holy creed that America is best." Critic Benjamin DeMott raised the question of "whether the status is deserved, whether the sick comic's efforts result in the kind of protest that clarifies moral and political issues. . . . At its best the school is exhilaratingly funny. . . . Examination of particulars, however, raises doubt as to whether the promise is confirmed."[7]

Such carping mattered not a whit. To the 1950s generation, their "sick" humor refracted their suspicions of the rapidly growing gap between expectations and realities. It was no coincidence that much of the humor focused on certain sanctified institutions, since these were the very ones being buffeted by severe change. The driving emphasis upon personal striving and sacrifice—in short, the insistence on individual needs over communal requirements—severely dented familial and religious institutions. "It could be said that the history of the Baby Boom generation," argued the editor of the *National Lampoon*, Tony Hendra, "has been one of seeking stability out of chaos, the chaos that was the underbelly of postwar prosperity, and which was made even more confusing by having all the hallmarks of stability but none of the substance."[8]

It is not surprising, then, that the first major joke cycle in the post–World War II period involved the wrenching of relationships. "All of these jokes," noted folklorist Brian Sutton-Smith in his analysis of the cycle, "have in common a disregard for sentiments which are usually taken very seriously. The afflictions of others which are normally treated with considerable sensitivity or tenderness, the love for children which is regarded as 'human nature,' the respect for religious institutions and revered persons which is customarily thought to be basic, are in these jokes made the subject matter of amusement."[9]

The disparity between the hallowed family unit and its antipodal tendencies within the affluent setting became the basis of the child joke cycle. The compulsion to attain "a place in the American sun" was a drive that had among its practical consequences two working parents, acceptance of mobility as a mode of existence, frequent residential moves, separate rooms for each child, and increasingly high rates of separation and divorce. The frantic drive to arrive in suburbia evoked anxiety from many quarters and a profusion of hostility as intimacy, role models, marital connections, and sibling relationships suffered. Expectedly, the child became the focus around which the cycle energized, the child as victim.

As overall expression, cruel jokes revealed a revulsion to a hostile family environment, especially to feelings of parental rejection, and possibly of violence. The opening phrase of the parent's response to the logical question posed by the curious child, "Shut up," expressed the harsh sentiment of an earlier period: "A child should be seen but not heard."

> Hey, Mom, why does Dad always lose his head?
> *Shut up, and sharpen the axe.*

> Mommy, where's Daddy?
> *Shut up, and keep digging.*

> Mommy, why are we pushing the car off the cliff?
> *Shut up, or you'll wake up your father.*

> Mommy, why is Daddy swimming so fast?
> *Shut up, and reload.*

> Daddy, why is Mother lying so still?
> *Shut up, and keep digging.*

Similarly, extended family relations came under generational assault, suggesting that the nuclear family possessed but a smidgen of ancestral sentiment:

Mommy, Grandma is starting to breathe again.
 Shut up, and get that pillow back in place.

Mommy, why can't I kiss Grandma?
 Shut up, and close the casket.

Mommy, can we play with Grandpa?
 No, you've dug him up enough already.

The actions of adults were repeatedly criticized as being hypocritical. This view of elders as two-faced would eventually find its way into the countercultural declaration, "Don't trust anybody over thirty."

Mommy, I want milk.
 Shut up, and drink your beer.

Daddy, why is it wrong to gamble?
 Shut up, and deal the cards.

Mommy, can I go out and play?
 Shut up, and deal.

Mother, can I put lipstick on?
 No, you look bad enough already.

Mommy, what is an oedipal complex?
 Shut up, kid, and come here and kiss your mother.

Parent–child antagonisms had their natural effect on sibling relationships suggesting the disintegrative state of the family. Swipes between brothers and sisters:

Johnny, quit pulling your sister's ear.
Johnny, quit pulling your sister's ear.
 All right, Johnny, give me your sister's ear.

Mommy, I tied Johnny to the railroad track.
Well, untie him.
 No, I like to see people with their head and body separated.

Son, will you quit kicking your sister!
 Oh, that's all right, she's already dead.

Not surprisingly, then, undergirding the jokes was the child's own sense of rejection, the intense fear of being ugly and unwanted:

Mommy, Mommy, why am I running around in circles?
   Shut up, or I'll nail your other foot to the floor.

Mommy, I'm cold.
   Get back in that refrigerator right now.

Mommy, why are we out in our boat at night?
   Shut up, and tie that cement block around your leg.

Mommy, why do I have warts on me?
   Because you are a toad, honey.

Mommy, what is a vampire?
   Shut up, and drink your blood.

Mommy, what is a werewolf?
   Shut up, and comb your face.

Mommy, Mommy, little brother is on fire.
   Then hurry and get a marshmallow.

Going from being unloved and unwanted to being totally rebuffed was part of a process that naturally led to the "dead baby" jokes. Making its appearance in the early 1960s, the "dead baby" cycle symbolized the family as lifeless. Babies were portrayed as mutilated, destroyed, even cannibalized. Here was black humor reaching its most apprehensive state regarding the viability of the family:

What's red and sits in a corner?
   A baby chewing [teething on, eating, sucking] razor blades.

What's green and sits in a corner?
   Same baby two weeks later.

What's red and green, red and green?
   A baby going through a lawn mower.

What's harder to unload, a truck full of bowling balls [or bricks] or a truck full of dead babies?
A truck full of bowling balls because you can't use a pitchfork.

What's the difference between a bowling ball and a baby?
You can't eat a bowling ball.

How you make a dead baby float?
Two scoops of dead baby and one pint of root beer.

How did the dead baby cross the road?
He was stapled to a chicken.[10]

It would be incorrect to assume that cruel jokes centered solely on the child and the child's nuclear and extended family. The jokes further encompassed significant others, those father and mother figures writ large, thus indicating that the *nation as community* was under siege as well. Gallows jokes directed at political and religious figures:

Aside from that, Mrs. Lincoln, how did your husband like the show?

Did your husband get his polio shots yet, Mrs. Roosevelt?

Happy Father's Day, Mr. Lindbergh.

Happy Easter, Jesus.

I don't care if your name is Santa Claus; get your hand out of my stocking.[11]

Closely related were the "doll" jokes that made their appearance at the same time. Excoriated were highly recognized individuals who in later decades would be identified as "celebrities." Here the jokes functioned to deflate personas. "In each case, the doll's supposed action sums up a popular conception about the historical person in question. In addition, when this person is a successful and eminent male, as is most often the case, then the summation usually subjects him to implied moral or ethical criticism."[12] The doll device was a clever, sharp jibe against policy makers and trendsetters. Pinpointed was an essential flaw:

1. Entertainers

Wind it up and it wrecks two marriages. What is it? The Elizabeth Taylor doll.

The Dean Martin doll: you wind it up and it gets drunk.

Wind up the Marilyn Monroe doll, and if it's on time, it's broken.

Wind up the Jack Paar doll and it cries.

The Miles Davis doll: you wind it up and it walks out on its audience.

The Oscar Levant doll: you wind it up and it cracks up.

The Frank Sinatra doll: you wind it up and it chases another doll.

No point in trying to wind up the Jayne Mansfield doll. It's busted.

2. Politicians

The Eisenhower doll: wind it up and it doesn't do anything.

Then there's the Nixon doll: wind it up and it goes through a crisis.

The Barry Goldwater doll: you wind it up and it walks backward.

3. Preachers

The Billy Graham doll: you wind it up and it saves you.

The Oral Roberts doll: you wind it up and it heals you.

4. Organizations

You wind up the elephant doll and it pins everything on the donkey.

The John Birch doll: wind it up and it points a finger at you.

At times, the jokes possessed a gallows flavor:

Did you see the new Helen Keller dolls? You wind them up and they
walk into walls.

The Lenny Bruce doll: wind it up and it laughs at the Helen Keller
doll.[13]

That all these jokes were aspects of a national disenchantment is
evident from the major script that immediately abutted the child cycle: the elephant jokes. Appearing in California in mid-1962, the elephant riddles quickly spread to almost every other region of the
country and even to other parts of the world. Within a year, the cycle
had become common fare as television shows, newspapers, magazines representing diverse readerships—*Time, Seventeen,* and *Saturday
Review of Literature*—and radio talk-show hosts repeated them.

The elephant as comic motif can be seen as a metaphor that alternately suggested both the magic and the terror of strength and power.
Though there was awe of the giant's size and amazing powers, there
was also amusement at its cumbersome movements. In these riddles,
comedy stemmed from the image of contradiction. Despite its bulk
the elephant possessed powers defying the laws of nature by climbing trees, performing acrobatic tricks, wiggling in and out of refrig-
erators, and accomplishing other fantastic feats. This type of humor is
naturally associated with children, who are supposed to fancy such
nonsensical twists.

But why the elephant, and why did it loom so large in the early
1960s? That the animal possessed symbolic significance is certain, but
what provoked its emergence? An intriguing interpretation linking
societal change with Freudian undertones was proffered by folklorists
Roger Abrahams and Alan Dundes. "One cannot help but notice . . .
that the rise of the elephant joke occurred simultaneously with the
rise of the Negro in the Civil Rights movement." As the epitome of
giant animality, and consequently of sexual prowess, "one might say
that the elephant is a reflection of the American Negro as the white
sees him and that the political and social assertion by the Negro has
caused certain primal fears to be reactivated." Triggered by the civil
rights movement, then, anxiety defined blacks as a "phallic force to
be reckoned with." Juvenile joking, however, neatly neutered the sexually potent creature.[14]

Positing an entirely different view was Mac E. Barrick, who argued that the animal had to be seen within the context of a society obsessed with rationalist policies and programs. "The illogical nature of many elephant riddles suggests that they represent a revolt against a scientific-minded society overly concerned with statistical analysis and reasoned assumptions. The popularity of these riddles among the younger generation suggests that there is still hope for the world: man has not lost his sense of humor, but can still find something funny in this grotesque world."[15]

But if the elephant possessed symbolic meaning, it was because the language of male giantism had long infiltrated American culture. This was not the first time that the elephant had conveyed some larger meaning. In his gold rush diary written more than a century earlier, *Overland to California with the Pioneer Line*, Bernard J. Reid described the names painted on covered wagons that were about to travel from St. Louis across the arid regions of the Southwest: "Prairie Bird," "Tempest," "Albatross," and *"Have You Saw The Elephant?"* The bad grammar perfectly corresponded with its intended meaning. "To see the elephant" was an expression coined as early as 1834 and meant confronting a severe hazard or gaining experience through an ordeal. During the 1850s gold rush the elephant connoted a frenetic quest for gold. When one San Franciscan related to a friend that he had decided "to see the elephant," it was to point out not that he was "going on a toot, but that he intended to take a flier at the mines."[16]

Almost a century and a half later, in the 1980s, whimsical scholars proposed the elephant as a session focus for an upcoming Modern Language Association convention on issues confronting cultural studies: "The Elephant as 'Physical Other'"; "The Elephant: Interrogating Multi-Cultural Rhetoricities"; "The Elephant as Eurocentric Object"; "The Elephant as (Post) Modern Construction." Related questions included "Tracking the Elephant Through Texts: Western Visuality vs. Olfactory Perception," "Garage Sales and Elephants: A Dialogue of Contested Spaces," and "Situating the Paradigmatic Other: The Elephant in Weight-Loss Discourse."

The elephant of the joke cycle derives from another idiosyncratically American source. Throughout the nineteenth century particular frontiersmen were viewed as possessing giant strengths, enduring specific physical hardships, and matching their skills with high moral qualities. Johnny Appleseed, Mike Fink, Casey Jones, Davy Crockett, John Henry, Paul Bunyan, and others were symbolic men to match actual mountains and mythical obstacles. Hyperbolic feats became storytelling fixtures. Tall tales, liar contests, exaggerated anecdotes, inventive situations characterized people's narratives.

Such proclivity toward exaggeration added more names to the lexicon of national heroes in the twentieth century, a mixture of real and imaginary figures: Superman, John "Duke" Wayne, Batman, Joe DiMaggio, Wonder Woman, Rambo, Frank Sinatra, the Terminator. While the prefix of Superman's name would assume preeminence in the post–World War II vocabulary, the idea of the American colossus was by this time culturally ingrained. In spectator sports it had already been fixed to baseball's World Series and boxing's Championship of the World. Hollywood presented *King Kong* (1933) and the futuristic *The Big Broadcast of 1938*, starring comedians Bob Hope and W. C. Fields, in which two mammoth ocean liners, *Gigantic* and *Colossus*, compete in a race.

It was World War II itself, however, with its global dimensions and massive technological requirements, that lifted the language into even loftier superlatives. The imaginal incentive required in mobilizing a diverse population of 120 million encouraged the reordering of words and phrases. Military developments produced a bounty of soaring descriptions. The skies were filled with "flying fortresses" capable of dropping "blockbusters"; the seas had "armadas" and "supercarriers"; "wonder drugs" combated diseases; bond drives demonstrated "super efforts." The future held such vast possibilities that, in Wendell Willkie's memorable phrase, nations could be melded into "One World." Then came the atomic bomb with the possibility of "global annihilation."

The expansive reworking of words and images to accommodate vast changes continued unabated in the postwar years. With the defeat of the Great Depression and the dictatorships, a heady populace embraced the arrival of the world's most powerful nation, a superpower. "Super" is defined in *Webster's Dictionary* as "that which surpasses all or most others of its kind, as in power or size, as in superstate," an apt description that summed up American military and economic power in the second half of the century.

Expectedly, the nation's language was swiftly altered to redefine its international place. Never modest in any case, American ideals, intentions, institutions, and materialism were elevated to higher planes, the words reflecting a technological giant. The prefix "super" and related words quickly became attached to the American universe. "Super" was promiscuously sprinkled throughout the consumer culture as products were labeled "extra large," "giant," "jumbo," with advertisements beckoning consumers with "super buys," "super sales," "gigantic giveaways," "stupendous closeouts." A chain store smugly offered "giant-size half-quarts." Tampons became "super absorbent," and body odors were eliminated by "super deodorants."

Colloquial expressions fixed on being "super." A positive response to almost anything became "that's super," "super-duper," or merely, "su—per." Special lists came into existence: an exceptionally hard worker was dubbed a super worker; a highly successful entertainer or athlete was anointed a superstar; those who went beyond the norm were "in orbit"; an exceptionally nice individual was supernice or supersweet. To be in a happy state was "supercalafragilistic-expialidocious," from the child/adult film *Mary Poppins* (1964). "Simply great" became one of the hyperbolic phrases that upgraded ordinary situations.

The vernacular landscape was similarly realigned. Grocery stores were expanded into supermarkets; six-lane highways became superhighways; a city and surrounding environs swelled into a megalopolis; the $64 question radio show (*Take It or Leave It*) became television's *$64,000 Question*; movie screens enlarged to Cinemascope; airplanes traveled at supersonic speeds; oil moved around the globe on supertankers; super drugs were proclaimed; supernovas and ominous black holes were discovered; football claimed ritualized status in its competition with boxing and baseball by initiating a Super Bowl championship played in a Superdome on Super Sunday; the soaring birthrate was described as a baby boom; *Playboy* magazine celebrated the first physically perfect female in an elongated centerfold; sexually active men were dubbed "superstuds"; and the A-bomb gave way to the more frighteningly destructive H-bomb. The effects of both bombs were displayed in dramatic and horror films: *On the Beach, The H-Man, The Blob, The Thing, Attack of the Crab Monsters, The Incredible Shrinking Man,* and *Godzilla* (a Japanese sea monster spawned by the weapon).

At the conscious level, "super" came to symbolize national and international might. Because excessiveness in one cultural realm affects other areas, it was not surprising that in an age of such linguistic extravagance, humor would respond with equal, if not greater, intensity. The elephant, in effect, became the symbol of the superstate incarnate.

Toward this type of symbol, as it has existed throughout mythology, a dual attitude emerged. Giants have been alternately viewed with awe and trepidation, adulation and anxiety, suggesting a lurking demon within the strength of a deity. Humans have alternately desired to emulate and to slay such giants set on a plane above ordinary mortals. For many centuries, as Bruno Bettelheim aptly noted in *The Uses of Enchantment* (1976), the fairy tale has enabled humans to cope with divergent feelings ranging from joy and desire to rage and despair.[17]

The elephant motif was an equivalent of the modern fairy tale, revealing the ambivalence of the 1950s generation toward the nation as superstate, the invincible elephant with its strengths and flaws. Unlike a traditional narrative form, however, the intent of the story is to be found within the joke cycle itself.

There was, first, the elephant's ubiquitous nature. His presence was everywhere in the burgeoning consumer culture:

How can you tell if there's an elephant in the bathtub with you?
   By the faint smell of peanuts on his breath or
   The water won't go down.

How can you tell if there's an elephant in bed with you?
   He has buttons on his pajamas this big.

How does an elephant get out of an elevator [or a telephone booth]?
   The same way he got in.

How can you keep an elephant from charging?
   Take away his credit card.

How can you tell if an elephant is going on vacation?
   He packs his trunk.

How can you tell if there's an elephant in the refrigerator?
   The door won't close or
   By the footprints in the butter [Jell-o, pizza, cream cheese] or
   By the "E" on his sweater or

His tusks are cold or
Look and see if his motorcycle is parked outside.

How do you make an elephant float?
With two scoops of ice cream and some root beer.

How do you know when you've passed an elephant?
You can't flush the toilet.

Because the elephant's youth and size overshadowed all other characteristics, he had to be taught some elementary rules of civility: "How do you housebreak an elephant? *Get fourteen copies of the New York Times—Sunday edition.*" It was essential to teach him language: "How do you talk to an elephant? *Use big words.*" Like postwar culture, the elephant was quite playful: "How do you raise an elephant? *Put a tack on his chair.*" He was clearly a prodigious eater: "How do you make a hamburger for an elephant? *Take 500 jars of mustard, 60 gallons of catsup, 90 pounds of onions, and then you get this big roll. . . .*" Clothing him required extraordinary measures: "How do you make an elephant fly? *Take a zipper this lonnnggg. . . .*" Toiletries were important: "Do you know where I can get a bowling ball and a magician? No, why? *I'm trying to make a roll-on deodorant for elephants.*" No other animal compares with the elephant: "What do you call a hippopotamus who's been carrying elephants across a river all day? *A tired hippopotamus.*" There is only one thing larger than an elephant: "What is bigger than an elephant and doesn't weigh an ounce? *An elephant shadow.*"

Despite his size, the elephant possessed magical properties. He could fly, disguise himself, effectively hide, expand and contract, and create others in his large image. "What's yellow, has four legs, weighs a thousand pounds, and flies? *Two 500-pound canaries.*" What's yellow and green, and weighs a thousand pounds? *Two 500-pound parakeets.*" He's a very tricky devil, this elephant. "How do you get an elephant out of a tub of Jell-o? *Follow the directions.*" "How do you get six elephants into a Volkswagen? *Three in front and three in back.*"

Many of the early riddles centered on his color, a sign of his ability to mask his true identity. "Why are elephants gray? *So you can tell them from the canaries.*" "What's red and white on the outside and gray on the inside? *Campbell's cream of elephant soup.*" Significantly, the issue of identity was a national quest in the 1950s. Presidential commissions, entrepreneurial groups, academics, and others struggled with such questions as what constituted national, business, or personal identity. One verb synonymous with cultural identity was "color," as in "color him" and "color me." This equation led to the success of coffee table publications using a children's format: *The JFK Coloring Book* and *The John Birch Coloring Book.*

Intriguingly, in the cycle the color red was most pronounced. Was there a connection between the McCarthyite atmosphere, the fear of subversion by "Reds" and "fellow travelers," and the jokes? President Harry Truman had earlier attempted to undercut the drive to uncover internal subversion by labeling it a "red herring." In the joke cycle there was indeed such a hidden threat: the elephant itself. "Why does an elephant paint himself red? *So he can hide in a cherry tree.*" "Have you ever seen elephants paint their toenails red? No. *See how effective it is.*"

Like all giants, it was the elephant who posed the true danger. "What looks like an elephant, flies, and is dangerous? *A flying elephant with a machine gun,* or *A flying elephant with diarrhea.*" "What's blue, up a tree, and kills you? *A blue machine gun barrel.*" "What's black, lives in a tree, and is dangerous? *A crow with a machine gun.*" "What is green, slimy, lives in swamps and ponds, and is dangerous? *A frog with a hand grenade.*" Clearly, the elephant was aggressive and attacked living things much smaller than himself. "Why do elephants walk sideways in the grass? *They're trying to trip field mice.*" "Why do elephants lie across the middle of the road? *To trip the ants.*" "Why do elephants lie on their back with their feet in the air? *So they can trip birds.*" "Why was the elephant standing on his head? *To squash a bug.*"

Elephants hid themselves in order to attack when least expected. "Why do trees have leaves? *For elephants to hide behind.*" "Why is it dangerous to walk in the forest between 1 and 2? *That's when elephants jump out of trees.*" "Why is it dangerous to walk in the jungle at night? *Elephants jumping out of trees can hurt you.*" "Why shouldn't you walk through the jungle between 7 and 8? *That's when the elephants are taking their parachute lessons.*" Few escaped the elephant's attacks, not even the comic-strip master of the jungle: "Did you hear what happened to Tarzan? *He walked through the jungle between 7 and 8.*" Other animals, dangerous in their own right, had to be wary. "Why are cheetahs the fastest animals in the jungle? *They need to be fast to get away from the elephants jumping out of trees.*" "Why are cheetahs so scarce? *They don't always get out of the way of elephants jumping from trees."*

The elephant's attacks on insects and other animals, his dangerous size and proportions, and his capability to reinvent himself reflected a disguised, deepening anxiety within the populace regarding American military prowess. Occasionally, the humor revealed the giant's offensive and malicious intent more succinctly. "What are elephants building nests out of? *Concrete blocks."* The elephant had specific targets, particularly in Third World countries: "What's that black stuff between an elephant's toes? *Squashed natives."* "Why do the natives run through the jungle? *To escape from elephants jumping on them."* "Why do elephants have big ears? *To hear the natives running through the jungle so they can jump on them."* "Why do elephants climb trees? *To look for natives running through the forest."* "Do you know why the natives are restless? *Because the elephants are climbing trees."*

Was it possible to restrain the monster that resided within American culture? Public concern over the elephant's propensities led to talk about how to control, or at the very least check, its unbridled powers. Perhaps he might just disappear: "How do you get something out from under an elephant? *Wait for the elephant to go away."* If not, then "How do you kill a blue elephant? *With a blue elephant gun."* Yet the essential problem remained: "What is the height of ambition? *A flea running up an elephant's leg with rape on its mind."* If America could not escape this fact of giantism, was it then doomed to lament, "What did the elephant say when he sat on a box of Girl Scout cookies? *That's the way the cookie crumbles."*[18]

Since humor often hides, or disguises, what do these joke patterns reveal about the postwar generation that had to grapple with the complicated changes of international place and social matrix in these decades? What is the connection between the rise of the nation as a superpower and the humor that focused on the youngest generation—the relationship of power to powerlessness?

The thrust of the humor suggests that there existed an undercurrent of deep anxiety about the giant's ability to wreak havoc with the world of the child—in other words, with itself. Aware that their fierce quest for status was undermining familial bonds, yet tuning out their responsibility for the breakup of relations, adults simply "joked" their way around it. In so doing, adults were essentially mocking themselves and using child-centered humor as a means of assuaging culpability. Thus the connection between the two joke cycles that emerged in the tumultuous decades of the 1950s and 1960s: the elephant acknowledged as a hurtful giant, the child as its potential victim.

Eventually the jokes became the property of children. But in initiating and sponsoring this humor, the older generation was intuitively groping for a way out of a dilemma: how to accept a lifestyle that centered so heavily on material accoutrement, that continually uprooted itself and disrupted the continuity of childhood, and that focused on "making it" in the workplace, to the detriment of the family place and the larger community as well. Subliminally understood was that the cost of attaining middle-class status was being paid at the expense of family stability, and that in attaining a desired existence they were in effect creating undesired consequences, namely, the fragmentation and alienation of intimate relations.

It is significant that the generation of the counterculture, separating itself from anyone "over thirty" and redefining American values and institutions, rejected the accent on materialism, lived with one another sans the sanctity of marriage vows, experimented with communal relationships, quested after spiritual values, plunged into the world of inner consciousness, and fought the elephant on the Vietnam War.

All this corroborated playwright Thornton Wilder's observation of the "silent generation" as possessing a mischievous mistrust about the direction of American society. A variation of a traditional nursery rhyme indicated their distaste for the socioeconomic changes that had so affected their well-being:

> Humpty Dumpty sat on a wall,
> Humpty Dumpty had a great fall.
> And all the King's horses and all the King's men
> Ate egg.[19]

6

Repression and Riposte

One of most steadfast canons in the pantheon of American beliefs has centered on political humor's place. It has long been argued that democracy is best sustained by a boundless, unimpeded, egalitarian humor. Malcolm Muggeridge, when editor of *Punch*, stated the proposition unequivocally: "Humor is an aspect of freedom, without which it cannot exist at all."[1] For this reason, humor is correctly assumed to be a characteristic defining societies: democratic states embrace critical humor; authoritarian ones forswear such openness.

This notion has understandably led to the conviction that the United States is one of those blessed societies in which power is subordinate to humor, not the other way around. While debate often turns on what society should be, few contest humor's relevance to being an American. In a survey undertaken by the federal government in the 1980s that queried individuals about qualities that best fit them personally, the only answer to receive a unanimously affirmative answer was to the question "Do you have a sense of humor?"[2]

The demise of political comedy in the post–World War II period came as a profound shock, occurring so quickly after the war pitting democracy against fascism. As if not wanting to believe that the impossible had occurred, many expressed bewilderment at the turn of events: "Why aren't the comedians puncturing the inflated false fronts of some of the preposterous politicians like they used to. . . . What has brought on the new silence?" plaintively inquired the trade journal of the entertainment industry, *Variety*, in the mid-1950s.

It was, of course, a feigned pose. *Variety* knew only too well who and what had produced the stillness. A frenzied response to the threat of Communist influence in the country, a peril woefully exaggerated and adroitly manipulated, had produced a fierce repression. Like others in the industry, the trade journal carefully avoided denouncing the instigators of the repression because the new version of the Red scare was playing too well across the country.

Essayists and humorists ruefully nailed obituaries of political humor's demise on the doors of popular culture. "Satire is *verboten* today," exclaimed Groucho Marx. "The restrictions—political, religious, and every other kind—have killed satire."[3] Humorist Corey Ford anguished that "something has happened to laughter in this country lately, and it's no laughing matter. Our output of comedy is disappearing, and so are the outputters. . . . Political satire is extinct, personal caricature is libel, parody is illegal, dialect jokes are strictly taboo. . . . We are afraid to laugh." Ford pointed to television comedian George Gobel's response to the charge of tastelessly making his wife the butt of jokes: "Because it's the only subject that's safe."[4]

Even Al Capp's popular comic strip *Li'l Abner* succumbed to the pressure. Despite his reputation for having stemmed the tide, Capp actually laid low, offering in defense a curious view of the satirist's role. "I really believe that it's the duty of the satirist to stay alive—to duck—until it's safe to come out and possible to be useful again." Explaining his position a decade later, Capp cited those "inconceivably terrible times. They got worse and worse, until eventually the only satire possible and permissible in this democracy of ours was broad, weak domestic comedy."[5]

Not all political humor was excised. While most of it went underground, thriving in various forms throughout the 1950s, there remained several outposts, especially Walt Kelly's comic strip *Pogo*, the editorial cartoonist Herblock, and outspoken pieces by humorist James Thurber. "A nation in which a Congressman can seriously ask: 'Do you think the artist is a special person?' is a nation living in cultural jeopardy," wrote a fearful Thurber. So apprehensive was Thurber that he questioned the depth and caliber of American humor itself:

> Americans pride themselves on being a nation of humorists, but I'm afraid that our sense of humor and comedy—certainly sense of humor—does not go very deep. America is the country of the gag, the hot foot, the pay-off, the belly laugh—and that kind of thing. But a basically imaginative humorous country could never have over-emphasized the way we have overemphasized "Americanism."[6]

Then, in 1958, came the publication of *The Realist*, a wildly irreverent magazine edited by the youthful Paul Krassner that broke
the shackles. Krassner, who had worked for *MAD* magazine and
edited Lenny Bruce's book *How to Talk Dirty and Influence People*,
welcomed "an open field mined with taboos waiting to be exploded. My vision was a magazine of 'free-thought criticism and
satire.'"[7] Although Krassner's assault occurred in the waning days
of the repression, *The Realist* became the "rogue uncle—if not the
father—" of media satire for the next several decades, including the
National Lampoon and *Spy*, the comic strip *Doonesbury*, and the television series *Laugh-In*.[8]

Political comedy's disappearance may have been the consequence
not only of political repression but of a cultural warp as well. In *The
Rise and Fall of American Humor* (1968), Jesse Bier argued that the powerful, if not unique, events of midcentury had truly tested humor's
capabilities. Enormous excesses and traumas had made their appearance on both the national and the international scene, and the
response was the "collapse of comic as well as tragic distance." Humans were overwhelmed, Bier maintained, and "if the world and the
nation lives [*sic*] in a succession of grim and farcical jokes, what is
humor to do? The worst result of all is the loss of the comic instinct."[9]
Susan Sontag's interpretation extended the scenario. "Ours is indeed
an age of extremity. For we live under continual threat of two equally
fearful, but seemingly opposed destinies: unremitting banality and inconceivable terror."[10]

Nonetheless, the contraction of political humor was mainly the
consequence of an anti-intellectualism spurred by the repression. Severely emasculated during the McCarthyite repression, public comedy barely spoke in a whisper. Humor in a democracy draws its
power from an intellectual underpinning, but the "atmosphere of fervent malice and humorless imbecility stirred up by [Senator Joseph]
McCarthy's barrage of accusations," wrote historian Richard Hofstadter, made even the most rudimentary comedy impossible.[11]

Two episodes in the late 1940s—the reaction to a modest film comedy
and the assault against the most influential film comedian of the first
half-century—signaled the repression. The film, *The Senator Was Indiscreet* (1947), coincided with the advent of the Cold War, a time when
the government and states were instituting loyalty oath programs and

self-anointed patriotic groups were demanding unwavering allegiance to "Americanism."

Written by playwright Charles MacArthur, directed by playwright George S. Kaufman, and starring popular actor William Powell, *The Senator Was Indiscreet* was a farcical treatment of the presidential nominating process. Mark Twain, Will Rogers, Al Capp, and Fred Allen were among others in the past who had lampooned Congress and politicians; some of their caricatures, like Capp's Senator Jack S. Phogbound ("good old Jack S.") and Allen's pompous Southern Senator Claghorn had become familiar to the public. Senator Melvin Ashton in *The Senator Was Indiscreet*, a holder of an honorary Ph.D. from the Edgar L. Eubanks College of Animal Husbandry and Modern Fertilizing Methods, was but another in a long line of such spoofing characters.

The movie's plot was altogether familiar, and the comedy's tone, while assaultive, was quite temperate. Motivated by the maxim that the presidency is within the grasp of any worthy American man, Senator Melvin Ashton embarks on a campaign for that coveted office. It is immediately apparent that our seeker of the presidency is high on charm, low on intellect, and cheerful in promoting issues crucial to the country, among them two hundred dollars a week in Social Security benefits, a Harvard education for everyone, and defending "against inflation, against deflation, but for flation." Highlighted is the senator's surprise at being criticized for his lack of ethical standards. He places his relatives on the payroll, and plaintively inquires about taxes, "How could I know that the income tax bill meant me, too?"

Without doubt the senator is a bumbler, but he is certainly no fool. An experienced and realistic politico, he lets it be known that in his possession is a little book, actually a diary maintained for over thirty years, containing more than a few "indiscretions" of party members. Just when it appears that dirty secrets will out, the diary is lost, and the senator's campaign fizzles out.

Time lauded the film's lighthearted humor, stating that "it is so rare to see any national institution really slapped around, on the screen, that the picture seems not only very funny but very audacious."[12] In the political climate of the period, "audacious" was a euphemism for "unpatriotic." Film critic Bosley Crowther noted in the *New York Times* that "Already we've heard the usual muttering that [the Senator] is 'Un-American.'" Crowther threw his support behind the film: "Unless the country lacks humor (which has been a moot question of late), it should get a great deal of amusement from *The Senator Was Indiscreet*."[13] Senator McCarthy called the movie "un-American and traitorous," and Claire Boothe Luce, wife of editor Henry Luce of *Time* and *Life* and a longtime friend of the producer and cowriter, exclaimed at a screening, "Was this picture made by an American?" The film was assailed by the American Legion and a unit of the Allied Theater Owners; a spokesman for the latter declared that "the picture will be recommended highly by *Pravda* and the party line." Appearing before the House Committee on Un-American Activities (HUAC), one of the organizers of the Motion Picture Alliance for the Preservation of American Ideals testified that "where you see a little drop of cyanide in a picture, a small grain of arsenic, something that makes every Senator, every businessman, every employer a crook . . . that is Communistic!" Subsequently the Motion Picture Association of America prohibited the film from being shown overseas in accordance with a 1945 State Department memorandum cautioning against offering materials "which create erroneous impressions about the United States."[14]

A few years later the film *Born Yesterday* (1950), derived from a 1946 Broadway play starring Judy Holliday and Broderick Crawford, was castigated by the Catholic War Veterans, who picketed and distributed leaflets indicting Holliday as "the darling of *The Daily Worker*."[15] Political film comedy had gone from being scarce to nonexistent.

Charlie Chaplin's *Limelight*, a 1952 film unrelated to political issues, also was singled out for suppression. The focus here, however, was Chaplin himself, who had never relinquished his British citizenship and whose film works had always rankled conservatives. In the early 1950s, the Attorney General James P. McGranery, the American Legion, and other patriotic groups accused Chaplin not only of being "un-American" but also of "consorting" with the Communist Party. McGranery depicted Chaplin as an "unsavory character" with "a leering, sneering attitude toward the country whose hospitality had enriched him."[16]

Limelight opened in several cities on the East Coast but was quickly withdrawn by the Fox West Coast theater chain in response to the threat of picketing by the American Legion. Joining in the opposition were other organizations, notably the Veterans of Foreign Wars and the Catholic War Veterans. These and other groups further pressured theater owners and television managers not to present Chaplin's classic silent films, several dating as far back as 1916–17.[17] When the attorney general refused to extend Chaplin's reentry permit—he was aboard the *Queen Elizabeth,* on the way to Europe—until he answered charges of a "political nature and of moral turpitude" before the Immigration Board of Inquiry, Chaplin resettled in Switzerland. He returned to the United States only once thereafter, to receive a special award at the Motion Picture Academy's Oscar ceremonies in 1972. By that time, fears that Chaplin and other comedians would subvert the country had become, to put it mildly, ludicrous.

Maligning and destroying political comedy and comedians was part of a much broader strategy directed at the entertainment industry. Influenced by *Red Channels* and similar publications, the industry dismissed thousands whose politics were in any way deemed "leftist." Throughout the country, American Legionnaires picketed films, major performers, writers, and directors whose names were listed in the vigilante publications, or had been circulated among Legion posts.[18]

Blocked from the public airwaves, political humor and social criticism moved underground. The "silent generation" preserved political humor by avidly consuming comic materials in magazines and on records, in particular embracing a new wave of stand-up comics and creating their own graffiti scenarios. Together with the older liberal and left groups, the new comics' banter was permeated with wit and ridicule, the very forms assumed to have been extinguished. Presidential candidate Adlai Stevenson's quip in 1952, "Eggheads of the world unite, you have nothing to lose but your yolks,"[19] became a comedic buoy in an ocean of vapidity. The dreaded Senator McCarthy was nicknamed "Low-Blow Joe."

The mimeograph machine and the long-playing record spread graffiti along the underground pathways. Located in labor union offices, colleges, and political offices, mimeographs cranked out flyers, essays, cartoons, jokes, and allegorical stories. At small Beat coffeehouses, gatherings, and parties across the country, mimeographed tracts were distributed among young, leftist, and alienated groups. Reinforcing them were compilations from a handful of writers and cartoonists, among them Al Capp's *Li'l Abner,* Walt Kelly's *Pogo,* and

Herblock. Later in the decade came Jules Feiffer, whose drawings in the *Village Voice* adroitly mirrored a swiftly changing cultural environment. Yet despite the public dissemination, Feiffer observed that "in a sense, we were members of an underground."[20] The publication of his book *Sick, Sick, Sick* marked the first time the term was applied in "an explicitly ironic sense."[21]

Capp, Kelly, and Feiffer plunged their characters into public issues, deriding conservative and right-wing politicians, businessmen, lawyers, doctors, military figures, and establishment figures. Capp presented Senator Jack S. Phogbound, and J. Roaringham Fatback, the latter a prototypical rich businessman who had the site of Li'l Abner's family, Dogpatch, moved because it cast a shadow across his breakfast egg. Kelly's critters of the Okefenokee Swamp beleagueredly maintained their stance against the reactionary onslaught: "Our most recent laughter," Kelly wrote in 1952, "has been somewhat nervous. We have been trying to keep an eye on all sides before we laugh, but the true humorist has found it well nigh impossible to laugh (and in such a state, how can we cause laughter?) while peering back over his shoulder."[22] Kelly created a fat-cat character, named Simple J. Malarkey, modeled after Senator McCarthy, and in one of the most oft-quoted comic strip lines, Pogo declared in the midst of the hunt for Communists that "We have met the enemy, and they is Us." Of the political cartoonists, Herblock (Herbert Block), who drew for the *Washington Post*, was the most luminous. His caricatures of McCarthy, Nixon, HUAC, military hawks, and the Bomb, underscored by pithy captions, were frequently reproduced and quoted, elevating him to towering status.

From the bottom of the entertainment world, moreover, a new generation of comics rose. Prevented from reaching the mass audience by cowed radio and television networks, the comedians performed in small, out-of-the-way coffeehouses and nightclubs. Spots like the Purple Onion and the hungry i in San Francisco, the Blue Angel in New York, Mr. Kelly's and the Gate of Horn in Chicago, the Crystal Palace in St. Louis, Crescendo and Interlude in Los Angeles, and Freddie's in Minneapolis were filled by the "silent" generation." In the following decade, the list of places would expand to include the Bitter End, Troubadour, and a host of others across the country.

White comics and improvisational groups introduced a scathing humor replete with social class and ethnic observations, much of the content deriving from folk sources. The African-American comedians Dick Gregory, Godfrey Cambridge, Nipsey Russell, Redd Foxx, and Moms Mabley joined them in the following decade.

Experimenting with innovative techniques, rejecting traditional boundaries, and employing unconventional language, the new wave of comics was instantly acclaimed by the baby boomers. The opening salvos were Lenny Bruce and Mort Sahl's leaps into satirical consciousness. Bruce was the catalyst who leaped the language barrier and pried open the vault containing society's taboos. "The Humorist as Grand Inquisitor," wrote journalist Nat Hentoff of Bruce because his routines posed a danger to "many of our most fundamental defenses and self-evasions." Hentoff pointed out that Bruce was exceptional even within the tiny group of new satirists: "As a whole, the topical satirists do not question the foundations of our society. They simply caricature surface oafishness and hypocrisy; they do not attempt to subvert. Therefore, of course, they do not get in trouble with the police."[23]

Prying into restricted areas led to a series of arrests and charges of obscenity and indecency against Bruce, who focused on organized religion, racial hypocrisy, cultural myths, and the law, and in the course of his discourses spotlighted stereotypes and words covertly expressed. He thought of himself as a neologist, one who either invents new words or discovers new meanings for existing ones. And as the words and phrases rapidly cascaded throughout the clubs, the astonished audiences were at first shocked, then released in open laughter, saving them from embarrassment but putting them on notice as well.

Bruce's expanded humor landscape included characters from the sanctity of popular culture. In "Thank you, Masked Man," a takeoff on the *Lone Ranger* radio program of the 1930s and 1940s, the New York City boy got his revenge on the Western cowboy. Reminding the audience that the Lone Ranger was the epitome of do-gooder individualism, "so good that he never waited for a thank you," Bruce assaulted the props of American values:

What's with that putz? The schmuck didn't wait! Momma made a cake and everything! I got my hand out like some jack-off—he's on his horse already! What an asshole! I'm standing there with the mayor and a plaque and everything. I'm gonna punch the shit outta him if I ever see him again![24]

Bruce was in the mode of the comedic shaman, one who uses laughter as a means of confronting taboos and hidden forces, providing a cultural cathartic while enlarging the grounds available for shared beliefs. Many performers in the later decades of the century, including George Carlin, Richard Pryor, David Steinberg, and David Frye, acknowledged his immense legacy. The fictional presence of Archie Bunker, the irascible bigot in producer Norman Lear's CBS television series *All in the Family* (1970s), who represented society's pejorative ethnic impulses, derived from Bruce's comedic excursions.

By century's close, the terms and subjects that had brought Bruce into social and legal conflict had become commonplace fare among the stand-up comics of both sexes. His autobiography, published a year before his death, was whimsically entitled *How to Talk Dirty and Influence People*, a double-edged biting thrust at his problems and at Dale Carnegie's best-selling homage to the power of salesmanship published in 1936, *How to Win Friends and Influence People*. It became an underground icon and was purloined from libraries across the country.

Sahl was Bruce's political counterpart. Like Bruce, he argued that comedy should derive from and appeal to the intellectual senses. "I am not denying that suppression exists," Sahl discerningly argued, "but the ultimate taboo is not against racial jokes or off-color jokes but against intellectual content."[25] Sahl literally leapfrogged into the fray in 1953 at the hungry i. Dressed in a V-necked sweater and open-collar shirt, nervously twisting a rolled-up newspaper, he was the American idealist who half-smilingly walks into the political lion's den and grabs the lion by the tail. By substituting an idea for an event or anecdote, "he was the first to take tremendous license in leaping about from one aspect of that idea to another, as he pleased, until its possibilities were exhausted."[26] Hence his effective put-down of Senator McCarthy—"Joe McCarthy doesn't question what you say so much as he questions your right to say it"—and the actions of the House Committee on Un-American Activities (HUAC): "Every time the Russians throw an American in jail, the HUAC retaliates—by throwing an American in jail."

Complementing these two figures was Tom Lehrer, whose biting messages were first disseminated through the new technology of the long-playing record. Lehrer was a mathematician who taught at several Boston-area universities, including Harvard. Before small, local crowds, he plunked out highly familiar tunes with ironically disturbing lyrics about many sensitive topics. In 1953, at his own expense and at the exhortation of a number of friends, he recorded a number of his songs on a ten-inch long-playing record and distributed them privately. Within a few years, as word spread along the underground grapevine about the satirical messages, he was besieged for copies. Without publicity, sales reached an astonishing four hundred thousand, and eventually a commercial company brought out a longer record with additional songs. In the 1970s Lehrer became one of the key writers and performers on the satirical television series *That Was the Week That Was.*

The decade's most unusual satirical record, however, was produced in Canada. It was, further, the only one that directly confronted Senator McCarthy prior to Edward R. Morrow's heralded CBS Television program that indicted the senator for his intimidating, repressive tactics. *The Investigator: A Political Satire in Documentary Form* (1954) featured an actor who cleverly mimicked McCarthy's raspy voice, his nervous laugh, and his bullying behavior as chairman of the Permanent Investigations Subcommittee of the Senate Committee on Government Operations. Circulated throughout the country, *The Investigator* took its place, alongside Lehrer's ten-inch chronicle, among the most striking political satires of the period. The story opens as the Investigator is killed in an airplane crash and finds himself transported to "Up Here." In order to become an official resident, he must present his credentials before the Head Gatekeeper and the Permanent Investigation Committee on Permanent Entry. The advisory members of the Permanent Committee are among history's most notorious reactionaries: Titus Oates, the English conspirator; Torquemada, the Spanish inquisitor; Cotton Mather, instrumental in the Salem witch trials; and Baron George Jeffreys, the hanging judge of the Bloody Assizes.

The members of the Permanent Committee are delighted with the latest arrival, especially impressed with his knowledge of modern techniques of inquiry and intimidation. Once ensconced as a member, the Investigator immediately launches a political inquiry "Up Here," questioning the loyalty of everyone and condemning the laxness of entry standards. Attacking the Gatekeeper as being too lenient, the Investigator forces his resignation and convinces the Permanent Committee to reopen the files of all previous entries. Recalled before the committee, now headed by the Investigator, are the apostles of freedom and liberty: Socrates, John Milton, John Stuart Mill, Martin Luther, Baruch Spinoza, Galileo Galilei, Percy Bysshe Shelley, Giuseppe Garibaldi, Abraham Lincoln, and Thomas Jefferson. Each is found guilty of subversion and immediately deported from "Up Here" to "Down There." All persons named Karl Marx are deported, and others are declared guilty by association. Among the latter are Bach, Beethoven, Wagner, and Chopin, who had formed a string quartet; all are sent "down" because Chopin, in his youth, composed the "Revolutionary Etude."

However, the Investigator's tenure comes to an abrupt halt. Growing more obsessed with power, he decides to investigate "The Chief." This step is too much even for the Permanent Committee, and they deport him "Down There." McCarthy's downfall began in similar fashion. Initially supported by the Republican congressional hierarchy, McCarthy overextended himself when he launched an investigation into Communist infiltration in the U.S. Army and held hearings on television that impugned "the Chief," the former five-star general of the army, President Dwight D. Eisenhower.

"Down There," the Devil is beside himself—he doesn't want the Investigator either. He complains that the deportees the Permanent Committee sent to him are making his life miserable because of their constant demands for freedom. It becomes clear that no one wants the Investigator. An applicant who is wanted neither "Up Here" or "Down There" is returned to the point of entry. Accordingly, the Investigator is returned to Earth, where he is found alive but raving about being "Up Here." A medical diagnosis discloses a permanent inability to deal with reality. Intriguingly, one year after the record was released, McCarthy was censured by the Senate, and he died several years thereafter.[27]

With the lessening of domestic and international tensions, the success of the small nightclubs and coffeehouses, sales of records, and television's constant need for new faces and material, the situation gradually eased. Newer fare avoided political themes, but productions such as *I Love Lucy* set standards that would catapult women comics, including Carol Burnett and others, beyond stereotypical boundaries; and the innovative *Your Show of Shows* and *Caesar's Hour* provided a new generation of writers, including Carl Reiner, Mel Brooks, Larry Gelbart, Lucille Kallen, Selma Diamond, Mel Tolkin, and Woody Allen, who widened the areas of comedy by introducing new types and combinations.

By the end of the 1950s, the queasiness involving untouchable subjects dissipated, and with the winding down of anxieties, the media became animated with political commentary. Yet what was taken at the time as a revival of political comedy was for the most part an airing of the underground's comedic scenarios developed throughout the decade.

On Broadway, a political musical opened in 1959 that a decade earlier would have been charged with being "un-American." *Fiorello!* centered on the most colorful mayor in New York City's history, Fiorello La Guardia, and on polarized political energies: idealism and corruption. A satire on the Jimmy Walker administration that had preceded La Guardia's was a musical byplay in "Little Tin Box," performed by a judge and indicted officials of Tammany Hall.

The end of the 1950s was in marked contrast to its beginnings. Sales of record albums by the new stand-up comics clearly denoted an open environment. *Inside Shelley Berman* (1958) was a best-selling record and headed the list in 1960. Among the 150 best-selling monaural records in 1961 were over a dozen comedy albums, half of them in the Top 40; they included the routines of Elaine May and Mike Nichols, Jonathan Winters, Dick Gregory, and Bob Newhart.[28] Even television unblocked its cameras to these "unknowns"—but not to Lenny Bruce. Several years later, Mort Sahl joshed of "selling out" as he stood at an Academy Awards ceremony dressed not in his usual sweater and slacks but in a tuxedo.

No longer fearful of reprisal, colleges and universities invited humorists and stand-ups with minimal interference from administrations and trustees. On the podium at the University of Southern California, an institution he attended on the G.I. Bill for several years after the war, was the young columnist Art Buchwald. He delivered a wry, liberal speech to an overwhelmingly responsive turnout. The vice president for academic affairs, a historian who had been on the faculty for several decades, found the talk "most enjoyable" but objected to Buchwald's occasional use of four-letter words: "It was uncalled for and had I known in advance I would have asked him to monitor the speech."[29]

Although the repression lingered on—HUAC continued its hearings although the committee was defiantly confronted in San Francisco, the blacklist remained in force, and Bruce was repeatedly hounded by local police—nonetheless the political climate had dramatically changed and the way was paved for a most unusual chapter in American social humor. The members of the counterculture of the 1960s and early 1970s would offer a fervent comedic challenge to the society that had raised them.

7

Guerrilla Satirists

His wry retort was typical of the man, and on target for the times. The Cold War was raging and the national debate in the postwar decades was on surviving a thermonuclear attack from the USSR. In 1961, Willard Libby, a former Atomic Energy Commission member, constructed a "poor man's shelter" in his backyard. Built with sandbags and railway ties for the paltry sum of $30, it exemplified Libby's intent not merely to show how a simple, inexpensive measure could preserve lives but also to assuage a frightened nation. Not long thereafter, though, a brushfire swiftly incinerated Libby's shelter, fortunately empty at the time. Nuclear scientist Leo Szilard, who was instrumental in developing the atomic bomb and a leading disarmament figure, caustically intoned: "This proves not only that there is a God but that he has a sense of humor."[1]

The 1960s opened with the expectation of violent death as a central presence in the world. Years prior to the Cuban missile crisis in 1962, there was the dreaded consciousness of devastation realized through a weapon laconically referred to as the "Bomb." The confrontation over Cuba that brought the two superpowers to the nuclear edge further confirmed the possibility of planetary disaster. The theme of violent death, moreover, would be confirmed over and over again throughout the decade by the assassinations of John F. Kennedy, Malcolm X, Medgar Evers, Martin Luther King, Jr., Robert Kennedy, and many civil rights workers, particularly Michael Schwerner, Andrew Goodman, and James Chaney.

The Bomb supplanted all other issues in the post–World War II years. In *By the Bomb's Early Light*, Paul Boyer delineated how the theme engulfed the country until the Cuban missile crisis slightly dif-

fused it. Only after the confrontation had ended in standoff and nego-
tiation was there a sharp dropoff in national attention to the awesome
weapon.[2]

Among the Bomb's unique features was its egalitarianism: its
devastating force effectively rendered meaningless any distinction between citizen and warrior, ruler and people, haves and have-nots,
white and colored, physicist and layman. No one was immune, save
the political and military elite who had possibly ensured survival of a
sort by constructing massive underground bunkers and using other
techniques.

The generation of the 1950s emerged in the wake of the Bomb.
"The bastards right now are only interested in seeing if they can blow
up the world," exclaimed a character in Jack Kerouac's *On the Road*
(1957).[3] "Is it possible that it is all going to be over?" physicist Richard
Feynman asked a group of students and faculty at the Massachusetts
Institute of Technology centennial a year prior to the Cuban episode.
"One of the most likely things, from a political and social point of
view, is that we have soon a terrific war and a collapse. What will
happen to physics after such a collapse? . . . Can physics slide back
temporarily and then recover? I don't think so."[4]

A graffito on college walls and elsewhere reflected the dread:

> A is for Atom
> B is for Bomb
> C is the world now
> Before it is gone.[5]

Disarming the terror was critical, and it was done partly through
trivializing. A fast-food stand in Salt Lake City placed on its menu a
"tasty uranium burger" and a "uranium sundae"; in *The Honeymoon-
ers*, a popular television sitcom starring Jackie Gleason, a boyfriend's
ardor was termed "atomic passion"; the Chamber of Commerce in
Las Vegas crowned a "Miss Atomic Blast" to coincide with the development of "cleaner bomb testing"; and in Tennessee, the opening of a
golf course included a blindfolded caddie with a Geiger counter who
located golf balls injected with cobalt-60 pellets by nearby Oak Ridge
scientists.[6]

Regardless of its potency, the Bomb was not the only factor in the
equation of mortality and technology. There was also the unraveling

reality of the Holocaust, the extermination of millions of Jews, Gypsies, political dissidents, and others because of presumed racial, religious, or ideological differences. Not unexpectedly, this monumental atrocity combined with possible annihilation to severely jolt the notion of an expansive postwar future. As Robert L. Heilbroner observed in *The Future as History,* the developing, terrifying technology presented the country with "an unprecedented need to revise its outlook for the future. With brutal abruptness the new war technology has knocked out the keystone of our optimistic philosophy by forcing us to confront the possibility of national extinction, an eventuality which has never before even remotely entered our calculations. As no other development of our age, the nuclear threat has torn down the barriers which have held 'history' at a remove from the American consciousness."[7]

Perched on the edge of cataclysm, people reached for humor as a direct means of mitigating the Bomb's sheer horror. Lenny Bruce was one of the earliest comics, but by no means the only one, to confront the issue. Excoriating the paucity of thinking regarding national policy, Bruce sarcastically jived, "The Bomb, the bomb—oh, thank God for the bomb. The final threat is: 'I'll get my brother—the bomb.' Out of all the teaching and bullshitting, that's the only answer we have."[8] Even the American military got into the gallows act by designating its thermonuclear policy MAD, an acronym for *m*utually *a*ssured *de*struction, one that played well for *MAD* magazine's readers.

The Bomb's liveliest dissection came in an American film of 1964, Stanley Kubrick's *Dr. Strangelove or; How I Learned to Stop Worrying and Love the Bomb.* Kubrick's deciphering of the Strategic Air Command's top-secret fail-safe strategy was dazzling in itself, but his scenario of the world on the brink of destruction was chilling satire. Kubrick and the film's writers had a wickedly wonderful time naming the characters deciding the world's fate: American officers (General "Buck" Turgidson, Colonel Bat Guano, Air Force Commander Jack D. Ripper), the Russian premier (Kissoff), and the German rocket scientist (Dr. Strangelove). And the film's concluding scenes with the Air Force commander straddling a 10-megaton H-bomb hurtling toward a Russian target, cowboy hat in hand, and the political and military survivors of the Doomsday weapon arguing about a "mineshaft gap" on a devastated planet, were virtuoso gallows humor. No other film, and no novel save Joseph Heller's *Catch-22* (1961), which dealt with individual survival, so satirically plumbed the possibility of extinction through technology.

The threat of annihilation unleashed an awareness of vulnerability through technology. Virtually all the verities of existence came under comic scrutiny once the possibility of death was publicly acknowledged. The literary response to this type of vulnerability was "black humor," a phrase initially employed by Bruce Jay Friedman in a 1965 collection excerpted from the novels, short stories, and plays of J. P. Donleavy, John Barth, Terry Southern, Joseph Heller, Kurt Vonnegut, Walker Percy, Thomas Pynchon, James Purdy, Donald Barthelme, and John Hawkes, which described the contemporary scene in ways previously considered grotesque.

Asserting that fiction employing black humor had its roots in the "chord of absurdity," Friedman questioned whether the continuing existence of boundaries separating the journalist's role from the novelist's any longer made any sense. "What has occurred is that the satirist has had his ground usurped by the newspaper reporter. The journalist, who in the year 1964 must cover the ecumenical debate of whether Jews, on the one hand, are still to be known as Christ-killers, or, on the other, are to be let off the hook, is certainly today's satirist. The novelist-satirist, with no real territory of his own to roam, has had to discover new land, invent a new currency, a new set of filters, has had to sail into darker waters somewhere beyond satire and I think this is what is meant by black humor."[9]

Within the body of works utilizing dark humor were characters who, in grappling with death and the moral ambiguities of modern living, largely veered toward death rather than life, pessimism rather than hope.[10] The laughter that arose from their entangled situations did not necessarily scare off death; rather, it created an environment in which death and social reconciliation could be resisted. In part this was because the humor was pitched "at the breaking point where moral anguish explodes into a mixture of comedy and terror, where things are so bad you might well laugh."[11]

Others offered bleaker causes for black humor's sudden emergence. Events too overwhelming to unravel or cope with led, in critic Michael Wharton's estimation, to "a world which is already Beyond a Joke."[12] A leading critic concurred: "Like Shakespeare's dark comedy,

Black Humor condemns man to a dying world; it never envisions, as do Shakespeare's early and late comedies, the possibilities of human escape from an aberrant environment into a forest milieu, as a ritual of triumph of the green world over the waste land."[13]

In people's humor, death and maiming were leading motifs in the "sick" or "cruel" joke cycle. By the early 1960s these themes in fact had a central place in several stand-up routines. Performing at the hungri i shortly after a plane crash had occurred in the San Francisco Bay area, Don Adams, a hitherto conventional comic, peered over his audience and suddenly began pointing. "Sitting over there, I see Mr. G. A. Thompson, who lost his wife and two children in the crash today. Let's give him a great big hand! Stand up and take a bow, Mr. Thompson. Thank you! Don't hog it!"[14]

The new comedic iconoclasm with its emphasis on dislocation and destruction produced an instant outcry. "Hardly a Laughing Matter," opined *Time* in a special essay in the mid-1960s: "The proliferation of comedy into every corner of American life, the spreading hipness and general joking seem to indicate one of the richest times for comedy in American history. But do they?" Answering its own question, *Time* disparaged the scene: "A closer examination of current comedy reveals neither a renaissance nor a reformation but the beginnings of what could, unless it is reversed, become the dark ages of American humor."[15]

More than a few literary critics lamented the new harshness. One scholar raised the question of whether, revolving as it did around "disillusion, pessimism, nihilism," such writing could be termed "humor at all."[16] Another asserted that black humor was a technique, not a form, that "engenders in the audience a therapeutic rather than cathartic effect . . . the black humorist does not seek sympathy or alliance of his audience but deliberately insults and alienates it."[17]

His book's title, *The Rise and Fall of American Humor,* was Jesse Bier's estimation. "We are in great part humorless as never before" because the vulnerabilities and excesses of the age had initiated a form that might more properly be termed "counterfeit humor, closer to annihilatory diatribe and invective than to deflationary comedy." Black and sick humor were but parts of the same phenomenon; one was "an expression of dark rage at miserable conditions or values and the other is a perverse enjoyment of the same." Bier saw the ant joke cited in Max Eastman's *Enjoyment of Laughter* (1936) as the model for black humor: "The tale is of a convict who has trained an ant over twenty years to do tricks. After release from prison, he takes him in a match box to a bar, has a drink, releases the ant and calls to the bartender, 'Hey, see this ant. . . .?' 'Oh, that,' the bartender says, squashing the ant at once, 'sorry.'"[18]

The flaw in these arguments is that humor either expands to meet changing circumstances or suffers loss of relevance and communal purpose. Unexpected social and technological transformations at this particular point in time had prompted innovations in people's humor, alterations that simultaneously reflected conditions and resisted negative impulse. By concentrating too intently on Thanatos, the critics were oblivious to black humor's impact on at least one particular segment of the population. Anticipating the generational explosion, Beat poet Kenneth Rexroth in the mid-1950s had lashed out at adults for failing to heed their children's alienation. "Listen you," he admonished, "do you *really* think your kids act like bobby soxers in those wholesome Coca Cola ads? Don't you know that across the table from you at dinner sits somebody who looks on you as an enemy. . . . If you don't, you're headed for a terrible awakening."[19]

The accent on dislocation and death did not lead to ennui within the 1960s generation. On the contrary, the historic moment captured their imagination, spurring them on with a sense of urgency and calling for reprioritizing values and reconstituting institutions. Like those coming-of-age generations across the centuries, the emerging youths were buoyed by energy, conviction, and ideology, and impelled by the imminent possibility of thermonuclear destruction.

"Our work is guided by the sense that we may be the last generation in the experiment with living," wrote the organizers of the Students for a Democratic Society in *The Port Huron Statement* (1962), the most significant political document of the age. Seeking to reverse the course of American history, the framers focused on the relationship between political and social values: "A first task of any social movement is to convince people that the search for orienting theories and the creation of human values is [sic] complex but worthwhile. We are aware that to avoid platitudes we must analyze the concrete conditions of social order. But to direct such an analysis we must use the guideposts of basic principles. Our own social values involve conceptions of human beings, human relationships, and social systems."[20]

In *The Making of a Counter Culture*, Theodore Roszak argued that

the ensuing scene was undergirded by an imaginative, ecstatic rollick-
ing rarely found in American protest or radical movements. Throwing down the cultural gauntlet, the counterculture assaulted the
components of bourgeois society: its accent on materialism and banal
consumerism, its Darwinian emphasis on competition and violence,
its Victorian strictures on sexual attitudes and practices, and its constriction of spiritual embrace. Especially the hip radicals mocked tra-
dition and authority. Many with bearded faces and shoulder-length
hair, dressed in outlaw clothes, dancing to music and lyrics of their
own creation, frolicked in love-ins, be-ins, and flower-ins, experimented with drugs, invented new communal forms, lived together
without marriage, and plumbed the levels of consciousness in a
search for new visions. The rallying expressions and slogans of the
counterculture offered a spontaneous tone of whimsical immediacy:
"Tune in, turn on, drop out"; "Let's get it together"; "Move on or
move over"; "If you're not part of the solution, you're part of the
problem"; "Be yourself"; "Do your own thing"; "Love everyone";
"All power to the people"; "Right on"; and "NOW." These were artic-
ulations of the powerless declared unambiguously.

Intent on designing a "participatory democracy," and encouraged
by an underground consciousness, the counterculture sought a comedic approach to communicate their ideas and rebellion. They found it
in guerrilla satire, a form historically rooted, but seldom employed in
any major way, in American culture. Its outlets were oral and graphic
graffiti, the underground papers, a new form called "comix," and Yippie street theater. Graffiti was the counterculture's most spontaneous
idiom. Thousands of anonymous commentaries and judgments surfaced across the country, a veritable tableau of people's scribbling on
walls, flyers, placards that were repeated and recounted throughout
the movements. It was, moreover, a perfect fit to the mold of protest.
The joke of choice with riveting one-liners and witty rhyming coup-
lets, graffiti galvanized social consciousness through hit-and-write
tactics and offered to one and all participation in the comedic thrust.

So extensive were the writings that in a men's bathroom at the
University of California, Irvine, in 1968, someone scribbled across the
top of a stall covered with graffiti: "This wall will appear . . . in paper-
back in the fall."[21] In 1970 the city of Boston succumbed to the graffiti
artists by placing four large, blank walls at the edge of the historic
Boston Common on which people could scrawl, draw, or leave mes-

sages. The anonymous messages were reported in diverse publications, among them *Saturday Review of Literature, Time, Newsweek,* and *Harper's.* "Usually graffiti has ranked one rung below limericks on the literary scale," wrote *Newsweek,* "but lately the message sages have gained a new respectability."[22] The idiom was subsequently analyzed by major writers, dissected in papers at an American Psychiatric Association convention, and disseminated commercially in paperbacks and on bumper stickers. Playwright Edward Albee indicated that an inscription in a Greenwich Village lavatory first suggested the title of his *Who's Afraid of Virginia Woolf?* A gourmet sampling of graffiti thus became the most unusual comic offering in the history of American humor. Although graffiti usually were hard-core sexual or scatological, the counterculturists' graffiti were far removed from this type; they passed judgment on wide-ranging critical issues while jocularly lambasting bourgeois values.

As was to be expected, trepidation about the possibility of thermonuclear war was an early focus, eventually fusing with the anti-Vietnam protest. "Ban the bomb," went a caustic, challenging declaration, "save the world for conventional warfare." A pronouncement about life after World War III: "Knock-knock. Who's there? *[Silence].*" Radiation was mocked in an old tavern drinking toast: "Eat, drink and be merry, for tomorrow you may be radioactive." And a refashioned nursery rhyme:

> Ring around a neutron
> A pocket full of protons
> A fission, a fusion
> We all fall down.

Perhaps the most sardonic line that brought the point across: "In the event of nuclear war, will the last person to die please turn off the lights?"[23]

Antagonism toward the superstate was high on the counterculture's agenda. "I am an enemy of the state" went one line on a wall on the Lower East Side of New York City; appended underneath was an even harsher sentiment, "I am an enema of the state." Comments derided its ineptitude and corruption. "Flush twice," was the opening expression on a UCLA bathroom wall, "Washington is a long way from here." On government efficiency: "Eliminate government waste no matter what it costs." An anecdote involving payoffs by the CIA and American corporations to Latin American governments with anticommunist policies:

> In 1963, a contingent from the State Department journeyed to South America for a conference of the Organization of American States, where the U.S. hoped to achieve unanimity among the member nations for a condemnation of the government of Cuba. When the Americans returned to Washington, one junketeer submitted a supplementary expense account:
>
> | taxicabs | $14.30 |
> | lunch with Guatemalan delegation | $600,000,000[24] |

The most frequently targeted politicians were conservatives and spokesmen of the radical right. "J. Edgar Hoover sleeps with a nightlight"; "Ronald Reagan eats peanut butter"; "Reagan for the *Late, Late Show*." Derided were Senator Barry Goldwater's ideas expressed in the 1964 presidential election: "Goldwater, he'd rather be far right than president"; "Goldwater in '64, hot water in '65, bread and water in '66." His campaign theme "In your heart you know he's right" became "In your heart you know he's *far* right" and "In your guts you know he's nuts." To Goldwater's "I'd like to lob an A-bomb into the men's room at the Kremlin," college students replied with a reworked title of Kubrick's film: "Dr. Strangelove, or How He Became a Conservative and Learned to Love the Bomb."

Richard Nixon's politically cynical and unethical tactics and dour demeanor brought him a special place in the guerrilla campaign. A slogan in the 1968 presidential election linking him with used-car salesmen became a counterculture favorite: "Would you buy a used car from this man?" The issue of distrust appeared in a subway stop in New York City: "Nixon is XYY." His awkwardness generated considerable sexual byplay. A rhetorical question in a men's toilet at Rutgers University, Newark, was posed by many: "How can anyone hate a president with a name like Dick?" In a women's lavatory at Bernard Baruch College, New York, but found in many places: "Lick Dick." "Can You Imagine?" became a parlor game at gatherings: "Can *anyone* imagine Dick making love to Pat?" which led to "Pat Nixon, the only virgin in the White House."

Nixon's selection of Spiro Agnew, governor of Maryland, as his running mate spawned a variety of acerbic responses. "Dick and Spiro add up to zero." One version spanned several administrations: "Nixon is the first president to have an asshole for a vice president," to which was added, "No, Eisenhower was." Agnew's conservative posture, and his snide and alliterative phrases attacking the protesters—"effete snobs," "radiclibs," "troglodyte leftists," and "nattering nabobs of negativism"—produced a plethora of pique. Students at the University of Michigan countered with "Spiro Agnew has hoof-in-mouth disease." Scrawled in the New York subway and other locations around the country: "A pox Agnew," "Mickey Mouse is wearing a Spiro Agnew watch," "No news Agnews," and a lengthy poem at the University of Maryland:

> Gag a goat.
> Frig a pig.
> Spear a steer.
> Ball a wall.
> Bang an orangutan.
> Assault a Renault.
> Rape an ape.
> Intercourse a horse . . . of course.
> Jog a dog.
> Plug a bug.
> Bump a stump.
> Tool a mule.
> Shaft a giraffe.
> Screw Agnew.[25]

Although many graffiti focused on conservatives, opposition to the Vietnam War and President Lyndon Johnson's policies was equally fierce. Anger over the war—in effect, the elephant run amok—was revealed in the frequency and sardonic nature of the comments:

Commit LBJ, not the U.S.A.

Bombing can end the war—bomb the Pentagon.

Escalate minds, not war.

End the boys in Vietnam, Bring the war home.

War is good business—Invest your sons.

Support peace or I'll kill you.[26]

Apart from political issues, a major portion of the graffiti centered on social mores and practices. Issues of sexual activity, gender roles, drugs, psychotherapy, education, and a smattering of related concerns filled the walls. Challenging the older generation was particularly relished: "The whole world is going to pot." Several gibed at bourgeois culture: "Mary Poppins is a junkie" and "Psychedelize suburbia." And a variety of observations were intended to contrast lifestyles: "With booze you lose, with dope you hope." Hence the positive side of drugs was forcefully asserted: "Grass is nature's way of saying 'high'"; "Acid indigestion can be fun"; "Acid—takes the worrying out of being"; "Be placid with acid"; "LSD = Love-Sex-Dreams"; "Take LSD and see." There was a cynical wryness about the carcinogenic environment wrought by the older generation: "Cancer cures smoking"; "Cigarette coupons pay for cancer operations"; and, on a subway placard that advertised cigarettes, "Smoke-Choke-Croak."[27] But the protesters were not above spoofing themselves: "LSD is fattening" and, on a lawn sign at the University of California, Berkeley, campus, "Please Don't Smoke the Grass."

The celebration of openness especially extended to sexual liberation. Here women's support of the new openness was pivotal. On the loss of virginity: "Vote yea on propositions"; "Virtue can hurt you"; "Never be led astray onto the path of virtue"; "Boys marry virgins; men marry women." A play on metaphors appeared in a Boston subway car: "Virginity is like a balloon—One prick and it's gone." Many graffiti belittled abstinence: "Chaste makes waste"; "Chastity is its own punishment"; "Be creative, invent a sexual perversion"; "Think dirty."

Liberation from the fear of pregnancy was acclaimed in the popular declaration "Have pill, will." To the criticism "Girls who use men sexually for power are really abusing themselves," someone countered, "Groovy abuse." Proclaimed as well was the open expression of sexual desire: "Hooray, hooray / It's the first of May / Outdoor fucking starts today" and "Candy is dandy but sex won't rot your teeth." Some women indicated that indiscriminate sex had become the norm in their lives: "Before Freud sex was a pleasure; now it's a necessity" and "Help me! I'm a sex junkie."[28]

Yet not all change was warmly greeted. Fears of venereal disease and pregnancy continued. "Carry me back to old virginity," wrote one college student. In the ladies' room in a New York City restaurant someone penned, "Please don't let me be pregnant." Many of these apprehensions, however, were allayed by comic responses. To the charge that "Sex is beautiful but unsanitary," someone replied, "So wash." Known practices rarely publicized were offered: "I want to seduce my history teacher," wrote a female at Hunter College, to which someone added, "I did, and got an F."

Criticisms of male behavior abounded. On the narrowness of men: "The thing most men learn too late—sex is of interest to both sexes" and "Men, once they possess women, either throw them away or use them until they are no good to anyone." On fulfilling male demands: "Think about him, talk about him, but don't go down for him." On women's psychological needs: "Men are like bathtubs—as soon as you get used to them, they're not so hot." More than a few graffiti became movement rallying trumpets:

When God made man, she was only joking.

Eve was framed.

Adam was a rough draft.

A woman without a man is like a fish without a bicycle.[29]

At times, the graffiti encompassed larger issues. A late 1970s flyer, "Double-Crossed by the Double Standard," dealt with gender inequities in the business world:

A businessman is aggressive; a businesswoman is pushy.

A well-dressed businessman is fashionable; a well-dressed businesswoman is a clotheshorse.

He loses his temper because he's so involved with his job; she's bitchy.

He gets depressed from work pressures; she has premenstrual tension.

He's a man of the world; she's been around.

He's confident; she's conceited.

He drinks because of excessive work pressure; she's a lush.

He's a stern taskmaster; she's impossible to work with.

He's enthusiastic; she's emotional.[30]

Closely allied to sexual and gender matters was the mind–body connection, a relationship partly spurred by the rise of growth therapies in the 1950s and 1960s. The expanded psychological field that included Gestalt, psychosynthesis, EST, primal scream, Rolfing, bioenergetics, yoga, and transcendental meditation reflected the acceptance of therapy as a guide to personal salvation. Contained within the movement was an accent on deliverance from one's psychological problems: "Alienation can be fun"; "Make your psychosis work for you"; "Masochists: you're only hurting yourselves"; and a jaunty four-line couplet:

> Neurosis is red.
> Melancholia is blue.
> I'm schizophrenic.
> What are you?[31]

A gnawing concern centered on the establishment's plotting to do the counterculture in, an apprehension borne out with the disclosure of massive unconstitutional activities conducted by state and national law enforcement agencies. Sly double entendres eased the anxiety: "Help! The paranoids are after me"; "Even paranoids have real enemies"; and the oft-repeated "Just because you're paranoid doesn't mean they're not after you." One caustic comment directly assailed the bureaucracy: "I am a masochist; please spindle, fold, or mutilate."

It was to be expected that the 1960s protesters, galvanized by mind-expanding drugs and imbued with plumbing the depths of inner consciousness, would grapple with the meaning of existence. Preceding them in this pilgrimage were the Beats, who laid the foundation with drugs and cosmic questions during the conformist 1950s. Kerouac's *On the Road* captured the nub of their quest in the single image of the road, the metaphoric American highway that runs toward new possibilities. The Beats were always on the move, seeking "It" but never quite attaining that mythic place. The hip radicals, by contrast, made the internal road their common denominator, a yellow brick road that would reunite all at its end.[32]

Those involved in spiritual and mystical matters grappled with society's most sacred canon, the existence and meaning of God. The public debate of the period manifested the intense quest for meaning in a time of vast social transformation. At its height the polemic produced intellectual and religious debates, an obituary for God in the *New York Times*, a *Time* cover story entitled "Is God Dead?" and, at the 1979 international conference of scientists and theologians in Cambridge, a scribbled note on the announcement board: "Please invite me to your conference. I want so much to help you. God."[33] So prevalent were the discussions that William F. Buckley, Jr., editor of the *National Review* whose book *God and Man at Yale* (1951) had brought him instant prominence, sarcastically observed that any person who mentioned God more than once at a New York dinner party was not invited again.[34]

The very phrase "God is dead" piqued whimsical repartee. "God is not dead!" was countered by "He is alive and autographing Bibles today at Brentano's"; "He just couldn't find a parking space"; and "He is just trying to avoid the draft." Many rejoined with "God is alive—everybody else is dead." Some responses were highly personal: "My God is alive, sorry about yours." One script was a byplay of authors: to the declaration "God is *dead*. Nietzsche" came the response "Nietzsche is dead. *God*."

But if God was alive, why was He not involved in matters crucial? One graffito quipped that "God nibbles," to which someone else shruggingly noted, "One does what one can." Yet many other graffiti were harsh indictments of God's aloofness: "God isn't dead—he just doesn't want to become involved"; "God is not dead, he is just very, very sick"; "Walt Disney turned me against God and made me believe in Mickey Mouse"; "God is omnivorous, he loves chitlins, bagels, pizza, even enchiladas," to which someone posed, "Napalm, too?" And on occasion, God's son was invoked: "Call on Jesus" read a sign on which another appended, "If no one answers, leave a message at the candy store."

Yet if God was truly dead, there was still room for hope in the world's most optimistic society. In the men's room of the central

Cleveland police station came the faithful pronouncement: "God is dead, but don't worry, the Virgin Mary is pregnant again."[35]

Guerrilla graffiti combined with another counterculture stratagem, improvisational street theater. The possibility of political and cultural change originating in the streets arose in the minds and actions of the Youth International Party, "Yippies," of whom Jerry Rubin and Abbie Hoffman were the high practitioners. Stephen Whitfield discerningly observed that for Hoffman, "show business was not the antithesis of leftism but something that could *change* and radicalize politics."[36]

Rubin and Hoffman held no reverence for traditional protest methods. "There is no program," announced Abbie Hoffman grandly in *Revolution for the Hell of It* (1968). "Program would make our movement sterile." Rubin and Hoffman envisioned street theater as realizing the essence of democracy. "Yippies are a participatory movement," wrote Hoffman. "There are no ideological requirements to be a yippie. Write your own slogan. Protest your own issue. Each man his own yippie."

Thus the reconstruction of America could be achieved through the transformative power of people's theater. Rubin put it epigrammatically: "Revolution is Theatre-in-the-Streets."[37] Confronting America in the streets would be the first order of the day. "Yippies believe in the violation of every law, including the law of gravity," exclaimed Hoffman. Why the streets? Because, he argued, "the Street has always been an intriguing symbol in middle-class American life. It was always the place to avoid. . . . It was always 'let's keep the kids off the streets' as honkie America rushed from inside to inside. It is in the streets that we will make our struggle. The streets belong to the people!"[38]

With cunning awareness of the media's thirst for offbeat stories, Rubin and Hoffman embarked on a campaign of guerrilla satire that took them into the heart of the enemy, to their symbolic streets. Rubin proposed "to use the media and guerrilla theatre humor, fun and rage to expose Amerikan injustice to young people."[39] In 1967 the gleeful pair showed up at the New York Stock Exchange. From the visitors' gallery—guards who initially denied them entrance on the grounds of their being "hippies" relented when Hoffman explained it was not "a good idea to keep a Jew out of the Stock Exchange"—they scattered dollar bills in the air, sending the brokers on a madcap chase of the swirling money.[40]

A year later they were both subpoenaed by the House Committee on Un-American Activities (HUAC), then investigating the Vietnam Day Committee. Hoffman was handed the legal papers before Rubin, an act that provoked in the latter "that old sexual anxiety again. Subpoena envy." When HUAC agents caught up with him, Rubin hooted: "It was the biggest, most beautiful subpoena in the world!"

"We are hippie guerrillas," Rubin announced as the episode was unfolding in the press, and the pair proceeded to the House Office Building. Rubin was attired in a Black Panther beret with Panther and Yippie buttons, Egyptian earrings, a Mexican bandolier with live .303 British Enfield bullets, a toy M-16 rifle, black silk Viet Cong pajamas, jangling ankle bracelets, beads, and a headband; psychedelic designs and peace symbols adorned his face, chest, and bare feet. He was promptly denied entrance and dragged down three flights of stairs until he relinquished the live bullets. Hoffman wore a red, white, and blue shirt. He never made it inside the building and was arrested for desecrating the American flag. Before an infuriated judge who assailed him for the "Viet Cong flag" painted on his back, made visible when the police ripped off his shirt, Hoffman impishly explained that the flag was "Cuban, your honor." On another occasion they went to the Justice Department, where they pounded on the doors with boxing gloves, challenging Attorney General John A. Mitchell to come out and fight fair.[41]

In 1968, the Yippies focused on the Democratic National Convention in Chicago—the "Theater of Chicago," in Hoffman's words. Unaccustomed to guerrilla humor, Chicago and Democratic Party officials were thoroughly intimidated by the Yippies' puckish threats to place LSD into the city's water supply and to kidnap delegates—Yippies dressed in Viet Cong outfits would take them, in camouflaged taxis, to Wisconsin. The Yippies mocked the convention by nominating "Pigasus," a pig, for president. "It was the perfect symbol," said Hoffman, "Everything is Pig . . . [Daley, cops, authority]."[42]

These impromptu activities—a type of free-associational play that found its place, in one form or another, on many communes—derived from different comedic sources. Hoffman, as Whitfield noted, was probably the first American radical heavily influenced by a comedian, specifically Lenny Bruce, to whom his *Woodstock Nation*

(1969) was dedicated, and for whom "show business was not marginal to society but was its microcosm."[43]

Improvisational comedy also had a defining influence. Its roots—ironically in light of the 1968 Chicago antics—dated to Chicago's Hull House of the 1930s, where tough teenagers were enticed into acting by a method of spontaneity. It was developed by Viola Spolin and enlarged by her son Paul Silas, who observed that "True improvisation is a dialogue between people."[44] In 1956 he founded the Compass Players, whose alumni include Mike Nichols, Elaine May, and Shelley Berman.

Improv comedy had another notable source, one that connected to African-American music, in "jamming," a string of associations thematically related to jazz sessions. Both jazz riffs and oral improvisation were dominant in the routines of the Second City Review, as exemplified by May and Nichols.[45]

In the early 1960s, other troupes followed: the Committee in San Francisco, Proposition in Boston, and Premise in New York. By the 1970s, the Second City branch in Toronto developed the talents of Dan Aykroyd and Bill Murray, both of whom formed the basis of the long-running satirical television program *Saturday Night Live.*

Both satire and the satirist have, for good reason, stood suspect throughout history. Robert C. Elliott noted in *The Power of Satire: Magic, Ritual, Art* that the satirist is "of society in the sense that his art must be grounded in his experience as social man; but he must also be apart, as he struggles to achieve aesthetic distance. His practice is often sanative, as he proclaims; but it may be revolutionary in ways that society cannot possibly approve, and in ways that may not be clear even to the satirist."[46]

Guerrilla satire in the 1960s and early 1970s highlighted societal fault lines and posed an American Dream along radically different lines. The writings and theater revealed conviction: "I am an incurable optimist who daily raises my head to the beat of human existence!"; employed wry twists to convey its messages: "We hate all people regardless of race, creed or color," "Do unto others—then cut out," "Love thy neighbor but don't get caught,'" and a favored line, "Support mental health or I'll kill you"; and on occasion expressed ambivalence regarding the attainment of its goals: "If I had a wish, I would wish that people would stop beating each other's brains out."

Graffiti's satire would reverberate in people's humor throughout the century in the cultural conflicts over the definition of American democracy. But the counterculture movement dissipated, its energies running down and out in the mid-1970s.

8

"Is There Life Before Death?"

On a summer's day in 1970, shortly after city officials in Boston had erected four blank billboards at the corners of the historic Boston Common, there appeared an exasperated query about the craziness of swirling circumstances: "Is there any intelligent life on earth?" For several days the space underneath remained blank, then someone scribbled, "Yes, but I'm only here for a short visit."[1] That witticism presaged the shift in expectations across the country that by mid-decade had been replaced by an anguished downsizing.

Across the national landscape tumultuous events one after another—the ongoing Vietnam War, the assassinations of Robert Kennedy and Martin Luther King, Jr., Black Power and urban rebellions, police violence at the Democratic Party convention in Chicago, student killings at Kent State University and South Carolina State College in Orangeburg, and Watergate—led to an anguished period rivaling any in the century since the 1920s. For those who had envisioned a radically restructured society there was exhaustion, exasperation, and recoil. The opposition pointed to the nation's ills as the outcome of counterculture values and behavior; and they initiated a campaign to defame the protesters, one that impacted on national politics up to the end of the century. Indeed, efforts to derail the counterculture had been under way during the 1960s as J. Edgar Hoover's FBI, state law-enforcement agencies, and conservatives devised and deployed myriad legal and unconstitutional tactics. With the election in 1968 of a Republican president whose constituency and policies were antithetical to the counterculture's style and aims, the establishment was poised to impede not only the protesters' symbols but also their media support. Themes and slogans were trivialized, at times ridiculed. To their expected ire, President Richard Nixon and his advisers smilingly flashed fingers in the "V" symbol for peace in parodying counterculture messages. Corporations issued edicts affecting dress, hair length, and language. The U.S. Navy overturned its relaxed policy regarding hair length and issued a policy restricting men to four inches, and women to a length no greater than the bottom of their uniform collars.[2]

Barely a year after President Nixon assumed power, moreover, the opposition forced the cancellation of CBS Television's *The Smothers Brothers Comedy Hour,* an old-style variety show overlayered with political conviction that had been running for two years. The problem was not audience ratings—its popularity was never in question—but its lampooning of tobacco advertising and lung cancer, religious issues, and particularly the Vietnam War had rankled conservatives and riled the White House. A skittish network capitulated to the pressure. Notice was once again served of the difficulty of employing transformative humor on commercial media.

By the early 1970s it was clear that the country's metaphoric glass of water was being perceived not as half full but as half empty. Graffiti communicated the bewilderment about deteriorating conditions. One query prominently displayed at the entrance of a New York subway station in 1972 whimsically inquired, "Is there life before death?"[3]

Then with a suddenness that was as swift as it was jolting, the nation was besieged by a torrent of economic problems. The initial trigger was a major economic contraction, the first since the Great Depression. Beginning with a wrenching gasoline shortage in 1973, it was followed by soaring energy prices, a careening job market, and an inflationary spiral. Despite President Nixon's upbeat rhetoric that the United States was the "greatest country in the world"—a metal American flag pin in his lapel proclaimed his patriotism—the claim was undercut by somber reports of economic reversal. Within three years after his ignominious resignation resulting from the Watergate scandal came the baleful news: a 1976 survey by the Organization for Economic Cooperation and Development, an association of the twenty-four richest nations in the Western world, noted that in terms of per capita income the United States had dropped to third, behind Switzerland and Sweden, and if trends persisted, it would plunge to fifth place.

Introduced into daily existence was a gnawing trepidation that the ballooning interest rates, long lines at the gasoline pumps, and unemployment were signs of decline. Reinforcement of the foreboding was provided by a massive electric power outage in 1977 that plunged New York City into total darkness, accompanied by thousands of arrests for looting. "The ensuing mood," wrote Richard Barnet in *The Lean Years*, "was no conventional pessimism, but rather a loss of faith rooted in a sense of betrayal." A rapid succession of economic shocks, noted Barnet, "had ushered in a politics of austerity. Suddenly the word on every lip was *scarcity*."[4]

The political radicals of the 1960s had touted the notion of scarcity as one artificially devised by a capitalist system within a competitive ideology. With considerable persuasiveness they contended that technology had long ago created a possibility of bountifulness in which cooperation would be the prime determinant in human and business relationships. But their position was immediately undermined by the mounting economic disorders. Instead of a "people of plenty" there was persistent talk of a "society of scarcity." The term *progress*, so prized in the vocabulary of the American Dream, lost its luster. Politicians and businessmen who had routinely placed their faith in the entrepreneurial system abruptly steered clear of employing the term. Gone was the General Electric ad with its familiar slogan, "Progress Is Our Most Important Product." Not until President Ronald Reagan's unabashed optimistic oratory in the 1980s was the notion of an unbounded future partially reclaimed.

Public discourse came to be marked by increased hesitancies. *Caution* became the policy maker's favorite byword: businessmen reinvested capital warily; universities expressed anxiety about enrollments as they pared down tenured positions; stockbrokers urged discretion in investments; public utility companies advised prudent use of electricity; Congress enacted the 55-miles-per-hour highway speed limit; and clothing manufacturers harkened back to 1950s styles. Polls taken during the decade indicated that a substantial number of people felt that the nation's problems could not be readily solved. Daily existence was expected to become more precarious.

By the mid-1970s, the period of the national bicentennial celebration, there appeared a bevy of semicomic stories about worsening economic conditions facing the ordinary citizen:

Mary Wendell stuffed two cents into the hand of a stranger wrestling with a parking meter behind her tan Toyota on Main Street in Concord, and waved aside the offer of a nickel repayment.

"That's okay," she said with a laugh, "those are only worth one-eighth of a penny anyway."

Some joke.

Although no one has calculated the exact inflationary value of a penny these days, the Federal Reserve Bank has reported recently that today's dollar is worth half of what it was ten years ago.[5]

Yet the issue of scarcity touched on matters beyond monetary concerns. It went to the core of the national identity itself, to the quality of consumer existence. Flawed goods, obsolete appliances, and shoddy workmanship spoke to the policy of "planned obsolescence" by manufacturers that severely undermined confidence in the statement "Made in the U.S.A." "An engineer's principal purpose as an engineer," declared Elisha Gray II, chairman of the board of Whirlpool Corporation, a decade earlier, "is to create obsolescence. Any attempts by various people to toady up to the public by saying they are against planned obsolescence is so much commercial demagogy."[6]

Corporate policies deeply affected workers' attitudes. Essays in *Time* ("Is the Work Ethic Going Out of Style?") and *Newsweek* ("The Work Blahs: Who Wants to Work?"), and books such as Studs Terkel's *Working* (1974), reflected the workforce's increasing alienation. Thousands of graphics circulating in offices across the country resonated disgruntlement:

> Doing a good job here is like working in a whorehouse. . . . The better we perform, the more often they screw us!"

> It has been brought to the attention of this office that many employees have been dying while on duty for no good reason. Furthermore, some employees are refusing to fall over after they are dead. This, in some cases, has resulted in much *UNEARNED OVERTIME* payments.
>
> *Effective immediately, this practice must be discontinued.*
>
> On or after this date, any employee found sitting up after he or she has died will be dropped from the payroll *at once*, without investigation, under Regulation No. 20, Section 'Nonproductive Labor.'[7]

A typical complaint on a company bulletin board in Cambridge, Massachusetts:

> To err is human,
> To forgive is not company policy.[8]

Resurrecting the cult of individualism as the embodiment of the American ideal, conservatives offered a reconstituted social Darwinism as the driving force in public policy. To the counterculture, "do your own thing" had involved the creative self in relation to a wider community; in the 1970s it was the economic self to the exclusion of others. Peter Marin asserted that the new direction signified "the deification of the isolated self." Novelist Tom Wolfe excoriated the 1970s as "the 'ME' Decade," an apt description of the incoming Yuppies. Over the airwaves came Frank Sinatra's emphatic rendition of "My Way."

The new accent on entrepreneurship immediately revived the issue of social welfare. Downplaying its complexities, conservatives redefined the argument as one of workfare versus welfare. Ubiquitous phrases of the period—"reordering priorities," "taking stock," and "reassessing values"—were euphemisms for revamping the welfare system by emphasizing individual initiative and restoring minimum government. When the secretary of the treasury in President Gerald Ford's administration categorized food stamp recipients as "chiselers," he echoed a charge that had been leveled against welfare programs since their inception. Over the decades, in his gubernatorial and presidential campaigns, and later as president, Ronald Reagan constantly denounced "welfare queens" and "welfare parasites," regaling his audiences with tales of poor families living in fancy hotels, their lifestyle more luxurious than that of most workers. Minorities recognized these phrases as code words with an antiethnic and antiurban animus.

Economic uncertainties were further intensified by a loss of fiduciary trust in the political system. A series of investigative reports in the media recounted corruption at every level of government, the most extraordinary being the indictment—and subsequent resignation in 1973—of Vice President Spiro Agnew for kickbacks, some of which he brazenly collected in the basement of the White House, followed shortly thereafter by the near impeachment and resignation of the president himself. Involved in the Watergate imbroglio were President Nixon's closest advisers, many of whom served prison terms for their part in the clandestine operations. So stupefying was Watergate that the designation appeared in revised dictionaries. Capping the episode was the pardoning of the ex-president by President Ford—who had been selected as vice president by Nixon—even before actual charges were filed. Presumption of a deal, the one going free while the other assumed the highest political office, was widespread.

Mistrust lingered into the next administration. Despite President Jimmy Carter's unquestioned ethics and piety, a joke circulating in mid-1977 focused on the president's flamboyant, beer-drinking brother, Billy, and the director of the Office of Management and Budget, Bert Lance—who had been forced to resign because of financial improprieties: "Billy Carter and Bert Lance are going into business together— they're marketing a new beer called Overdraft."[9]

Further impairing the government's reputation were disclosures that the Federal Bureau of Investigation under J. Edgar Hoover had resorted to illegal wiretapping, burglary, eavesdropping, mail openings, second-story men, fake letters, falsified documents, and other nefarious acts in an effort to destroy the counterculture and the civil rights and Black Power movements. The FBI placed under surveillance thousands of individuals it had arbitrarily deemed dangerous to the social fabric. Stage and film comedian Groucho Marx, then in his seventies, was among those investigated as a risk by the FBI, CIA, and other government agencies after an underground newspaper reported that he personally welcomed President Nixon's demise. When questioned about the statement, Marx's rejoinder became an instant classic: "I deny everything because I lie about everything and everything I deny is a lie."[10]

Language reflects the leitmotiv of a period, and the darkening uncertainties produced new words and phrases. Prior to the mid-1960s there had existed no separate listing for "violence" in the *Reader's Guide to Periodical Literature*, the main bibliographical reference for published articles. Following the assassination of President John F. Kennedy, however, the theme of violence replaced "force," which had been in usage for more than sixty years. As personal crimes and ethnic revolts by blacks and Hispanics in cities mounted during the 1960s, there had been a corresponding mushrooming of articles.

There may have been "nothing new in our violence, only in our sudden awareness of it,"[11] as historian Richard Hofstadter argued at the time, but public anxiety over safety spiraled and a new fearful phrase, "crime and violence," swept into the public's vocabulary. Indeed, the theme became the media's preoccupation. Crime serials and police shows became prime-time fare on television networks, films showed the infinite possibilities of personal attack, and print media ran articles on ways to protect oneself and family. Millions of urban dwellers ordered extra bolts for their doors and peered cautiously out of peepholes.

"Violence is becoming a way of life in the nation's cities," stated the *Boston Globe* in December 1972. *Newsweek* published a corroborating feature essay, "Living with Crime": "Crime's grip on America today is both a reality and a state of mind. Few citizens actually die of fear, but its chilling effects have become part of the daily life for millions in and around the nation's cities."[12]

As vulnerability inserted itself in the national psyche, "law and order" became the domestic counterpart to international communism as a dominating political issue. Responding to the internal threat, the government established a substantial number of presidential commissions. From the mid-1960s to the 1970s, five commissions focused on its various dimensions: the assassination of John F. Kennedy (Warren Commission); civil disorders (Kerner Commission); law enforcement and the administration of justice (Katzenbach Commission); causes and prevention of violence (Eisenhower Commission); obscenity and pornography (Lockhart Commission). In addition, a bevy of other agencies analyzed related issues, marijuana among them, and state commissions focused on local violence, such as the Governor's Commission on the Los Angeles Riot (McCone Commission). The result was the expenditure of hundreds of millions of dollars, the publication of hundreds of volumes offering invaluable testimony, penetrating analysis along with social policy recommendations, and a minimum of follow-through.

Hampering social discourse was the deliberate misuse of language emanating from government agencies. Neil Postman summed up the process as "disinformation," that is, "information that creates the illusion of knowing something but which in fact leads one away from knowing."[13] Hence the invasion of Cambodia in 1970 by American forces during the Vietnam War was labeled an "incursion" by President Nixon, and his secret, massive bombings of North Vietnam, later disclosed, were justified as "protective retaliation strikes." President Reagan designated a particular superweapon as the "Peace Keeper," paralleling the illuminated sign at the entrance to the Strategic Air Command headquarters in Nebraska, "Peace is our Profession." When the Central Intelligence Agency reported that it arranged to "terminate with extreme prejudice" by means of a "non-discernible microbinoculator," it meant that the organization had planned to kill an individual with a poison dart gun.[14]

The National Council of Teachers, hoping to counter the problem, initiated a Double-Speak Award, the phrase from George Orwell's novel *1984* in which the state's power over the populace is largely maintained by word imagery. The 1975 award went to an agency for its policy description of a consumer affairs coordinator as one who would "review existing mechanisms of consumer input, thruput and output, and seek ways of improving these linkages via the consumer communication channel."[15]

Distinguishing image from reality, problematic at best, became increasingly difficult during the 1970s as the media devised new techniques of reporting events. On television newscasts, a magazine-style format created a series of fragmented frames unconcerned with and unrelated to historical continuity. The consequence was a smorgasbord of incidents "separated in content, context, and emotional texture from what precedes and follows it."[16] The viewer, in short, was challenged to decipher news's priorities. After listening to a field reporter extol chimney safety in the pre-Christmas season, an exasperated local news anchor in Boston blurted out, "We'll be back with more alleged news in a moment." His action resulted in his immediate firing, the station manager insisting that "We do not put on 'alleged news.' We put on real news."[17]

That things were coming apart, splitting, even disintegrating, had produced a broad malaise. As he prepared for the traditional springtime planting in Maine in 1975, essayist E. B. White took stock of the foreboding mood. Placing his fingers on the nation's pulse, White pondered its prospects. "With so much that is disturbing our lives and clouding our future, beginning right here in my own little principality, with its private pools of energy (the woodpile, the black stove, the germ of the seed, the chick in the egg), and extending outward to our unhappy land and our plundered planet, it is hard to foretell what is going to happen." What *was* certain, White noted with some relief, was the inevitability of seasonal change. On a "not too distant night, somewhere in pond or ditch or low place, a frog will awake, raise his voice in praise, and be joined by others. I will feel a whole lot better when I hear the frogs."[18] White's idyllic pond was far removed from people's woes.

Evidence of hardening attitudes appeared in graffiti declarations across the country. A flyer circulated among the elderly: "Avenge Yourself: Live Long Enough To Be A Problem To Your Children"; diamond-shaped yellow cards dangled in automobile rear windows: "Husband In Trunk"; an anonymous business office tract made the rounds, "Always Be Sincere—Whether You Mean It Or Not"; a notice for parking-space hoggers:

PARKING VIOLATION

_____	_____
PROVINCE OR STATE	AUTOMOBILE LICENSE NUMBER
_____	_____
TIME	MAKE OF AUTOMOBILE

This is not a ticket, but if it were within my power, you would receive two. Because of your Bull Headed, inconsiderate, feeble attempt at parking, you have taken enough room for a 20 mule team, 2 elephants, 1 goat and a safari of pygmies from the African interior. The reason for giving you this is so that in the future you may think of someone else, other than yourself. Besides I don't like domineering, egotistical or simple minded drivers and you probably fit into one of these categories.

I sign off wishing you an early transmission failure (on the expressway at about 4:30 p.m.). Also, may the Fleas of a thousand camels infest your armpits.

WITH MY COMPLIMENTS[19]

Graffiti recorded fortification from gnawing events. Wrote a university student in Boston:

> Some folks need killer weed,
> Some folks need cocaine.
> Some folks need a little speed,
>   to purify their brain.
> Some folks need two women,
> Some folks need alcohol.
> Everybody needs a little bit of somethin'
> But Lord, I need it all.[20]

"Humor can only exist," wrote the novelist Milan Kundera in *Immortality*, "when people are still capable of recognizing some border between the important and unimportant. And nowadays this border has become unrecognizable."[21] Emblematic of the uncertainty was a rudderless humor that roamed over the landscape in search of a purposeful theme. Acts of comedic nonsense cropped up, the Pet Rock craze, an occasional graffito:

> To do is to be—Nietzsche
> To be is to do—Kant
> Do be do be do be—Sinatra
> Do be or not do be—Hamlet with a Cold
> Do be a good do be—Romper Room teacher
> I am not a do be—Richard Nixon
> What is a do be?—Gerald Ford
> Do me do me do me—My girlfriend[22]

Shrewdly sensing the public's need for laughter, AT&T in New York in 1974 offered a new public number, 999–3838: Dial-a-Joke. Leading off the two-minute patter was the recognizable, raspy voice of Henny Youngman with a rapid string of one-liners. In its first month of operation the number logged 3.3 million calls, for a net profit of $275,000 in preinflation dollars. Following Youngman came comics Morey Amsterdam and Phyllis Diller, also practitioners of the one-liner. The telephone company held a gala reception at Sardi's restaurant on the service's second anniversary; it was attended by comedians, writers, and others who regaled each other in a contest of one-upmanship.[23]

Concomitantly, brilliant satire appeared on prime-time television—*M*A*S*H, All in the Family, Saturday Night Live*—and in the breakthrough film *Blazing Saddles.* These existed side by side with a variety of sitcoms that made the nostalgic leap back to the 1950s, recalling its dress and hairstyles and projecting a kind of kitsch sentimentality.

Such wild extremes revived the lament about humor's doleful condition, the earliest of such declamations appearing in a *Time* essay in 1970, "We Are Not Amused—and Why." *Time* identified a new disease overtaking the country, "cataplexy," which made its victims physically unable to laugh despite a desperate desire to do so. "At the moment, the silent absence of laughter is deafening, though the will to laugh is agonizingly there." How to alter the dire situation? "Bring on those '70s clowns. A touch of madness may save us from the real thing."[24] The magazine did not have long to wait.

The clown proved to be Steve Martin, who became the decade's most publicized and publicly echoed comedian. To his youthful audiences Martin was the anarchic Marx Brothers reincarnated. "In philosophy I started to study logic and they were talking about cause and effect," said Martin of his college career, "and then you start to realize 'Hey! . . . there is no cause and effect! There is no logic! There is no anything!' "[25] Wearing a white suit with tie, he paradoxically identified himself as a "wild and crazy guy," at one time or another during his monologue appearing with an arrow through his head, juggling oranges, plunking a banjo, begetting a herd of bizarre balloon animals, politely sipping a glass of water and then spitting it out, appending bunny ears, and careening across the stage in "happy feet." Phrases like "Well, excuuuuuse me! and "Naaaaaah!" quickly entered the younger generation's vocabulary.

In an ironic way, however, Martin's routines were subtle jabs at the new narcissism. Presenting himself as the successful entrepreneur and his audience as the sucker, Martin assumed the role of latter-day P. T. Barnum. A typical skit would open with overstated sincerity fashioned to the ticket price and his profit:

Hi, folks, my name is Steve Martin . . . and it's great to be here, tonight. I know that sounds phony, because every entertainer in the world comes out and goes [arms open widely] . . . "HEY, IT'S REAL-LLLLLY GREAT TO BE HERE." But I am *sincere when I say* . . . "HEY, IT'S REALLLLLLY GREAT TO BE HERE." So listen, how much was it to get in?

. . . Five bucks? . . . [chuckles smugly] . . . . Just for fun, I figured out what my gross would be if I filled a 3,000-seat hall at $800.00 per ticket. Two million, four hundred thousand! That's what I'm shooting for . . . a one-man show and goodbye![26]

Martin satirized the ultimate consumer. "I bought some electric socks, a dog polisher, a fur sink. . . . Sure, I bought some dumb stuff too." As his wealth increases, the capitalist in him must invent new ways of spending, so Martin begrudgingly lends his mother fifteen dollars for food: "And now she calls me up and says she can't pay me back for a while! I said, 'What is this bull———?' So I worked it out with her. She's gonna work on my transmission and if she can't fix that I'll have her move my weights up to the attic."[27]

This wealth enables circumvention of social responsibility. On *Saturday Night Live*, Martin suggested that transgression of any sort could be made acceptable if only two words were offered: "I forgot." "I forgot to pay my taxes." "I forgot robbing a bank was illegal." His most widely repeated phrase was the definitive escape, a wildly embellished "Well, excuuuuuuuse me!"[28]

On the people's level, comedy subverting cherished rituals emerged in the Occasional Doo Dah Parade, a parody conceived in 1977 by a group of artists and counterculturists in Pasadena, California, as a counterpoint to the Tournament of Roses parade. While both parades epitomize ceremonies that renew community existence and reaffirm identities, they clearly resonate to different sensibilities.

The traditional Tournament of Roses parade is largely indifferent to social change, and remains steadfast to its past. It was initiated in the 1890s by affluent Midwesterners who decorated their horses and buggies with flowers in celebration of the coming year. The sponsors gradually added chariot races and then college football, thereby laying the groundwork for the contemporary Rose Bowl spectacle in which sixty flower-decorated, self-propelled floats, twenty-two bands, and equestrian units are viewed by millions via television. Adorning the occasion are a celebrity grand marshal, the Rose Queen and her court, and the awarding of special prizes for the floats, marching bands, and equestrian units.

The Occasional Doo Dah Parade, by contrast, totally overturned its ritualistic counterpart by mirroring, indeed celebrating, the turmoil and chaos of the period. The name itself derived from the satiric rock group the Bonzo Dog Doo Dah Band, and the parade is a ragtag occasion. Scorned are rules, themes, prizes, judging, even a marching order. Over succeeding years the procession has attracted students, professionals, schools, service agencies, mainstream agencies—in short, any individual or group attuned to its zaniness.

Its first queen was an elderly ballroom singer transported in a shopping cart; the official language was Swedish; and the committee's emergency telephone number connected to Dial-a-Prayer. "The Czar" orchestrates and coordinates the event. At one time or another there have appeared a two-hundred-member Red Shoes Dance Supplies Store Tap Troupe; a Toro! Toro! Toro! World's Premier Lawnmower Drill Team; a one-hundred-person All-City Waitresses' Marching Band dressed in aprons and uniforms; a Couch Potatoes group reclining vegetable-like on sofas, watching television; a food coop clothed as vegetables; and a flamboyantly painted male wearing a blond wig, his balloon breasts filling a satin dress. On occasion the marchers assail political figures: a sign on a Nixon impersonator reiterated Nixon's famous "I'm not a crook"; in the 1980s Reagan masks adorned a group leading blind marchers carrying a "Trickle Down" sign; a Nancy Reagan figure bore the placard "Let Them Eat Ketchup," a reference to the Reagan administration's categorizing ketchup as a vegetable in the school lunch program.[29]

Sensing the disgruntlements, in 1978 *Time,* in "How to Raise the U.S. Mirth Rate," offered yet another analysis on the state of humor and proffered a remedy: "Happy days could be here again," claimed the author, if only "Americans will discover that the public itself is the butt of some of the biggest jokes around. In such case, laughter might be reduced. Still, half a laugh is better than none."[30]

Turned in against itself, the public did indeed accept itself as the butt of humor. The lightbulb joke cycle that made its appearance in the waning years of the decade bared a society in conflict with itself.

A spin-off from an earlier Polish joke, "How many Poles does it take to screw in a lightbulb?" "*Three [or more, in some versions], one to hold the bulb and two [or more] to turn the ladder,*" the bulb sally was a harbinger of the people's script for the remainder of the century.

Grappling with its significance, folklorist Judith Kerman deduced that the series represented a "whimsical meditation on the ways Americans make social decisions and get things done." In her estimation, the cycle was propelled by the technical requirements of social organizations and their decision-making requirements. These were, then, "jokes the groups tell about their *own* decision-making complexity."[31]

Alan Dundes took a different tack. Why "the choice of the act of screwing in light bulbs as the basis of a series of jokes?" So much metaphoric action for a single "stroke" suggested a sexual connotation—in other words, a problem of national impotence. Pinpointing scarcity emanating from the 1973 energy crisis as the cycle's impetus, Dundes noted the "widespread malaise Americans have about energy supplies and the power that comes from energy." Screwing in lightbulbs was, in effect, laughing at "our own potential lack of sexual and political power."[32]

Anxiety over natural and economic resources, however, was but an aspect of a much more severe distress. It extended to a growing perception of the "scarcity of quality" in American life. There was a palpable uneasiness involving the deteriorating caliber of work, goods, politics, language, and sheltered safety. Everything, it was felt, was contracting, including options.

The lightbulb jokes reflected society railing against itself by scorching every group. When no one can be fingered for fault, all are at fault. In this way the series echoed the counterculture aphorism, "If you're not part of the solution, you're part of the problem." Notice the perceived flaw of each association involved in the cycle:

How many Californians does it take to change a lightbulb?
Eight [or more]. One to change the bulb, the others to hold a therapy session [or conduct a sensitivity session].

How many Californians does it take to screw in a lightbulb?
None. Californians screw in hot tubs.

How many psychiatrists . . .
One, but the bulb must want to change.

How many real men . . .
None. Real men aren't afraid of the dark.

How many WASPs . . .
Two. One to mix the martinis, the other to call an electrician.

How many football players . . .
One, and he gets four credits [or a scholarship] for doing it.

How many Harvard students . . .
One. He sticks it in and the rest of the world revolves around him.

How many feminists . . .
That's not funny or
This is no laughing matter.

How many doctors . . .
It depends on how much health insurance the lightbulb has.

How many bureaucrats . . .
Three. One to do the paperwork, one to announce the daring move, and the third to actually screw the bulb into the socket.

How many New Yorkers . . .
None of your goddamn business.

How many Republicans . . .
Two. One to change it and one to complain about how much better lightbulbs used to be.

How many Puerto Ricans . . .
Three. One to do the work and two to hold the boom box.

How many law students . . .
Two. One to do the work. The other is there to kick the stool out from under him.

How many radical social workers . . .
It's not the lightbulb that needs changing.

How many gays . . .
Seven. One to do the work, five to hold the chandelier, and one to shout about how marvelous it looks.

How many Teamsters . . .
Seventeen. You have a problem with that, buddy?![33]

Thus the catalyst of people's joking was deteriorating conditions compounded by an embrace of social Darwinism that buffeted the social compact. With the compact in tatters, a rancorous and fragmented society was an inevitable outcome. The upshot in humor was the emergence of joke wars on a massive scale.

9

The Undeclared Joke Wars

In 1820 Percy Bysshe Shelley noted that "in periods of the decay of social life . . . comedy loses its ideal universality: wit succeeds to humour; we laugh from self-complacency and triumph instead of pleasure; malignity, sarcasm and contempt, succeed to sympathetic merriment; we hardly laugh, but we smile."[1] There was no better validation of the poet's insight than the undeclared joke wars in the later decades of the next century.

That the national mood was mired in a merriment of "malignity, sarcasm and contempt" could be discerned from the cynical graffiti that accompanied the opening of the 1980s:

> What are the four biggest lies of the 1980s?
>   1. My mortgage is assumable.
>   2. My Mercedes is paid for.
>   3. It's only a cold sore.
>   4. I'm here from the government to help you.[2]

Another implied a state of permanent estrangement:

> What's the difference between Herpes and true love?
>   *True love isn't forever.*[3]

Christopher Lasch, historian and critic, assayed the social climate at a 1986 conference, "The Search for Civic Community." Citing "the revival of Social Darwinism under Ronald Reagan, the decline in public spirit reflected in decreasing voter turnout, the growing influence of special-interest groups, and the general fragmentation of society," Lasch popped an urgent question: "How can there be a public philosophy in a society lacking any cultural consensus on common values?"[4]

"It begins to look as if the 1980s will have to be remembered," wrote novelist James A. Michener at the same time, "as The Ugly Decade, because so many distasteful things have surfaced in the first six years and may continue into the last four. . . . I hope it doesn't get worse."[5] Michener's hope went unrealized. "Mean-spirited" and "nasty" were terms publicly affixed to President Ronald Reagan's and George Bush's domestic programs, and even the premier humor magazine, *The New Yorker*, concluded that "anger is to our time what angst was to the nineteen-fifties."[6] Wrote a male in a bathroom at Boston's Logan Airport in 1983:

> The World Is A Shit Sandwich!
> The More Bread You Have
> The Less Shit You Have To Take.[7]

With the Reagan–Bush policies of a market economy based on the vaunted concepts of individualism and competition—its "trickle down" mechanism proving to reward the wealthy classes while excluding the middle and punishing the lower classes—the frayed trust in the "just state" dissipated. "The dominant ethic," Irving Howe opined, "has been a heartless Social Darwinism, reinforced by the weary myth that the sum of individual selfishness would be a collective beneficence. . . . The ideological right kept shrilling that nothing good could come from government, and did its best to prove it."[8]

The immediate comedic response to the intense social friction was the unusually high number of joke cycles that made their appearance. Following closely on the heels of the lightbulb cycle were the Jewish American Princess (JAP), White Anglo-Saxon Protestant (WASP), and numerous disaster scenarios. Although each cycle addressed a different matter, overall they posited societal axes of confrontation and contentiousness. And as if these were not enough, recast throughout the period were racial-, ethnic-, and gender-derogatory jokes that had been dormant during the 1960s and 1970s.

While few recognized it at the time, an unusual type of cultural war had erupted, its intensity approximating the ethnic and racial joking that had occurred at the turn of the twentieth century. Yet to distinguish the various antagonists, as theater folks are wont to say, it was necessary to consult a program.

The JAP series began as in-group insult humor, a form that operates "to strengthen the morale of those who use it and to undermine the morale of those at whom it is aimed."[9] Before long, though, the script wended its way beyond the Jewish community, as a result of commercial tracts—*The Jewish American Princess Handbook,* by Debbie Lukatsky and Sandy Barnett Toback, and *The Official J.A.P. Handbook,* by Anna Sequoia (née Schneider)—and of the letters *JAP* being emblazoned on bracelets, hair clips, T-shirts, sweatpants, undergarments, greeting cards, and posters. In 1986 talk-show host Johnny Carson, whose ear was cannily tuned to the people's grapevine, gibed about a sexy nightgown in a Frederick's of Hollywood shop displaying the sign "Do Not Disturb." A "Druish Princess" was accompanied by a robot maid toting a stack of Gucci luggage in Mel Brooks's film *Space-Balls* (1987).

The JAP joke was a fusion of traditional Eastern European motifs with American middle-class impulses, and involved more than one generation of mothers and daughters. As Alan Dundes perceptively noted, the joke could not be understood in isolation from the folk contours of the Jewish American Mother as an overly protective, solicitous, anxious, demanding, and martyred parent. In effect, the daughter was an extension of her mother's persona. Despite, or in response to, the advancement of substantial numbers of Jewish women into the professional and managerial classes in the second half of the century, the joke focused on the spoiled, self-centered traits. Depicted as narcissistic and materialistic, the Jewish American Princess is a shallow figure whose excitement over the accumulation of goods is matched by her indifference to sex and household chores. Aspects of this character had previously appeared in literary form, in Abraham Cahan's story "The Imported Bridegroom," Herman Wouk's *Marjorie Morningstar* (1955), and Philip Roth's *Portnoy's Complaint* (1969).

As they circulated throughout the country—at a Christian wedding in Oklahoma in 1985 and at a stockbrokers' meeting in Atlanta a year later—were these banters: "How does a JAP commit suicide? *She jumps off her shoe boxes*"; "What is the new Jewish disease? *Maids. You die if you don't have one*"; "How can you tell the widow at a Jewish funeral? *She's the one wearing the black tennis outfit*"[10]—outrage in the Jewish community mounted. By maintaining "that only American Princesses are Jewish," wrote Rabbi Jeffrey Salkin in 1982, "it provides a tremendous opportunity to recast the old money-grubbing Jew stereotype—shylock in Drag. . . . Gentiles believe it, too." Moreover, added the rabbi, the jokes were misogynist, a kind of "kosher sexism." "It is a pernicious marriage of racism and misogyny. It is time for us to expose the ugliness that masquerades as humor."[11]

A study of the joke's phenomenon and the mechanism by which it was transmitted supported these charges. "We conclude from an analysis of our data," argued a Syracuse University team, "that the JAP-baiting phenomenon is directed primarily at Jewish women and, as such, is both sexist and anti-Jewish. The content of the humor contains a stereotype of women that communicates a sense of a place, appearance, and perceived moral failings."[12]

Countering these assertions was Bernard Saper, who contended that the cycle constituted neither a *"trend, fashion,* or enduring and widespread *movement*—an organized, concerted effort to defame certain Jewish women. There is *seldom* the progression from joking to violent antifeminism, or anti-Semitism." If the joke is unreinforced "by the hearer's withholding of attention, interest, praise, laughter, or repetition—the telling or laughing at that joke will soon extinguish. It will perish from neglect or disinterest."[13]

The JAP series was but an opening salvo in a major backlash against the women's movement, one that rumbled from historic male resentments. There has existed "a rampant misogyny in all our humor." Mother-in-law jokes, for example, as sociologist George P. Murdock pointed out, are indigenous only to American culture; this type of comic relationship between a male and his mother-in-law is unheard of in any other society throughout the globe.[14]

Thus, it became evident that the attack was not only about third-generation, college-educated, professional Jewish American women but, rather, women sui generis, those who were demanding a restructuring of social and political matrixes. At work was nothing less than a male counterinsurgency, which explains why the cycle, as it intensified over the years, perpetuated the themes of narcissism, materialism, and asexuality. "It may be more than a coincidence," Dundes rightly conjectured, "that the joke cycle came into favor at a time when women's liberation and feminist ideology were becoming increasingly well known (and may have been regarded as threatening by old order male chauvinists)."[15]

By the late 1980s Susan Faludi was quite certain of the humor's design. *Backlash: The Undeclared War Against American Women* (1991) names the sexist joking by comics as one of the "more subtle indicators" in the popular culture that often "receive momentary, and often bemused media notice, then quickly slip from social awareness."[16]

The issue seemingly most troublesome to men was women's sexual energies, as indicated by the jokes criticizing them for being asexual. Thus their sexual indifference, and especially revulsion to oral sex:

> What do you call a JAP's nipples?
>   *Tip of the iceberg.*

> What is Jewish foreplay?
>   *Two hours of begging.*

> How do you know when a JAP is having an orgasm?
>   *She drops her emery board.*

> What do you get when you cross a computer with a JAP?
>   *A system that won't go down.*

> What's the difference between a JAP and poverty?
>   *Poverty sucks.*

> What's the difference between a JAP and the Bermuda Triangle?
>   *The Bermuda Triangle eats seamen.*

Traditional joking during the period echoed a similar refrain. Sexual aversion:

> Three guys during a golf game were discussing the problem of getting onto the green early in the morning hours.
>   Said one, "I gave my wife a diamond ring."
>   Said the second, "I gave my wife a $30,000 car."
>   Said the third, "I didn't have to give my wife anything."
>   "How did you convince her?" they asked.
>   "Simple," he said. "I woke up my wife at 3:00 A.M. and asked her: Honey, golf course or intercourse?"
>   My wife quickly answered, "And don't forget to take your sweater."[17]

Sexual desirability:

> What's an 11?
>> *A 10 with a headache*
>> *A mother who owns a liquor store* or
>> *A 4 with a six-pack.*[18]

> What's the difference between a fox and a dog?
>> *Five drinks.*[19]

Lesbians:

> What's the definition of a lesbian?
>> *Just another woman trying to do a man's job.*[20]

Immediately following the selection at the 1984 Democratic Party convention of Walter "Fritz" Mondale and Geraldine Ferraro—the first woman nominated to a national ticket as vice president—came a series of one-liners:

> Fritz & Tits.

> Wally & the Beaver.

> No tits on the ticket.[21]

Likewise, the appointment of Sandra Day O'Connor as the first woman on the U.S. Supreme Court generated

> What has 18 legs and a pussy?
>> *The Supreme Court.*[22]

Vitriolic voices sprang as well from the "shock comics," a group of performers in the late 1980s and early 1990s whose routines were predominantly sexist and homophobic. Media descriptions of Andrew "Diceman" Clay, Sam Kinison, and others less known ranged from "the comedy of hate," to "attack comedy." For their part, the comics sought the label "rebel comics" or "outlaws of comedy." Their audiences cut across the spectrum, from teenagers and college students to blue-collar males.

Appearing in clubs, colleges, HBO specials, and rock venues—

over twenty thousand attended a Diceman concert in Queens, New York, in 1989—the self-styled rebels singled out gays and women and recently settled Asian immigrants as the nemeses of society. So offensive was their language that "audiences often gasp before they laugh," wrote one reporter.[23] Breaching the boundaries of taste was intentional. "The ruder Kinison got, the more his fans approved," noted a music critic. "Call it a hate-in."[24]

Clay, in particular, referred to women as "pigs" or "hooers," sarcastically praising them as good for dating, laundry, and impersonal sex. He exulted in having given his girlfriend a broom at Christmas one year, a dustpan the next. A substantial part of his routine was detailed sexual insult.[25]

All this vehemence signified resilient mysogyny exacerbated by male uneasiness piqued by sexual and political concerns. References to passivity and frigidity constituted an attempt to neutralize women's demands for equality. Fearing, as many female comics chided at the time, that they might not be capable of "rising" to the occasion produced repercussions that not only sharpened anxieties about potency but further convinced men of women's "voracious" appetites. A case in point was oral sex. Few men had ever complained about the stimulation—indeed, it was one of the most sought-after forms of sex—so long as they were its recipient. But their chiding women in this regard was subterfuge. Retaliation came through the following quip:

What are the three lies men most often tell women?
   1. I like kids.
   2. I love you.
   3. I won't come in your mouth.[26]

Similarly, the traits of dependency and irresponsibility couched in the JAP sally and in other jesting references were attempts to sustain a nostalgic connection to the past.

What does a JAP tell her asshole in the morning?
   She tells him to go to work or
   She sends him out with the garbage.

What do JAPs make for dinner?
   Reservations.

How do JAPs design a house?
No kitchen and no bedroom.

How do JAPs call their kids for dinner?
Get in the station wagon!

Classicist Mary Lefkowitz assessed the male twist in this banter: "Feminists will note that the JAP doesn't want to be liberated or even independent; instead, she always remains someone's pampered little girl."[27]

In further retaliation, men resurrected the "dumb blonde" series, a combination of JAP and traditional numskull joking. With the sudden death of Marilyn Monroe in 1962 and her subsequent elevation to mythical status, the beautiful-but-blonde jests seemingly lost their luster. But their revival in the early 1990s was emblematic of a considerable degree of male vengefulness:

Why do blondes write "TGIF" on the end of their shoes?
To remind them "Toes Go In First."

What does a blonde say after you blow in her ear?
Thanks for the refill.

Would you be impressed by an IQ score of 150?
For 15 blondes?

Why do blondes have more fun?
Because they don't know any better.

How many blondes does it take to make chocolate chip cookies?
Three. One to make the batter and two to peel the M&Ms.

Similar quips directly confronted women in the workplace, particularly those in managerial positions. Daniela Kuper, the owner of an advertising agency in Colorado, was the lone female at a conference of Realtors gathered to generate a major development project. Describing possible locations and features on blueprints tacked to a large board, the organizer pointed to a line that stretched across the plans. "Daniela," he declared, "that's where the choo-choo will go." Several men laughed "hard and long," some looked uncomfortable, and others displayed indifference.[28]

Other traits were invoked in the "dumb blonde" series. A light-bulb motif alluded to sexual behavior:

> How many blondes does it take to screw in a lightbulb?
> *None. Blondes screw in convertibles.*
>
> Okay, so how many blondes does it take to change a lightbulb?
> *What! And ruin her nails![29]*

In the aftermath of past women's movements, as Faludi observed, there had often occurred "a masculinity crisis" that produced, among other responses, all-male retreats and activities.[30] In August 1983 a Manhattan lawyer founded the National Organization for Men (NOM)—its title intended as a counter to the National Organization for Women established in 1966—to further "equal rights for men." The organization's telephone number was 686-MALE. The first comprehensive study of men's reaction to the women's movement, furthermore, corroborated the intensity of the backlash. Anthony Astrachan noted in *How Men Feel: Their Response to Women's Demands for Equality and Power* (1986) that although the proportion of men who approved of their wives or daughters and sisters holding full-times jobs had increased to 88 percent by 1980, the percentage supporting women's "claims to overall equality" was barely 35 percent. In short, resistance to full equality persisted despite the steady increases in the number of men who generally accepted social change.[31]

No sooner had the "dumb blonde" jokes faded than the "Hillary" jokes came into national play. Barely two months after Bill Clinton was sworn in as president in 1993, his wife, Hillary Rodham Clinton, became the focus of intense jesting. On the surface the jokes seemed to elevate rather than denigrate women. Gone were the themes of vapidity, sexual play, and narcissism; they were replaced by issues of power and strength.

> What would happen if Hillary Clinton passed away?
> *Bill would become president.*
>
> Why does Hillary Clinton have so many Secret Service agents assigned to her?
> *Because if anything happens to her, Bill would become president.*

Why does Bill Clinton have so many Secret Service agents assigned to him?

Because if anything happened to Hillary, he'd become president.

Longer variations of the same refrain:

Bill and Hillary were driving down a country road in Arkansas when they stopped at a filling station. Hillary noticed that the man pumping gas was her former boyfriend.

"Boy," said Bill, looking him over, "if you had married him, you'd probably be pumping gas, too."

"No," she replied, "*he'd* be president."

Chelsea Clinton was sick in school. The principal wanted to phone her mother. "Oh, please don't call my mother," Chelsea pleaded. "She's very busy working on health care and all sorts of other important things. Call my father."[32]

Hillary Clinton's presence, intellectual force, and ambition truly caused alarm. For many males, the women's movement was succeeding *too* well. "All of this reflects the fact that people often make jokes when something makes them uncomfortable," observed Jill Ireland, the president of the National Organization for Women. "They're trying to take a threat, and their fear of it, and make a joke. Many men are threatened by strong women and by women who are achieving a measure of political power."[33]

Political power was one thing; physical assault was quite another. Throughout the period there had been media reports of the increasing number of battered women who had killed their abusive spouses and lovers. Then in the early 1990s there occurred an episode that brought the issue into sharp focus, an act of castration by a young wife who had been sexually and psychologically abused for years. Following a sexual assault by her husband with a kitchen knife, Lorena Bobbitt severed his penis while he slept, drove with it in her hand, and eventually threw it out the car window. The penis was retrieved and, after a lengthy operation, reattached. In the several trials that ensued, both husband and wife were acquitted of charges, the former for assault and the latter for malicious intent to harm, though she was sentenced, after a nationally televised trial in 1994, to a forty-five-day hospital stay for psychological evaluation.

Conversations across the country revealed a complex of responses separating the sexes regarding the act of castration. While many women argued that the deed, though harsh, should not have been prosecuted, not a few men expressed unrestrained anger. "In terms of its legal significance," wrote a journalist im the *New York Times*, "the case will probably never merit more than a footnote, but its social impact has been far more profound. Wherever men and women found themselves in the same room . . . sides were drawn and differences were sharp."

On the popular *Today* show, Sidney Stiller of NOM pointed out that there was "a lot of glee from radical feminists" following the verdict to acquit on grounds of temporary insanity, and argued that the issue extended beyond the United States, noting that an Ecuadoran group had threatened to cut off a hundred penises if Lorena Bobbitt were found guilty. Also indicting feminists was William Margold, a porno star, who related that "What you're doing is licensing the feminists to come and slice our [penises] off." Within minutes of the verdict a male passed out flyers at a Boston mall that warned of the "clip and flip" syndrome and offering to sell penis insurance. John Wayne Bobbitt seized the moment to commercialize himself by appearing on television selling T-shirts bearing the inscription "A Cut Heard Around the World."[34]

The jokes, at the very least, suggested male wariness:

John Wayne Bobbitt was driving along the highway, when he spotted a cop signaling him to pull over. The cop came up to the car, and Bobbitt opened up the window.

"Did you know you were speeding?" the officer said.

"I'm sorry, officer," Bobbitt replied, "I must have lost my head."

What is Lorena Bobbitt's favorite drink?
Slice.

Lorena Bobbitt. What a bitch. I was talking to her on the phone and she cut me off.

Do you know why Lorena Bobbitt only got forty-five days in jail?
The evidence wouldn't stand up in court.

Lorena Bobbitt's next husband will be a woman.

And a quip that linked her to Jeffrey Dahmer, the serial killer who had cannibalized his victims:

> What did Jeffrey Dahmer say to Lorena Bobbitt?
> *Are you gonna eat that!*[35]

Further fueling the national tension was the growing insurgency of other minority groups. In this period of politicization women as targets were joined by blacks, gays, Hispanics, and the handicapped. Yet not all of the joking humor was motivated by animosities. Ethnic and gender humor as a barometer of assimilation has long demonstrated a degree of acceptance and incorporation into the larger community. Mary Jo Neitz noted of the relationship of immigration to joke patterns that "the history of the assimilation of immigrant groups into the American mainstream can be seen to a certain extent in joke patterns: closely following the waves of immigrants were waves of immigrant jokes; in part these jokes functioned as a socializing mechanism, pointing to what one could and could not do, what the immigrant did, and how the American would react."[36]

Consequently, as John Lowe persuasively argued, historically "ethnic humor has always formed a significant part of the world of American folklore and culture, partly because it provides pleasure, and partly because of its connection with mythical concepts of aggression, struggle, and our national passion play and ritual, 'Americanization.'"[37]

The public's embrace of Don Rickles, the stand-up comic whose insult routines in the postwar decades spared no one, attested to the dual aspect of ethnic joking. Arguably, the impact of pejorative humor during the 1980s and 1990s was problematic. "I think," submitted Lydia Fish regarding the "Polack" joke cycle, "that there is great doubt about how seriously these ethnic jokes are taken at any time," noting that jokes were "a real source of ethnic pride, a sort of humorous gloating that 'one of our boys made it.'"[38] Dundes observed the same process at work. "Despite the clearcut pejorative cast of most of the ethnic slurs, it is important to realize that most of the slurs were told and enjoyed by members of the group concerned."[39]

There is little doubt, for instance, that the laughter elicited from consensual and symbolic jokes during the period had a positive side to it. Bumper stickers and T-shirts bearing catchall slogans materialized, including "Kiss me, I'm Italian," and joke books by members of targeted groups proliferated, suggesting a benign acknowledgment of ethnicity writ large.⁴⁰ A wraparound joke located in ethnically diverse Los Angeles in the late 1970s opened with the question "How come the freeways are empty on Sunday mornings?" The inclusive reply: "*The WASPs are all playing golf; the Catholics are all at Mass; the Jews are all eating bagels and lox; the blacks are all in jail; the Japanese are all working in their gardens; and the Chicanos are all trying to start their cars.*"⁴¹ Racial styles were gently jived in another sally: "What's the difference between white and black fairy tales? The white fairy tale begins, '*Once upon a time. . . .*' The black fairy tale begins, '*You're not going to believe this shit. . . .*'"⁴² Woody Allen's classic film *Annie Hall* (1977) and concert performances by Jackie Mason, Richard Pryor, and Lily Tomlin, for example, contained cross-cultural and racial materials that simultaneously mocked and elevated diverse groups. Public letters gave further evidence of ambiguity. One such missive appeared in the widely read Ann Landers column in 1984:

> Am I a sourpuss, a grouch, totally devoid of a sense of humor? I'll leave it to you.
>
> My cousin told me her husband, Jerry, ran into my husband at a stag for a man who was retiring. Jerry asked my husband, "How is your wife?" He answered, "Better than nothing."
>
> Jerry thought it was hilarious. My cousin didn't think it was one bit funny. I am fuming. What do YOU think?

Answered the columnist:

> I think your husband's response was meant to be a joke. I also think your cousin has a big mouth.

Highly profitable paperbacks—*Truly Tasteless Jokes, Truly Tasteless Jokes Two, Gross Jokes, Outrageously Offensive Jokes,* and *The Complete Book of Ethnic Humor*—in whose pages blacks, Jews, Poles, homosexuals, and the handicapped were ridiculed, further spread the jokes. How to assess the impact of these various collections? Reactions at the time reflected mixed responses. "Everybody else makes jokes about other people," psychiatrist Martin Grotjahn contended, "but in all jokes there is a disguised aggression, and racial jokes could be an invitation to racial hatred." Historian John Hope Franklin was exasperated: "We should be coming to grips with the dignity of the human spirit, not embarrassing or shaming whole groups of people. The success of these so-called joke books is a sad testament to the taste of this country." Anthropologist Ashley Montagu viewed the scenario in a different light. Provided the jokes were told in the right spirit, they could be construed as a positive development. "Frequently, these jokes are funny even if tasteless. And on the whole, human beings are healthier for taking the view that nothing human is alien to them."[43]

The Helen Keller jokes that made their appearance following an NBC-TV presentation of William Gibson's *The Miracle Worker* in 1979 seemed to point to a constructive, albeit rather nominal, effect. Coinciding with the passage of the Education for All Handicapped Children Act, the television drama embraced and illumined the lives of the outcast handicapped. The show was aired as a wave of jokes about deformed or mentally retarded children was circulating around a U.S. Post Office slogan, "Hire the Handicapped," to which people appended, "They're fun to watch."

> Did you see Helen Keller's new house in Philadelphia?
> *Neither did she.*
>
> Miss Keller, how did you like the movie?
>
> Helen Keller's new book: *Around the Block in 80 Days.*
>
> How did Helen Keller's parents punish her?
> *They moved the furniture around.*
>
> What did Helen Keller's parents do when they caught her swearing?
> *They washed her hands with soap.*

Folklorist Mac E. Barrick was quick to posit that the Keller cycle "fulfilled an important social function. Like a classical drama, it has had a cathartic effect of erasing the pity normally felt toward the disabled, so that the joke-teller and his listener now accept these people on equal terms."[44]

However cathartic the Keller jokes, the various joke cycles, tasteless joke books, and proliferation of ethnic, gender, and racial stereotypical quips also signaled an antagonistic social milieu of considerable proportion. "A joke can be judged conservative or radical if," argued Joseph Epstein, "in its implications, it tends to reinforce the arrangements of society as it stands, or if it protests against current arrangements."[45] In this sense, the intensity and derogatory nature of joking aimed at the minorities constituted a decidedly reactionary swing and, significantly, were coincident with an increase in racial, gender, and sexual violence and in verbal epithets. Yet is it possible that communal relations would have been more frayed without such humor? Was further violence deterred by such insult jokes?

Malicious refrains sounded at social and political gatherings, along the computer superhighway, on the golf fairways, and in myriad intimate settings. But there was a distinctive difference from the past; the *open* relating of pejorative humor was severely and forcibly criticized. The combined force of social and racial movements, buttressed by a growing sensitivity within certain segments of the population, rendered shameful the casting of stereotyped images.

Criticisms notwithstanding, insult jokes were extensively employed during the Ronald Reagan–George Bush years, often told by members and supporters of the administrations. Presidential candidate Reagan lamely explained that the joke he narrated to reporters while campaigning in New Hampshire in 1980—"How do you tell the Polish guy at a cockfight? *He's the one with a duck;* How do you tell the Italian? *He's the one who bets on the duck;* How do you know the Mafia was there? *The duck wins*"—was actually intended to illustrate the type of humor he deplored. Quipped aide Edwin Meese, who was to be Reagan's attorney general, "There goes New Hampshire." The candidate's wife directed her anger at the reporter who broke the story. Disparagement was directed toward women, blacks, and gays. Conservatives in midlevel positions in President Reagan's first administration who opposed enforcing civil rights legislation peppered their discussions with racist jokes and ridicule. "I was shocked," wrote Secretary of Education Terrel H. Bell, "to hear their sick humor and racist clichés. For example, when the bill to establish a national holiday to honor Martin Luther King, Jr., was before the president for his signature or veto, these bigots referred to Dr. King as 'Martin Lucifer Coon! Ha Ha! We'll soon be able to celebrate Martin Lucifer Coon's birthday.'" And "they delighted in making other slurs. Arabs were called 'Sand Niggers.'"

Officials in higher positions offered similar humor. Secretary of Agriculture Earl Butz resigned in 1976 following published reports of jokes slurring blacks that he recounted during a dinner. At the occasion itself, Butz's candor was praised by the emcee: "We appreciate Earl Butz. He calls a spade a spade. We appreciate that he knows the difference. That is, unless he stumbles over a spade in the dark." Vice President Dan Quayle's press secretary retracted a joke he made about lesbians at a fund-raiser in 1991, declaring that "many of my gay and lesbian friends thought it was unfunny." Not all of the put-downs came from the political right. David Beckwith's quip to the criticism directed at a joke told by Democratic Senator Bob Kerrey, then campaigning for the presidency—and for which he apologized—was likewise lambasted: "The good news is that the lesbians are upset with Kerrey. The bad news is that they'll be coming our way to support us."

The Reverend Jesse Jackson, who campaigned in the presidential primaries in the 1980s, was a lightning rod for many such quips. New Hampshire State Senator John Chandler, an honorary county chairman for Jack Kemp's presidential bid in 1987, was fired when he publicly stated before friendly crowds, "Did you hear that Jesse Jackson has dropped out of the presidential race? He found out that his grandmother had posed for the centerfold of the *National Geographic*." Unlike other political figures, Chandler refused to apologize for the remark, citing the right of free speech: "I'm not going to apologize for anything I said because this is a free country, and I believe I have a right to express my opinion." Mayor Emory Folmar of Montgomery, Alabama, who directed George Bush's reelection campaign committee in 1992, "drew laughs from Bush supporters" when he declared that he had a "bad dream" about Governor Bill Clinton as president and the Reverend Jesse Jackson as vice president: a Democratic Congress held a special session to pass a $500 billion tax increase "to buy everybody below the poverty level two Cadillacs."

Gender politics were especially mocked. Title IX, the federal law guaranteeing equal opportunity for women in education, was labeled by President Reagan's aides as the "lesbians' bill of rights" because it was enacted "to pacify masculine women who wanted women's athletic programs in schools and colleges." As a result of the Tailhook sexual harassment scandal that engulfed the U.S. Navy in 1992, the promotion of Vice Admiral Jerry O. Tuttle, whom President Bush had nominated to become chief of naval aviation, was canceled because of one-liners he had personally incorporated into his command's newsletter: "Beer is better than women because beer doesn't get jealous when you grab another" and "Beer is better than women because beer never has a headache."[46] The admiral explained that his "intent was certainly not to offend!" Hawley Atkinson, Republican chairman of the Maricopa County Board of Supervisors in Arizona, created a furor with a "facetious remark" that he "didn't think would get in the newspaper." Atkinson suggested that "homosexuals and lesbians from San Francisco" should be used for experiments instead of animals from the pound. Arizona Governor Evan Meacham, who had publicly opposed the national commemoration for Dr. Martin Luther King, Jr., scorned gays and women in a speech before the Phoenix Kiwanis Club in 1988, then directed his remarks to a gift of golf clubs he had presented to a major Japanese bank. "And Japanese like to play golf. And their eyes really light up when you say we've got over 200 golf courses in Arizona. My goodness, golf courses. Suddenly they got round eyes." As some in the audience tittered, Meacham added, "I hope that wasn't out of line." A similar expression of triteness was uttered by J. Peter Grace, the seventy-nine-year-old chairman and chief executive of W. R. Grace & Company, who had moved his company from New York City to Boca Raton, Florida. At the opening of a chocolate factory in Milwaukee, Wisconsin, in 1992, Grace told the audience "in jest" that where he came from, "We have Cuomo the homo, and then in New York City, we have Dinkins the pinkins." (Mario Cuomo was the governor of New York, and David Dinkins was the mayor of New York City.)

These remarks highlighted the shift in cultural decorum by the resignations that followed. Earl Butz and James Watt, secretary of the interior in President Ronald Reagan's cabinet, both left office. Despite Reagan's insistence that Watt was not insensitive to minorities, the secretary constantly regaled audiences with belittling jokes. Before several hundred members of the U.S. Chamber of Commerce, he derided ethnic "political correctness," referring to a commission created to review his embattled coal-leasing program: "We have every kind of mix you can have. I have a black; I have a woman; two Jews and a cripple." One of the commission members was Richard L. Gordon, a University of Pennsylvania professor whose right arm was paralyzed.[47]

Cutting through the period were Polish jokes, undoubtedly the most durable of all the cycles. First making their appearance in the late 1960s, they survived well into the 1980s, although, as indicated by the Reagan quip, the conundrum often encompassed other ethnics:

If Tarzan and Jane were Jewish, what would Cheetah be?
   A fur coat.

If Tarzan and Jane were Polish, what would Cheetah be?
   Gifted.

If Tarzan and Jane were Italian, what would Cheetah be?
   The other woman.

What did Christ tell the Mexicans?
   Don't do anything till I get back.

What did Christ tell the Poles?
   Play dumb till I get back.[48]

The widespread popularity of the joke has been puzzling because of its seeming lack of connection to domestic and international strains. "Why does this particular group, nationality rather, persist as a butt?" inquired Jesse Bier in 1990. "The era of Polish immigration is long over; the economic or demographic pressure, if ever there was one, was never as singular or threatening as others'—and is no apparent factor now." Bier surmised that the Polish joke was an anomaly "more truly activated by mutual and covert fear than by sheer egotism and aggrandizement."[49]

Other minorities with whom the Polish immigrants competed for jobs and housing devised invectives to describe their behavior. In one study of a small Midwestern industrial community in the 1940s, workers referred to their neighbors as "Polacks," despite the fact that over 50 percent were American-born.[50] Pejorative portraits formed around the ridicule. Popular expressions conveyed early in the century evoked a physically hulking, mentally retiring male, a "bohunk," "honkey," or "behemoth."

Hence the image of the Polish-American athletes recruited from the steel mill and coal mine town to play for college football powerhouses surfaced in stories, cartoons, and films. James Thurber presented an agonizing tale of just such an athlete in his semiautobiographical *My Life and Hard Times* (1933). A tackle named Bolenciecwcz enrolled in an economics class at Ohio State University in the pre–World War I years. Asked by the professor to name a means of transportation, Bolenciecwcz found his mind singularly blank, despite clues from his classmates: "choo-choo-choo," "toot-toot-tootoooooot," and "ding-dong, ding-dong." With a pronounced "chuffa, chuffa, chuffa," the professor inquired how Bolenciecwcz had come to the university. "M'father sent me," replied the tackle. "What did you ride on?" "Train." "Quite right," said the professor, ending the inquiry.[51] The football image firmly intact, the jokes were unending: "What is the first thing a Polack father buys his son? *Booties with cleats.*"

Unlike other cycles, the Polish formula extended over many decades. Dundes surmised that the joke persisted because it "takes the heat off the Negro. Lower-class whites are not militant and do not constitute a threat to middle-class white America. . . . With the Polack cycle, it is the lower class, not Negroes, which provides the outlet for aggression and the means of feeling superior."[52] Seen in this light, the Polish joke also became the archetypal cycle for otherness in this era of minority politicization. Although the term "Polack" persisted, the joke's force in essence was directed elsewhere.

Yet no ethnic group could displace the animosity directed toward the African-American, an enmity that mounted after the 1970s and continued to century's close. Imagaically contouring blacks as either Sambo or savage, white culture had for centuries elevated the former in the popular culture as a means of thwarting violent retaliation. With the demise of Sambo in the post–civil rights/Black Power period—past reminders persisted throughout this period as performers in blackface pranced at fraternity and business functions, and pledges at the all-white Phi Alpha Psi fraternity at Rider College in New Jersey were forced to talk in caricatured black speech while cleaning the fraternity house—the jester was replaced by the savage.

A surge of oppressive joking was the counterpart to the violent assaults on black males in the white communities of Howard Beach and Bensonhurst, New York, in the mid-1980s, and countless less publicized incidents throughout the country. Quips heard in the late 1970s and early 1980s reflected anxiety propelled by affirmative action programs: "What did Lincoln say after a three-day drunk? *I freed the who?*" and "What does MARTA stand for? *Moving Africans Rapidly Through Atlanta.*"

Numerous jokes connected to the numskull pattern by accentuating white intellectual and cultural superiority. "That's because stupidity is as cathartic as wit," noted Margo Jefferson. "It lets us feel smart without having to act smart or be smart, and it is the key to ethnic, racial and sexual insult humor."[53]

What do you get when you cross Billy Dee Williams and Bo Derek?
The ten of spades.

What's long and hard on a black man?
Second grade.

The Harlem High School cheer:
Barbecue, watermelon, Cadillac car / We're not as dumb as you think we is.

One black scholar greeting another,
'Is you done your Greek yet?'

A companion theme involved laziness:

What do Kinney Shoes, or Thom McAn, and the post office have in common?
One thousand black loafers.

Why don't blacks like blow jobs?
They don't like any jobs.

What has Mayor Harold Washington [of Chicago] done that no other black has done?
He died on the job.

What causes sickle-cell anemia?
Glue on the back of food stamps.

In the process, black speech patterns were lampooned:

What has six legs and goes, "HO DEE DO, HO DEE DO, HO DEE DO?
Three black guys running for the elevator.

Why did a black man dress up for his vasectomy?
Because if he was going to be impo-tent, he was going to look impo-tent.

The new toy store for black children:
We-B-Toys.

Who are the two most famous black women?
Aunt Jemima and Mother Fucker.

And black culture was shredded:

> What's another definition of confusion? or
> What's the definition of humor?
>> *Father's Day in Harlem.*

> How many pallbearers does it take to bury a black man?
>> *Seven. Six to carry the coffin and one to pack the stereo.*

> What do Washington and Jefferson have in common?
>> *They're the last two white men with names like that.*

> What do you get when you put a groundhog and a black man together?
>> *Six more weeks of basketball.*

> What do you call a black man in a wet suit?
>> *Jacques Custodian.*

The galvanizing code phrase "crime and violence" was linked to blacks:

> What do they call a black man in a two-million-dollar Beverly Hills house?
>> *A burglar.*

> What do you call a black man with a new bicycle?
>> *A thief.*

> How do you keep five black guys from raping a white woman?
>> *Throw them a basketball.*

One riddle posed the encompassing question "What do you get when you have . . . ?"

> 1 white, 2 blacks?
>> *A victim.*

> 1 white, 5 blacks?
>> *A basketball coach.*

1 white, 10 blacks?
  A quarterback.

1 white, 100 blacks?
  A boss.

1 white, 10,000 blacks?
  A warden.[54]

Blacks were but part of the major assault directed against minorities. Latinos were frequently coupled with blacks: "A Puerto Rican [or a Mexican] and a black man jump from the top of the Empire State Building. Who lands first? *Who cares?* or *The black man—because the Puerto Rican [or Mexican] spray paints his way down.*" Often, however, Latinos had higher ranking in the jokes: "What do you call a black man who marries a Mexican in Texas? *A social climber.*" Yet theft and laziness entwined them:

What do you call two white guys in a white Cadillac?
  Rich whites.

What do you call two black guys in a black Cadillac?
  Black Power.

What do you call two Chicanos in a red Cadillac?
  Grand theft auto.

Why don't blacks marry Chicanos?
  They're afraid the children will be too lazy to pick up the welfare checks.

What do you get when you cross a Mexican with a black?
  A car thief who's too lazy to steal.

Demographic changes triggered many jokes: "Why will there be no Mexicans in the next Olympics? *Because anyone who can run, jump, or swim has left the country.*" With their numbers dramatically increasing—Latinos became the largest minority in the country in the 1990s—they became the latest of the immigrant groups to be festooned by the idiot and indolent motifs:

A Mexican marries a Pole. What do they call him?
    Retarded.

Why don't Mexicans become doctors and lawyers?
    Because spray paint won't fit on the checks.

Why don't Puerto Ricans use checkbooks?
    Because they can't spray paint their signatures.

A Puerto Rican walking down a street picks up a bottle and rubs it.
Out pops a genie who says that he is granted four wishes. "What is
your first wish?"
    "My first wish is to be white."
    "What is your second wish?"
    "My second wish is to own Cassini designer clothes."
    "What is your third wish?"
    "My third wish is to own a Rolls-Royce."
    "What is your fourth wish?"
    "My fourth wish is never to have to work again."
    Whereupon the genie turned him back into a Puerto Rican.

Cracks centered on the automobile. Unskilled laborers seeking
employment rely heavily on cars to seek employment. In the Hispanic
section of Los Angeles and other communities, males were observed
hovering under car hoods, tuning and repairing their vehicles. Recall
as a starter the final line of the quip turning on empty freeways on
Sunday mornings in Los Angeles, "The Chicanos are all trying to start
their cars."

What's the shortest thing in the world?
    A Mexican funeral with one set of jumper cables.

What are the two major Mexican holidays?
    *Cinco de Mayo [Independence Day] and October 27th, the day the
    new Chevies come out.*

Did you hear about the six Mexicans who were on the television
program *That's Incredible?*
    They all had automobile insurance.

Did you hear about the two Puerto Ricans on *That's Incredible?*
    One was an only child, the other had car insurance.

And a broader racial swath:

> Did you hear that *That's Incredible* is coming to Salt Lake City?
>   *They found a thirteen-year-old virgin, a black with a job, and a Mexican with auto insurance.*[55]

Others derived from particular circumstances. In response to the Second Vatican Council's declaration in 1964 repudiating the idea of collective Jewish responsibility for the death of Jesus Christ came a New York joke that mirrored the ethnic pecking order:

> Two elderly Jewish ladies met on the street after a long separation. "How are you, Sadie?" asked her friend.
>   "How should I be?" replied Sadie warily. "I'm fine, thank goodness. I've been watching television."
>   "Television?" said her friend.
>   "Yes. I've got lots of time, so I watch all the programs."
>   "So what have you watched lately?" asked her friend.
>   "Well, I saw a news program about the Vatican. It said that we Jews are no longer responsible for killing Christ."
>   "Is that right?" said her friend. "Well, if we didn't kill Christ, who did?"
>   "I don't know," replied Sadie, "probably the Puerto Ricans."[56]

Intensifying the invective throughout the period was the added dimension of gay and lesbian visibility. With the legislative and public debates over the complex issues of sexual preference and definitions of "couple" and "family" came a taunting humor; concerns were heightened by the unexpected emergence of acquired immunodeficiency syndrome (AIDS). A stream of quips, their virulence increasing with rising publicity over AIDS, surfaced from diverse quarters. Gay males were quickly indicted as the group most dangerous to the nation's health. "By joking about AIDS, one can distance oneself from the disease and from homosexuality," Dundes posited. "To the extent that the anxiety level of the general public remains high concerning the dangers of contracting the disease, it is likely that this joke cycle will continue to flourish. Only when some kind of temporary or permanent cure is finally discovered will AIDS jokes fade from the scene."[57]

Although the humor offered some psychological refuge, it did not radically offset the jokes' vindictiveness, which in part was magnified by a vendetta waged by the conservatives, who contended that the counterculture was the initiating culprit for the nation's woes. These jokes were in effect a scapegoating ritual in which the Moral Majority and other conservative groups were delegated the task of "declaring war" on symbolic representatives of the search for pleasure during the 60s and 70s, and specifically homosexuals (with their legendary promiscuity) and drug addicts. For this reason a portion of the humor contained elements of smug satisfaction, in effect declaring that homosexuals were getting what they "deserved": "What does GAY stand for? Got Aids Yet?"

The gay and lesbian community's drive for social acceptance and constitutional rights produced a blistering set of jokes:

Did you hear about AIDS?
> *That's the disease that turns fruits into vegetables.*

AIDS
> *Assholes in Deep Shit.*

Did you hear about the new gay Cabbage Patch doll?
> *It comes with AIDS and its own death certificate.*

What do AIDS and turkeys have in common?
> *Neither will make it to Christmas.*

What do you call a fag on roller skates?
> *Rollaids.*

They've developed a new drug for AIDS.
> *Trynoassatall.*

How do you keep from getting AIDS?
> *Sit down and shut up!*[58]

And one connecting to the century's most terrifying atrocity: *AIDS: The Lord loves Holocausts.*[59]

Entertainers who succumbed to the disease—"celebrity sick jokes" in folklorist Mac E. Barrick's terminology—became the focus of such jokes as well. The deaths of actor Rock Hudson and pianist Liberace in the mid-1980s were among the earliest reported:

How did Liberace gets AIDS?
  By not cleaning his organ between shoes.

Liberace had trouble leaving his friend's behind.

Rock Hudson was born in Texas and reared in California.

How did AIDS come to America?
  Up the Hudson.

Did you hear Rock Hudson is to be buried upside down?
  That way his friends will recognize him.[60]

Public figures who revealed their sexual preference were instantly added to the list. Representative Gerry Studds of Massachusetts, whose district included Cape Cod, disclosed his sexuality on national television in July 1983, and was reprimanded for having conducted a homosexual relationship with a congressional page early in his career. From Boston, and extending to Los Angeles, came the gibes:

What did one Congressman say to the other?
  So what page are you on?

Why don't Congressmen use bookmarks?
  Because they'd rather bend over their pages.

Gerry Studds is writing his autobiography and all he had to do is turn the pages.

Gerry Studds is going to China on a fact-finding mission.
  He's going to check out the Yellow Pages.

How did Gerry Studds know he was gay?
  His AIDS told him.[61]

On occasion the joke became a metaphor for bureaucracy: "Why isn't AIDS a problem in Eastern Europe? *The policy is to sit on it and keep your mouth shut*" and "There's a new form of AIDS. *You get it from listening to assholes.*"[62]

Dominating the cultural scene in the 1980s and early 1990s, then, were a series of comedic assaults triggered by affirmative action programs, social realignments, and multiculturalist agendas. All wars possess inherent contradictions, and this one was no exception. Its most palpable irony centered on the issue of free speech couched in the ambiguous phrase "political correctness," which saw minorities openly and defiantly ridiculing their oppressors while demanding the termination of derogatory humor. Years of comedic oppression had produced the controversy, and at this historic juncture the minorities resolved to end their victimization. Not only did they refuse to accept the role of culprit, they publicly roiled their adversaries with a reflective comedy inconceivable barely a decade earlier.

10

Comedic Correctness

With the collapse of the counterculture, the establishment was out from under lampooning portraiture. Here and there publications, *The Peter Principle* (1969) and *Up the Organization* (1970), by Laurence J. Peter; a film, *Fun with Dick & Jane* (1977); intermittent cartoons in *The New Yorker*; and sporadic skits on television's *Saturday Night Live* focused a humorous light on its mentality and modus operandi. By and large, though, the establishment prevailed against comedic scrutiny.

Then in the late 1970s and 1980s came the emphatic WASP script, followed by Michael Moore's satiric film *Roger & Me* (1989), a stinging rebuke to General Motors' plant closing in Michigan and Moore's wry, unsuccessful attempt to persuade Chairman Roger Smith to "spend a day with me in Flint and meet some of the people who are losing their jobs." In the summer of 1994, Moore continued his unique, clever foray in a brief and one-of-a-kind television series, *TV Nation*, in which he continued to skewer American corporate policies and arrogance. In 1991 came Robert Townsend's *Riverhead: Tales from the Assembly Line*. By way of the people's grapevine came the WASP jokes, and as sudden as it was rankling, the white Anglo-Saxon Protestant was the cycle of choice. And the targets were not in the least amused.

Just as humor has been used as a weapon of insult and intimidation by dominant groups, so has it been employed for resistance and retaliation by minorities. Sigmund Freud was convinced that humor is "highly suitable for attacks on the great, the dignified and the mighty who are protected by internal inhibitions and external circumstances from direct disparagement. . . . By making our enemy small, inferior, despicable or comic, we achieve in a roundabout way the enjoyment of overcoming him."[1]

Humor reviling the Yankee classes had long circulated around the edges of American culture. A well-known, derisive couplet of the nineteenth century:

> You can always tell the Irish,
>> You can always tell the Dutch,
> You can always tell a Yankee,
>> But you cannot tell him much.[2]

In his *Jokebook About American History* (1974), Ray Ginger proffered an anecdote as "a direct rebuff to the analysts who deny the presence of class conflict in America":

A Detroit businessman had been buying new Fords every couple of years from the same dealer. Then his income rose to the point where he could afford a Cadillac, so he thought: Why not? He bought the car. When he had driven only a few blocks from the agency he heard a rattle. He went back and explained the problem. The sales manager announced in a haughty voice: "Cadillac's do not rattle."

Furious, the man drove his Cadillac to the Ford agency where they knew him. They scoffed at him for deserting them, but agreed to check out the problem. Having test driven the car, and rocked it back and forth by hand for a minute, and squirted around with an oil can, they concluded that the noise was coming from within the door.

Service Manager: "We'll have to open up the upholstery."

Owner of Car: "If you must, you must."

They did. There inside the door was a half-pint milk bottle of the type sold by caterers' carts inside factories. The bottle held a coiled note. They fished out the note and opened it. It read:

"Here is that rattle, you filthy rich bastard."[3]

In the workplace and at intimate social gatherings, antiestablishment jokes and stories were disseminated largely out of earshot of authority. When the humor did confront, workers and minorities frequently resorted to subterfuge, relying on the tactics of mimickry, gibe, and taunt. African-Americans, in a singsong fashion and employing double entendres, comedically had befuddled masters, then bosses. Dialect jokes employed by Eastern and Central European immigrants provided communal sanctuary as well as a means of retaliatory jiving. Whenever the opportunity presented itself, workers laughed up a storm behind bosses' backs.

Then in the late 1970s the cocoon was shattered, the opening crack coming with the script bearing the insect-evoking WASP, an acronym deriving from E. Digby Baltzell's scholarly treatises *Philadelphia Gentlemen* (1958) and *Protestant Establishment: Aristocracy and Caste in America* (1964). As William Safire acutely observed, "Words, like spies, can be taken prisoner, turned and used against the enemy."[4]

The WASP cycle became the joke of the moment. On Johnny Carson's *The Tonight Show* in mid-1979, comedian Buddy Hackett asked, "How many WASPs does it take to change a lightbulb? *Two—one to call the electrician, the other to make sure the martinis are chilled.*" Jim Pietsch, a New York cab driver who collected and exchanged jokes with passengers, recounted a story typical in the 1980s:

> Two WASPS are making love. Afterward the man says to the woman, "What's the matter? Didn't you like it?"
>
> The woman says, "Of course I liked it. What gave you the idea that I didn't?"
>
> "Well," says the man, "you moved."[5]

The WASP series was more than a single assault against the upper class. It was one facet of the fierce joke wars that swept through the decade. Since the key to the pejorative joke resides in a set of stereotypical images, the minorities returned the favor. The establishment was portrayed as heirs of seventeenth-century Puritanism: elitist, uptight, penurious, asexual; and their immunity to and detachment from life's daily pains and problems were definitely galling. President George Bush's gaffe at a supermarket visit during the 1992 presidential campaign—he was surprised by the scanner at the checkout counter and asked how it worked—lent substance to their pique.

The WASP cycle highlighted the most obnoxious traits in their perceived character.

1. Elitism:

> What do you get when you cross a WASP with an orangutan?
> *I don't know, but it won't let "you" into its cage.*

What's a WASP's idea of mass transit?
The ferry to Martha's Vineyard.

2. "Smart dealing":

What do WASPs give their children to play with?
Trust funds.

What do you call 12 WASPs sitting around a table?
Price-fixing.

3. Stinginess:

How do you tell the WASPs in a Chinese restaurant?
They're the ones not sharing the food.

Especially ridiculed were lifestyle conventions.

1. Cleanliness:

What's the definition of a WASP?
Someone who gets out of the shower to urinate.

2. Sexuality:

What's the WASP's idea of an orgy?
Shares splitting.

How can you recognize a WASP at a nudist colony?
He's the one with the Wall Street Journal *on his lap.*

What do you call a WASP woman who makes love more than once a month?
A nymphomaniac.

Why do WASP men make terrible lovers?
Because by the time they've hung up their trousers and put the trees in their shoes, the woman has usually lost all interest.

3. Wealth:

Why did God create WASPs?
Because someone has to buy retail.

4. Self-centeredness:

> Why do WASPs smile at lightning?
> *Because they think they're having their picture taken.*[6]

Compared with the life span of the Polish or JAP series, the WASP chain was brief. Nonetheless, the establishment recoiled as if unsportingly ambushed. *Yankee* magazine complained that the term *WASP* cut just as harmfully as other ethnic epithets: "It's a deep character insult that shouldn't be permitted," wrote its editor. In an op-ed essay in the *New York Times*, Edward Hoagland called upon the media to "quit using the jeering word 'WASP' in their pages." The "ethnic epithet is often employed in print (and conversation) with a prejudice that is intended to sting." Worse, Hoagland argued, the word has no "honest meaning" because "all Anglo-Saxon Protestants are white, so 'WASP' is redundant at best." John Sears's protest was specifically grounded. Since the upper classes no longer possessed many of their past privileges, they did not deserve the bashing: "Since we WASPs no longer enjoy many of the original prerogatives, we tire of the same old privilege jokes."[7]

In light of the changing social order, many contended, it was unfair for the upper classes to have the limelight all to themselves. There was "no reasonable excuse for having one ethnic slur in general circulation while forbidding all others," insisted Hoagland, a position supported by Sears, who lamented that "we WASPs don't have the protection of other minority groups." Less and less was there a "difference between bashing Puerto Rican immigrants and bashing orange-headed gubernatorial candidates." "Orange-headed" was the caustic description of the Brahmin Republican candidate, William Weld, used by his Democratic opponent, John Silber, in the 1992 gubernatorial campaign in Massachusetts.[8]

Pursuing this argument further was sociologist Peter Berger, who contended that WASPs had indeed become the outsiders in the nation's unwritten rules of "liberal appropriateness." Berger faulted a "liberal cultural elite" for undermining humor's subject matter. A polite culture, he contended, tends to expunge ethnic language that offends the feelings of the underprivileged, a list encompassing gays and lesbians, the disabled, women, the overweight, racial minorities—every group, in fact, save the upper classes. "Pluralism creates an atmosphere of generalized tolerance," the exception being the establishment "minority." "Since most people agree WASPs are still a privileged sector of society, we assume no great harm is done joking about them."[9]

Raillery directed against the propertied classes was in retaliation for a history of comedic abuse as well as for the public upsurge in ethnic and gender slurs—driven underground in the 1970s by the combined forces of Black Power, women's liberation, and liberal energies—that had openly intensified during the 1980s. Derogatory comedy had largely been driven from public discourse, a major exception being Norman Lear's television series *All in the Family*, which brazenly exposed ethnic, racial, and gender stereotyping. Harsh jokes coursed through the byways of the establishment locker rooms, fraternal organizations, dinner parties, and political meetings. Corporate managers, high-level businessmen, conservative presidents, cabinet members, and administrative appointees regaled audiences with stories of ridicule, apologizing only when the print media reported them.

Not only had the upper classes countenanced the flow of oppressive humor, they had benefited from it over the centuries. While "what goes around comes around" does not justify the WASP series, it serves to remind that the insult genre constitutes a substantial portion of humor. "During the melting pot era of emphasis on assimilation," noted anthropologist Mahadev L. Apte, "the members of ethnic minority groups had to grin and bear the humor of which they were the butt. In a sense, they conformed, at least outwardly, to the dominant value of having a sense of humor since they learned to tolerate and, on occasion, to force laughter at the disparaging humor initiated by the outsiders at their expense."[10]

Concomitantly, a considerable portion of prejudiced joking derived as well from those resentful of welfare programs, irritated by gender competition, angered by affirmative action policies, and fearful of gay and lesbian sexual politics. Nonetheless, not only did the establishment fail to reprove and deflect such behavior, they partook in the raillery and ironically insisted that they, too, were victims of "political correctness."

From the early 1960s, the belief in the assimilation of minority groups into mainstream culture had collided with the growing insistence on cultural pluralism.[11] And with minorities insisting on redefining American society along multicultural lines, the issue of humor's content had become palpably immediate and incendiary. A political struggle over who would control the content, character, and language of national humor, a matter that intricately impinged on free speech boundaries, became a major aspect of the debate.

In challenging the dominant cultural institutions, the minorities concertedly moved to make anathema the open narration of bigoted, and what was perceived as derogatory, joking. Joining with women, ethnic groups denounced comedic expressions experienced as repugnant and demeaning. Each sought the elimination of image-based slurs: "chick," "baby," and "girl"; "Polack" and "honkey"; "greaser" and "dago"; "boy," "auntie," "junglebunny," and "nigger"; "chink" and "Jap"; "homo" and "fag"; "dyke" and "bulldyke"; "kike" and "JAP."

With the expanding comedic venue arose a confrontational strategy. "Anti-Polish jokes are no joke," wrote the president of the eastern Massachusetts branch of the Polish-American Congress in a letter to the *Boston Globe* at the height of the "Polack" joke cycle in 1975. "The continuing slander of Poles on TV, through books, news media, on stage by hypocrites is called humor—very sick humor. I do not believe it is harmless."[12] The president of New Jersey's African-American Bar Association in 1991 angrily decried as "racially insensitive" a skit before hundreds attending a Christmas show in which a male lawyer in blackface and curly-haired wig sang "Ol' Man River" and four dressed up as Anita Hill, the black lawyer who had testified that year regarding sexual harassment by nominee Clarence Thomas at his Supreme Court confirmation proceedings.[13]

Deeply incensed over JAP jokes, the National Federation of Temple Sisterhoods added to the agenda at their 1987 convention the JAP joke: "What began as an object of sexist humor has now become a tool of the anti-Semite" and the jokes, "far from being harmless humor, are forms of negative stereotyping and prejudice which demean Jewish women." The conference instructed its affiliates to discontinue the sale of items bearing the letters "JAP" and to foster an awareness of "the subtleties of discrimination in our everyday lives."[14]

In 1990, after a sophomore at the University of Connecticut placed a sign on her dormitory door listing "people who are shot on sight"—among them "preppies, bimbos, men without chest hair, and homos"—she was charged by the gay community with violating the student-behavior code and subsequently ordered off campus.[15] Students at the Johns Hopkins University seized copies of the campus newspaper—an action repeated at other institutions in the early 1990s—that printed a cartoon showing a male Asian student sitting at one end of a couch and a white female student at the other, with the man exclaiming, "I only date Chinks."[16] Pop singer Sinéad O'Connor and Nora Dunn, a cast regular, in 1990 boycotted the appearance of stand-up comic Andrew Dice Clay on a *Saturday Night Live* television show; the comic responded by referring to Ms. Dunn as "Nora Dunce" and suggesting that her action was a publicity stunt.[17]

A climate of skittishness prevailed as minorities responded vigorously to what they regarded as insult. As early as 1972, reacting to protest from the Polish-American community, comedian Steve Allen publicly apologized for telling Polish jokes on an ABC broadcast. Some two decades later, a small Irish-American lobbying group, the Irish National Caucus, denounced a promotional advertisement sponsored by ESPN, the cable TV sports channel, a thirty-second clip that scrolled across the screen: "Last night . . . I was watching . . . this foreign film . . . about two sisters enduring . . . the Great Potato famine . . . and I thought to myself . . . what the hell am I doing? . . . There's a hockey game on." Its flippant referral to the nineteenth-century Irish famine, the president exclaimed, was "racist to the core, extremely insensitive and deeply offensive."[18]

Many blacks protested a New York Friar's Club routine jointly devised by comedian-entertainers Whoopi Goldberg and Ted Danson in 1993, in which the latter appeared in formal attire and blackface. "What's black and white and red all over?" asked Karen Grigsby Bates in the *Los Angeles Times.* "Whoopi Goldberg's and Ted Danson's faces, if they possess between them even a scintilla of propriety." Several persons walked out in protest, including Mayor David Dinkins and talk-show host Montel Williams.[19]

Heartened, other groups came forward to protest their idiosyncratic predicaments. After hearing 1988 Democratic presidential candidate Michael Dukakis referred to as a "shrimp and wimp," two female television producers in San Francisco, 5 feet, 1½ inches, tall and weary of being tagged "cute" and "feisty," founded the National Association of Short Adults, the "Alternative Space Agency," a whimsical reference to NASA. A decade earlier, Randy Newman's song

"Short People"—"Short people got no reason to live"—had generated controversy, and the composer explained that the lyrics were
"aimed not at short people but at shortsighted people."[20] The association's sardonic motto was "Down in Front," and the first issue of its
newsletter, *The Short Sheet*, called for an equal heights amendment to
outlaw hats and bouffant hairdos in movie theaters, and to lower the
seat level of chairs in public places by 6½ inches.[21]

Larger organizations also responded to self-perceived affronts.
Cleveland, a city besieged by jokes spoofing its supposed cultural
vapidity, defaulted 1978 loan, and polluted river that had caught fire,
complained about a projected advertisement in a convention plan-
ners' trade journal. The ad displayed two photographs, one a cloudy,
gray, industrial skyline bearing the legend "Cleveland, Ohio," the
other a woman attired in a swimsuit and floppy hat, surf lapping at
her feet, with the identification "Palm Beach County, Florida." Head-
lining the photos was the question: "Given the fact they cost the
same, where would you prefer to hold your business meeting?" City
officials winced, maintaining that the advertising was blatant stereotyping; that Cleveland was culturally vigorous, with a first-class art
museum, professional orchestra, and the Rock and Roll Hall of Fame.
At the same time, convention officials in neighboring Columbus,
Ohio, who were competing for convention business, needled Cleveland's promotional gift of horns by suggesting that visitors to the city
could use them to ward off criminals. When Cleveland's officials reac-
ted, the director of Columbus's agency maintained that "it was a joke.
I didn't think they'd be touchy about it."[22]

Legal actions across the country reflected heightened political
clout. In 1987 city employees in Long Branch, New Jersey, received
along with their monthly salary a legal directive outlining a ban on
ethnic and racial jokes in the workplace. "We'd rather be safe than
sorry. We can't afford another lawsuit," explained the city administrator, following litigation by a black woman who experienced humilia-
tion and anguish from racist jokes at work. In 1990, in Los Angeles,
Raul Serrano, a fifteen-year Mexican-American bus driver, was
awarded damages in a defamation suit. Serrano had been featured in
the regular cartoon in the company's newsletter, "Operator's Humor
Corner," which depicted him arriving late at a bus stop. The would-
be passenger, a skeleton dressed in a sombrero and serape, exclaimed,
"Is about time for Serrano to show up. I was ready to die." Serrano

claimed that he was not after a financial award: "I was furious when I first saw that cartoon. It was demeaning, it was uncaring, it was ridiculing and racist, and it was singling me out for not caring about the hard-working people that I drive. To this day, all I've ever wanted was an apology."[23]

In 1972, in a case rejected by the U.S. Supreme Court, the Polish-American Congress brought suit against the ABC television network for airing Polish jokes. But two decades later, a unanimous Court, in *Teresa Harris* v. *Forklift Systems*, established new definitions for sexual harassment in the workplace that specifically addressed the issue of "friendly ribbing." In the arguments, newly installed Justice Ruth Bader Ginsberg, the second woman on the Court, maintained that sexual jokes and uncouth behavior alone could be construed as discrimination against women. Writing for the Court, Justice Sandra Day O'Connor stated that the law is violated "when a workplace is permeated with discriminatory intimidation, ridicule, and insult."

Institutions across the country consequently grappled with the problem of "hate speech." At the University of Michigan in 1989, after gender, racist, and gay jokes were inserted into a computer program and relayed by a student disc jockey over the university radio station, the faculty passed a resolution punishing any speech on campus that "stigmatizes or victimizes." Observing that the term "foreign" carries a pejorative image, the Turner Broadcasting System in 1990 replaced it with "international" on its business correspondence and on its Cable News Network broadcasting.[24]

Also reacting to the situation were the hearing-impaired, who in the early 1990s achieved new ways of signing the words for minorities. "In American Sign Language," noted psychologist Elissa Newport, "politically incorrect terms are often a visual representation of the ugly metaphors we have about people." Substituting for the signed word "Japanese," which had been conveyed by twisting the little finger next to the eye, indicating a slanted eye, was the Japanese sign for themselves: pressing the thumbs and index fingers of both hands, then pulling them apart, and drawing the silhouette of Japan. Similarly, the words "Chinese" and "Korean," which had been made by forming the letters "C" and "K" around the eyes, were altered. The original gesture for "Negro," a flattening of the nose, was replaced by the sign for "black." "Africa" was conveyed by outlining the continent in the air with one's hand. The old sign for "homosexual" had

been a swish of the wrist, a suggestion of effeminacy; it was supplanted by a one-finger spelling, or by the placing the letter "q" on
the chin, for "queer." A stroking of an imaginary beard, indicating
Jewish stinginess, also was eliminated.[25]

Newly emerged groups joined in protesting discordant language.
Real Men, an antisexist group founded in Boston in 1988, circulated
"Stop Verbal Violence Against Women" leaflets and scored sexist, racist, and homophobic jokes. Drawing a correlation between the comic
and violence, maintaining that ferocity is legitimized and reinforced
when people laugh at the subordination and objectification of oppressed groups, the organization challenged a Boston comedy club's
invitation to Andrew Dice Clay. "The Comedy Connection has the
right to feature Andrew Dice Clay. But they also have a *responsibility*
to the community, and to women." The flyer listed the name and
telephone number of the club's owner.[26]

All this activity signaled the moment of triumphant cultural politics by minorities. By the late 1980s and early 1990s the public had
shied away from jokes and stories that might be construed as distasteful or demeaning. The transition from a state of victimization to
empowerment regarding humor's substance in the public domain recalled George Meredith's brilliant "Essay on Comedy." "Comedy,"
Meredith observed, "can be a means of mastering our disillusions
when we are caught in a dishonest or stupid society. After we recognize the misdoings, the blunders, we can liberate ourselves by a confident, wise laughter that brings a catharsis of our discontent. . . .
Unflinching and undaunting we see *where we are.*"[27]

There was, however, a downside affect to minority power-wedg-
ing. Having finally blunted much derisive and humiliating humor,
they were confronted with the charge of subverting traditional cultural motifs. The question of stifling behavior encapsulated in the
phrase "political correctness" did suggest a particular societal dilemma. "Therein lies a complex issue in today's arts and culture,"
Richard Bernstein observed in the *New York Times* in 1990, "the issue
of insult: when it's acceptable and when it isn't."[28] At the core of the
predicament was the question of whose ox is being gored, whose ex-
alted. One person's joke, goes a familiar dictum, is another person's
insult. But in this period of political correctness, historic sensitivities
boiled over and out.

Accused of jousting with the lance of "political correctness," and in so doing, restricting the avenues of social discourse, minorities were thus scored for fostering a repressive climate. In the name of pluralism, according to the indictment, the multiculturalists were in effect undermining First Amendment rights.

Ambiguities dogged the situation, and were not easily resolved. The imbroglio surrounding a parody of a 1992 article by a feminist legal scholar who had been brutally murdered typified the problem. At the annual banquet of the prestigious *Harvard Law Review,* coincidentally the first anniversary of the unsolved stabbing of Mary Joe Frug, who had been a professor at the New England School of Law, the editors mocked Frug's published but not completed article, "A Postmodern Feminist Legal Manifesto"—an analysis of the relation between law and women's subjugation. The spoof, "He-Manifesto of Post-Mortem Legal Feminism," supposedly originated "from beyond the grave" by the "Rigor Mortis Professors of Law at Northeastern School of Law." The ensuing uproar touched on issues dividing the Harvard Law School, among them the appointment of blacks and women to tenured faculty positions, but the parody itself produced a fierce debate. Several students nailed wanted posters for the authors of the piece and demanded punitive action. A third-year female student protested that the parody was "symptomatic of the hostility toward women who are taking over positions of power traditionally held by white males. This was their fraternity-like response to getting back at women who fought to publish Mary Joe's article." Professor Alan M. Dershowitz countered, asserting that "there is something very wrong at Harvard Law School, but it is not sexism or racism." On the one hand, "feminists can accuse all men of being rapists and radical African-Americans can accuse all whites of being racists," but they cannot accept "even an unintentionally offensive parody of a woman or blacks." With exasperation, Professor Elizabeth Bartholet noted, "These people just don't get it. To see so many people on our faculty belittle what we take seriously is what is creating the level of anger we have."[29]

It was clear that in large part the problem lay in the perceived slow response to impassioned summons. No longer willing to bear slights, minorities were acutely sensitive to slurs, no matter how unintended or "in good fun." Especially they were furious over the backlash. In their view the dominant groups had not only been unheedful of insistent prodding, delivered with gentle and benign humor, but now the prodders were being cast as the "politically correct" villains.

In an article on the front page of the *Boston Globe* in mid-1993, "Can't We Take a Joke Anymore? Losing Our Sense of Humor Is No Laughing Matter," the historic moment was typically misconstrued. "Today, there is evidence that America is becoming an increasingly brittle, thin-skinned society, where a joke is seldom funny unless somebody else is the butt of it—and perhaps not even then. More than an outbreak of so-called political correctness, this seems to be an epidemic whose main symptom is chronic loss of perspective, not anemic self-esteem."[30]

If the cost of repressing public expression by eliminating derogatory racial and gender slurs was circumscribed humor, the deficit was more than offset by the diminishing of ghettoizing stereotyping that had long plagued American culture. Rather than the loss of social perspective, there was an increased awareness of minority culture that had long been absent in the popular culture. Its positive feature was, in addition, the varied composition of performers in the entertainment world. By forcing shut the door to comic scorn, the minorities were opening the way to comic diversity.

Consequently, by century's close, national humor vividly refracted a tribal arrangement: "No longer Americans we are now Native Americans, African Americans, Italian Americans, Jewish Americans, unequal citizens in a commonwealth of tribal cultures."[31] The WASP jokes were just the opening salvo of comic repayment as minorities showered assaultive humor on their detractors, to let them know that control over public humor was no longer theirs exclusively.

11

Tribal Reprisals

Filtering through the cultural cracks in the post–World War II period were a spate of retaliatory jokes that gave the first hint of the open assault to come later in the century:

> Christopher Columbus came ashore in the New World and walked up to a pair of Indians standing at the edge of a forest.
> "¿Cómo está?" Columbus greeted them.
> "Oh God," said one Indian to the other, "there goes the neighborhood."

> The Lone Ranger and his faithful Indian companion, Tonto, were suddenly surrounded by a hostile group of Indians.
> "Good heavens, Tonto!" said the Lone Ranger. "There are two thousand wild and maddened Indians swooping down over the prairie and only we are here to stop them."
> Tonto replied, "What do you mean *we*, paleface?"[1]

Building over the centuries, the stockpile of minority humor beneath the cultural surface had gradually seeped into national consciousness. Jewish jokes with their ironic, caustic, and self-deprecating sallies came from the burlesque and vaudeville houses, Catskill resorts, film comedies, and television variety programs. African-American witticisms and tricksterisms, honed on bondage and segregation, trickled in from the minstrels and blues. Bits and pieces of women's narratives made their way into print. Rarely heard, however, was Native American humor and that of other minorities.

Then in the early 1960s a group of young black comics played their routines before white audiences, and as Dick Gregory, Godfrey Cambridge, Flip Wilson, and Bill Cosby quickly soared into prominence in the 1960s and 1970s—opening the way for older, veteran entertainers "Moms" Mabley, Nipsey Russell, Redd Foxx, "Pigmeat" Markham, Dusty Fletcher, George Kirby, and Timmy Rogers—minority humor finally emerged from the underground. In swift fashion, whites became privy to the complexities of African-American life through its twisting quips, role reversals, and imaginative wordplay.

Until the civil rights and Black Power movements pried open the cultural venues, few whites could have identified black comedians and writers, including the widely published Langston Hughes. Even the knowledgeable humorist Ogden Nash had expressed astonishment about the range and creativity of African-American humor in a review of Langston Hughes's *The Book of Negro Humor* (1966): "The range of humor here collected is a surprise. One would have not have expected so many kinds, from so many sources. There are the contemporary comics. . . . There are jokes having to do with jive and the blues. There are anecdotes from the pulpit. There are stories from Orleans and Harlem."[2]

Extracting from historical experiences and reflecting communal banter, black comedians delivered a running commentary about black as well as white society. While their acts reflected individual styles, each was sustained by a vast body of collective memory. Ralph Ellison highlighted this fount of lore in a dialogue with novelist-poet Robert Penn Warren. "When the country was not looking at Negroes, when we were restrained in certain of our activities by the interpretation of the law of the land, something was present in our lives to sustain us. This is evident when we look at the folklore in a truly questioning way, when we scrutinize and listen before passing judgment. Listen to those tales which are told by Negroes themselves."[3]

With the stand-up routines expanded by Richard Pryor, Eddie Murphy, Damon Wayans, and others came a broadening of racial perspective. Gregory's early routines reconstructed a perspective that had long enriched experiences over the centuries: "It's kinda sad, but my little girl doesn't believe in Santa Claus. She sees that white cat with the whiskers and even at two years old she knows damn well that no white man's coming to our neighborhood at midnight." Cambridge tackled the question of property values: "Do you realize the amount of havoc a Negro couple can cause just by walking down the street on a Sunday morning with a copy of the *New York Times* real estate section under the man's arm?" Redd Foxx mocked the fear of crime by piquing an unenthusiastic, predominantly Caucasian crowd: "Why should I be wasting time with you here when I could be knifing you in the alley?"[4] Several decades later, Richard Pryor, whose films and one-person concerts entwined the racial with the intensely personal, redressed the imbalance of comedy, as did Bill Cosby in the long-running television sitcom of the upper-middle-class Huxtable family from 1986 to 1992, which liberated television from its racially confining boundaries.

One thread woven through the commentaries in the 1960s and 1970s was the stark reality of continuing segregation against the backdrop of legal changes effected by the *Brown* v. *Board of Education* decision and the struggle to abolish Jim Crow practices. De facto conventions produced a succession of retaliatory jokes. Multiplied across the country, such sallies echoed a chorus of militancy. Blacks openly taunted and vilified whites, who for so long had been immune to open censure. Certain jokes were directed against individuals whose policies were blatantly discriminatory. Governor George Wallace of Alabama, who had defiantly stood in a doorway to prevent black students from desegrating the University of Alabama in the mid-1960s, was such a target:

> Governor Wallace went for his annual medical checkup. The doctor examined him thoroughly and told him to return for the results in a week.
> A week passed and Wallace returned for the doctor's report. "Well, Doc, how'm ah doin'?"
> The doctor looks at him carefully and says, "Governor, I got good news and bad news."
> "Good news and bad news?" repeats Wallace. "All right, give me the good news first."
> "The good news, Governor, is that you got cancer."
> Wallace blanches. "That the good news, that ah got cancer?"
> "That's right."
> "Well, if that's the good news, what the hell is the bad news?"
> "The bad news is that it's sickle-cell anemia," says the doctor.[5]

Several decades later, a joke set in the North enlarged the social enemy:

A black freshman student at Harvard University stopped a white faculty member on campus and inquired, "Where's the library at?"

"Young man, you don't end a sentence with a preposition," admonished the teacher.

"O.K., man," replied the student, "where's the library at, asshole?"[6]

As black stand-ups performed in mainstream entertainment venues, they strove to impart the gnarled history of race relations. Pryor, who made the issue of race both personal and universal,[7] played a *Saturday Night Live* sketch with Chevy Chase, a white comic, in which the pair collaborated in a dialogue encompassing the gamut of racial slurs. Pryor was interviewed by Chase for a custodial job and given a word-association test:

"White," says Chase.
"Black," Pryor replies.

"Bean."
"Pod."

"Negro."
"Whitey," Pryor replies lightly.

"Tarbaby."
"What did you say?" Pryor asks, puzzled.
"Tarbaby," Chase repeats, monotone.
"Ofay!" Pryor says sharply.

"Colored."
"Redneck!"

"Junglebunny!"
"Peckerwood," Pryor yells.

"Burrhead!"
"Cracker."

"Spearchucker!"
"White Trash!"

"Junglebunny!"
"Honky!"

"Spade!"
"Honky, Honky!"

"Nigger," says Chase smugly.
"Dead Honky!" Pryor growls.[8]

Black comics were in part motivated to enlarge the sense of com-
monality. Cambridge stated the need to acquaint whites with the
"normalcy" of the black world, "with letting people see the truth of
our lives." In Cambridge's, as well as in Gregory's, acts could be
heard a sly mocking of black conduct and of white prejudice. "This
one Negro, Dr. Jones," said Gregory in a routine about his moving
into a white community, "he says 'you gotta be careful in this neighborhood, and cool 'cause they're watching us.' I said, 'What you-all
doing, stealing something?' He said, 'No, you know what I mean.
They're going to look for you to depreciate some property.' I said,
'Buddy, they just charged me $75,000 for a $12,000 house. I'll depreciate this whole block if you let me.' "[9]

Pryor's comedy further expanded the boundaries of black and
national humor. Employing street language, Pryor crisscrossed personal and racial lines—a decided fear of animals, a heart attack, drug
addiction, and accidental self-immolation—with biting social criticism. To blacks he "spoke the unspeakable," thereby shifting the
"burden of murderously vengeful thoughts we'd buried without
laughter deep within ourselves to his own shoulders for preciously
few moments that seemed a lifetime."[10]

Pryor's openness paved the way for the next generation of comics.
In Los Angeles in 1992, a group of comics who performed at the
Comedy Act Theater—founded in 1986 in a district heavily trashed
by the violence in that year—dissected the community's actions during the massive riot of 1992. Embracing and criticizing the looting and
firebombing that followed the Rodney King verdict, which had initially exonerated the four white policemen of brutality, the comics
offered perspective. "The purpose of making jokes about the riots,"
stated Keith Morris, "is to make people realize what they've done. I
feel that the rioting was justified, but, then, it was *not* justified? . . .
You don't burn down things that we need in the community."

Morris's routines reflected the deep ambivalence felt by many
blacks regarding the rampage. "The riots showed them that we won't
take this shit anymore," he told his audiences. "And it showed them

that you're all stupid shits because you burnt down your check-cashing places." Even "babies were looting. They had babies stealing, had them pulling TV sets down the street while they were in their strollers."

Similar thoughts chorused from other performers. "You know," exclaimed a female comic with disarming seriousness, "I'm glad the riots happened, because those prices have just gotten to be so ridiculous! Some of the burning I didn't like. But they didn't have to burn down Fatburger. That just broke my heart. I mean, is there any justice in the world that people can burn down Fatburger?" Black pride was wrapped within the comic. The Fun House club displayed T-shirts with the words "100% Black Owned," mimicking the signs that had spared some stores. Several comics noted that white people had altered their attitude toward blacks since the riot. "I come to work now, and white people are playing rap music, serving watermelon buffets."

Jokes sprang from the inner city as well. "The rioting stopped because they had to figure out how to program their new VCRs" went one popular quip. At a high school, students with new shoes were teased with "Where's your sales slip?" And the marquee of The Laugh Factory club on Sunset Boulevard sported the message: "All the jokes were stolen. Please don't break in."[11]

Nor was this the only instance of black comics responding to the drama of their neighborhoods. In Boston in 1991, Jef T and others organized Comics Against Gang Violence after his seventeen-year-old brother was killed in a gang rif. The show featured fifteen black and white comics who performed to a near capacity multiracial audience containing ex–gang members who were part of a local advocacy group, Gang Peace. One duo rapped to the song "Senseless Homicide": "On the streets of Boston, something's going wrong . . . a brother got bopped and dropped . . . another added to the death list . . . and after that you ask yourself why this is a senseless homicide?" Because of the somber occasion, the show had moments of "intense hilarity, as comics avoided lectures . . . and just let the happening be the statement."[12]

Confrontations were mounted against the historic pattern of comic stereotyping. Racist artifacts that had inundated the popular culture over the centuries were exhibited in various places around the country. "Images of blacks in popular culture have been an important vehicle for the transmission of the myth of white superiority," noted the introductory placard for Black Memorabilia, a 1981 display at Dartmouth College. A collection of several hundred objects produced between the Civil War and World War I, including toys, games, sheet music, postcards, advertising, illustrations, and packaging, portrayed blacks as "slow, lazy, ignorant, stupid, amoral, criminal, unclean, bestial and generally subhuman." "Our intention is clear," explained Dianne Pinderhughes, a political scientist who organized the show. "It may be unpleasant to view these items and to bring out into the open what may be considered shocking examples of black stereotyping. . . . We want to show how comprehensive a set of stereotypes we have in American society, among blacks and whites, and we want to generate discussion about how we create and maintain stereotypes." Marguerite Barnett-King, director of the Institute for Urban and Minority Education at Teachers College, Columbia University, whose private collection made up the bulk of the exhibit, saw the past as cultural mirror: "When one comes to terms with this material, one sees that the image is not me but an oppressor's idea of me."[13]

In this self-reflecting social climate, a minority within a minority also sought recognition. Black gays in San Francisco, the Pomo Afro Homos—Postmodern African-American Homosexuals—produced a show in the early 1990s that traveled around the country. *Dark Fruit* (its biting title deriving from Lillian Smith's powerful play of 1942) was a collection of skits, monologues, and readings that explored the complexities of black gay culture, wryly observing, "If you're poor, black, feminine and gay, life is the wrong place."[14]

Until the 1970s, the comedic stage was an uncertain place for the majority of women because it had traditionally meant the absence of "an enlargement of possibilities."[15] Unlike blacks, women were denied even the rudimentary and essential quality of humor itself. The notion that women possessed no sense of humor was in itself ironic, inasmuch as they were required to complement a man's comic sense. "If females have no faculty for humor, how were they to know when and what to laugh at?" was an oft-repeated response. One notable consequence was that "the development of an open rebellious humor may not have been an option available" to women.[16]

Although denied a sense of humor, women were its oppressive object. Specific types abounded: the dumb blonde, the nagging wife, the unconscious driver, the illogical thinker, the headachy sex partner, the bitchy mother-in-law. Ludicrous stereotypes portrayed them as two-thumbed, excessively verbose, and dazzlingly obtuse. Obscured by all these cultural headlocks were the complexities and nuances of women's humor. In a slew of forms—the domestic tale, the skit, the fantasy—women relayed a realistic comedy reflecting common experiences that offered a perspective on their place as "victims of cultural expectations." The absurdity of their jokes provided a reflection of "the fundamental absurdity of oppression."[17]

Throughout women's private sagas ran rivulets of antagonism that by the mid-1960s came pouring out in response to the calls for political empowerment. Satirical criticism made its appearance in graffiti, poetry, feminist music, and stand-up routines.[18] Early on, graffiti filled the vacant walls in bathrooms, revealing shared outrages that called for putting men in their place: "Why is a husband better than a cucumber?" went a typical comment in a Northeastern University bathroom in the early 1970s. "Because he can take out the garbage." Jokes peppering the scene suggested a growing sense of power;

> At her afternoon bridge game, a matronly woman casually mentioned, "Tomorrow is my husband's birthday."
>
> Immediately one of her friends asked, "Well, what are you getting for him?"
>
> Replied the woman, "I don't know yet. I'm waiting for someone to make me an offer."[19]

No longer immune, men were skewered at public forums and conferences. Millicent Fenwick, the liberal Republican congresswoman from New Jersey from the 1970s into the 1980s who inspired the Lacey Davenport character in Garry Trudeau's *Doonesbury* cartoon series, had often been beset by stereotypical asides. Fenwick possessed a powerful wit. During the debate over equal rights for women, one male legislator declared, "I just don't like this amendment. I've always thought of women as kissable, cuddly and smelling good." "That's the way I feel about men, too," Fenwick quickly replied. "I only hope for your sake that you haven't been disappointed as often as I have."[20]

A chorus of mocking confronted male definitions and nomenclatures. After Fundamentalist Christians in Santa Cruz, California, contended that they should not be forced to hire or rent to homosexuals—who, they said, violate God's laws—lesbians retorted with the challenging line, "We are all equal in the eyes of the Goddess."[21] In 1978 the clerk of the Cambridge, Massachusetts, District Court received a letter from a woman regarding a minor traffic infraction:

> Enclosed is my check for $10 for a traffic violation plus a request for a waiver.
>
> I will not and cannot fill out the form on the reverse of the waiver for obvious reasons. You ask for my "maiden name"! What is a maiden name? I have a name which is on my check and which was on my traffic violation. If, for reasons of identification, you wish to know my family name, why not ask for it, rather than propagate sexist terminology?
>
> I also do not know why you need to know if I have a husband or wife, or both or neither, since I pay my own fines and am responsible for my debts.
>
> If you need to identify me, I would be more than happy to provide you with my Social Security number.
>
> P.S. Some further thoughts have occurred to me on your request for a maiden name. According to the dictionary a maiden has long meant the same thing as a virgin (and she was expected to lose this virginity when she entered marriage). I am not aware that I was called anything different before I lost my virginity. Did the Cambridge Chief of Police go by another name before he lost his virginity, assuming that has happened already?[22]

Inversionary jiving abounded. "What's so bad about PMS?" went a joke in the late 1980s. "What's wrong with acting like a man for three days a month?"[23] Columnist Ann Landers printed a letter from "No Dummy in Philly":

> I'd get a big kick out of it if you'd publish my response to "A Texas Question," the reader whose son asked why women are so dumb.
>
> As the story goes, there was a man sitting in his room. He began to talk to God. The man said, "God, why did you make women so beautiful?"
>
> God replied, "Well, so you would like them."
>
> "Oh," the man replied, "why then did you make women so soft?"
>
> Again, God replied, "So you would like them."
>
> The man was pensive for a moment and then asked, "God, why then did you make women so darned stupid?"
>
> God replied, "So they would like you!"[24]

A chain letter that first circulated in 1968 and resurfaced in the early 1990s offered not the usual monetary reward for a small token plus copies to others but an exchange of husbands:

> Dear Friend,
>
> This letter was started by a woman, like yourself, in hopes of bringing relief to tired and discontented women.
>
> Unlike most chain letters, this chain does not cost anything.
>
> Send a copy to five of your friends who are just as tired of it all as you. Then pack up your husband and send him to the woman whose name is at the top of the list. Then add your name to the bottom of the list.
>
> When your name comes up, you will receive 16,478 men, and some of them are dandies!!!
>
> Have faith and don't break the chain. One woman broke it and got her own Son-Of-A-Bitch back.
>
> Sincerely,
>
> A Discontented Wife
>
> P.S. At the time of this letter, a friend of mine has received 183 men. They buried her yesterday, but it took three Undertakers 36 hours to take the grin off her face.[25]

Raillery put men on the defensive in the war of jokes, effectively ending their domination in the public arena. Jokes that in the past would not have circulated in the community surfaced at social gatherings:

> Two women were walking down a New York street when they spotted a frog. The frog looked up and said, "I used to be a handsome, wealthy stockbroker. But I was turned into a frog. If one of you kisses me on the lips, I will be turned back to my original self."
>
> One of the women stooped down, picked up the frog and placed him in her pocket. The two friends walked on for a while, but the other finally got curious and said, "Aren't you going to kiss the frog on the lips and turn him back to what he was?"
>
> "Nope," she replied, "don't you know how much I can get for a talking frog these days?"[26]

Accompanied by his wife, a man in his seventies goes to a urologist with a problem. After the examination, the doctor tells him that he will die if he doesn't have sex within the next several weeks. The man, who is also hard of hearing, cups his hand over his ear and asks the doctor to repeat his diagnosis.

"I said, if you don't have sex within the next couple of weeks, you will die."

Once again, the man says that he couldn't hear all of what the doctor was prescribing. In louder tones, the doctor repeats his charge.

Finally, the man turns to his wife and asks, "What did he say?"

"He said," his wife replies, "that you're going to die."[27]

Not a few women, especially stand-up comics, subverted the sexual hierarchy by appropriating sexual jokes involving genitalia and castration. In her study of obscene humor related by females in 1971–72 in Chicago, Carol Mitchell noted that joking about male organs was not unusual fare. The difference was that for the first time women were jubilantly recounting such jokes at mixed social gatherings, to the consternation of the men present. One subject that elicited polar responses of glee and distress was the topic of male physical endowment:

There was this man who was an exhibitionist. And he was going to take a trip on this airplane. And there was this stewardess who was waiting at the top of the stairs that go onto the plane and she was collecting tickets. So when this man got to the top of the stairs, he opened his coat and exposed himself.

And the stewardess said, "I'm sorry, sir. You have to show your ticket here, not your stub."

When Lorena Bobbitt severed her husband's penis in 1992, jokes directed at men assumed a particular reality. "The very fact that 'castrating bitch' is the female counterpart to 'male chauvinist pig,' and that the epithet was frequently thrown at members of the women's movement during its early days," wrote sociologist Mary Jo Neitz, "may account in part for the women's use of the image in their humor." What made the castration joke so pleasurable to tell before mixed audiences, Neitz observed, was that in displaying sexuality and aggression long denied, women were conveying their own sense of empowerment.

A guy was on an airplane and he had to go to the bathroom very badly, but the men's room was all filled up. So, he asked the stewardess if he could use the ladies' room.

She said, "Well, I don't think so."

But he said, "Oh, please. I have to go really badly."

So she said, "Well, I guess so, but don't touch any of the buttons."

He went in and after he was through he started looking at the buttons and said to himself, "Well, there won't be any harm in this." So he pushed the button labeled "WW" and his butt was sprayed with warm water. He thought this was great, so he pushed the next button "WA" and his butt was dried with warm air. Next he pushed "PP" and he was sprayed with powder. Then he saw the button labeled "ATR" and he wondered what that could mean so he pushed it. The next thing he knew he woke up in the hospital, and he asked the nurse what had happened and told her that the last thing that he remembered was pushing the "ATR" button.

She then said, "Well, I don't know how to tell you this, sir, but that button was for the automatic Tampax remover and your penis is under your pillow."[28]

When in the early 1990s men frantically fashioned the retaliatory "dumb blonde" joke cycle, women were totally prepared and counterattacked elatedly. "Dumb men" jokes peppered the scene, spread by office graphics and fax sheets—one circulated among female members of Congress—gibing men in a way that had never before been so openly employed. Inverting the image, women portrayed men as irresponsible, narcissistic, shallow, and childish:

From your home office friend! / DUMB MEN JOKES / Strange . . . . . . But True!!

Why are all dumb blonde jokes one-liners?
So men can understand them.

What is the difference between government bonds and men?
Government bonds mature.

What's a man's idea of helping with the housework?
Lifting his legs so you can vacuum.

What's the difference between a man and E.T?
E.T. phoned home.

Why is psychoanalysis a lot quicker for men than for women?
When it's time for him to go back to childhood, he's already there.

What did God say after he created man?
I can do better than this.

What's the male idea of a 50-50 relationship?
We cook, they eat; we wash, they dirty; we iron, they wrinkle.

What's the best way to force a man to do sit-ups?
Put the remote control between his legs.

How do men exercise at the beach?
By sucking in their gut everytime they see a bikini.

What does a man consider to be a seven-course meal?
A hot dog and a six pack.

How are men like noodles?
They are always in hot water, they lack taste, they need dough.

Why is it good that there are female astronauts?
When the crew gets lost in space, at least the women will ask for directions.[29]

Prior to the mid-1970s there were only a few recognizable female stand-up comedians performing in nightclubs and on talk shows. The male-dominated hierarchy had effectively denied women entrance to the field of entertainment comedy. "When we first started seeing young female comics," said the co-owner of New York's Catch a Rising Star, "a lot of agents and managers who came into the club, even [television] network people, couldn't accept them . . . just no acceptance of a female doing comedy."[30]

Increasingly, however, as prime-time sitcoms in the 1970s and 1980s centered on independent and resourcefully delineated comedians—the breakthrough performers included Carol Burnett, Mary Tyler Moore, and Bea Arthur in sitcoms and Joan Rivers on talk shows—women made their way to center stage. Even then, the organizer of New York's Improvisation Comedy in 1989 estimated that only 15 percent of the stand-up comics were women, though that figure may be compared with the less than 1 percent when he founded the club twenty-five years earlier.[31]

The new comics were chided for the direction of their material. In a review of *Wisecracks* (1992), a full-length documentary of two dozen young performers, film critic Janet Maslin observed that they tended "to joke more scathingly about matters of beauty and self-esteem than their male counterparts, and to sound more self-deprecating in the process."[32] But these self-assurance allusions obscured an important aspect of their comedy. "Today's female comics are, if anything, *more* likely than men to rely on comic conventions," observed Ellen Hopkins.

> And why shouldn't they? The ruling class's humor isn't the same when its victims become its mouthpiece, magically transforming offensive material into a brash form of social commentary. The sexual revolution may not be fully realized—that'll be the day the PMS joke dies. But the world has changed, and proof can be found in woman and her mike. Power doesn't just reside in *not* being the target of a comic's jokes. Real power is being the one who's telling them.[33]

An enlarged awareness of the past thus became for many women a primary objective. "We must construct a women's culture with its own character, its fighting humor, its defiant celebration of our worth," argued playwright Naomi Weisstein in 1973. The "public presentation of such a humor," she insisted, was crucial to female esteem.[34] By 1989, Women in Comedy at the Catch a Rising Star club in Cambridge reflected a newly emerging pattern. Their routines about PMS, dating, hair spray and hair gel, weight and appearance were couched in defiance and self-assuredness. Playing Sigmund Freud's girlfriend, Wendy Liebman admonished, "No, Sigmund, you have it all wrong. It's not envy, it's pity." A mockingly demure Janeane Garofalo said to the audience, "I'm sorry to spit. That wasn't very feminine," after she borrowed wine from a patron, sipped it, and then expectorated.[35]

Decidedly female vistas surfaced as women not only invaded the turf jealously protected by male comedians but also, like Elayne Boosler—introduced by a male comic in the mid-1970s as "the Jackie Robinson of my generation . . . she broke the mold for most female comics"[36]—insisted that audiences comprehend a woman's point of view. To her boyfriend's suggestion that they take a midnight walk by the river: "What, are you nuts? I'm wearing jewelry, I'm carrying money, I have a *vagina* with me." Another subverted the male issue of PMS to advantage: "Taking hostages on a day when I'm retaining water?" says the president of the country, a female, to hijacking terrorists. "This is going to go very badly for you."[37] Diva Bette Midler roiled male fantasies of large breasts in her show *Mud Will Be Flung Tonight:* "Tits, bazooms, fun bags, medicine balls, pachangas, my world—welcome to it! . . . I don't have to be well-informed, just well endowed. . . . I tell you, if I was a guy and I had this much extra flesh, I'd have dick down to my ankles."[38] Roseanne Barr in her stand-up routines undercut male complaints about marriage: "You know, there's some stuff that bugs me about being married—you know, like having a husband." Not a "housewife," Barr chidingly explained, she was a "domestic goddess." Insofar as the traditional relationship to children and home, Barr sarcastically intoned:

> When my husband comes home at night and my kids are still alive, I figure, hey, I've done my job!
>
> I know what bothers me most about men. It's that they never lift a goddamn finger to do anything around the house! Nothing! They just sit around like unconscious lumps! Listen, ladies, you may marry the man of your dreams, but fifteen years later you're married to a reclining chair that burps!
>
> My husband and I have found a method of birth control that really works. Every night, me and my husband, before we go to bed, spend an hour with the kids.[39]

Lily Tomlin enlarged the comedy of possibilities for women in her one-person show *The Search for Signs of Intelligent Life in the Universe,* written by her longtime collaborator, Jane Wagner. Opening on Broadway in 1985, the show ran for 398 performances and toured across the country. A series of monologues about the frailties and resilience of women in differing circumstances portrayed various personas: Ernestine, the telephone operator; Trudy, the bag lady; Edith Ann, the devilish five-year-old; Mrs. Beasley, the Tupperware queen; Angus Angst, the teenage performer; and Wanda V. Williams, the country singer.

In 1989 Tomlin received an award from the 9 to 5 office workers' organization in Boston. She had performed with Jane Fonda and Dolly Parton in *Nine to Five* (1981), a rare film of female humor. Introduced by Boston's Mayor Ray Flynn, who had been commended for his child-care programs, Tomlin turned to the mayor and sweetly inquired, "Ray, honey, would you get me a cup of coffee?" "Would you like cream or sugar?" responded a blushing Flynn.[40]

The exchange was symbolic. A decade earlier Mary Jo Neitz had conjectured about the future of gender relationships: "Laughter in this sense is only possible between equals when men and women can both tell jokes, and can both laugh together. Perhaps the content will reflect the change, with neither needing to assert superiority over the other through their jokes, or in other patterns of interactions."[41]

At the national level, the comic assertions of blacks and women further informed the humor of other minorities. An expanded commonwealth of tribal cultures poured forth their comedic visions in the latter decades of the century. On marquees and storefronts in the late 1970s and 1980s in San Francisco's gay community were signs of flaunting. Adorning a flower shop: "San Francisco is great. It's the only city in the world where a man can aspire to become a Queen." At the height of the first Medfly crisis in California—when authorities sprayed farm areas to eradicate the fruit-devouring insect: "Please Don't Spray Our Fruits."[42]

Spurred on by assault, and impelled by AIDS, the gay community cojoined humor's nurturing and retaliatory elements. While repartee and satire had long been utilized as a defense against censure and rampage, gay stand-up comedy in mainstream entertainment was virtually nonexistent. Mainstream comedy, in fact, had overwhelmingly inveighed against gays. In the late 1980s and 1990s, the vacuum was partly filled by individual comics and by groups, such as Funny Gay Males, a polished, fast-talking trio who broached gay themes with wisecracking intonation adapted to a traditional format. Flaunting the pejorative images of athletic wimps and swishy decorators, Funny Gay Males offered personal backgrounds conveying their individual experiences of "us" and "them": growing up in an uptight household where "the tree house had a breakfast nook," the drama class as a kind of Head Start program for homosexuals, instructing on "How to Be a Sissy in Gym Class," and caricaturing Joan Rivers in a blonde wig and Bette Davis as Dorothy in *The Wizard of Oz*.

Humor for gays had long served to deflect dangers inherent in situations. When a menacing trio taunts the title character in Paul Rudnick's comedy *Jeffrey*, declaring, "We've got knives. What do you have?" the response is "Irony, adjectives, eyebrows." It was the onslaught of AIDS that produced a full-fledged gallows humor. Goaded by the crisis, many located in comedy a salvation in confrontation. Gay writing was enlivened by camp, irony, and epigram in order to "if not defeat the virus, at least to scorn and contain it. AIDS is not the end of gay life or gay laughter. If people can't giggle in hospitals, or at memorials, all they can do is weep."[43] "Writers have been cautioned against employing wit in the face of tragedy," noted Paul Rudnick in 1993 as a close friend was in the hospital dying of the disease. "Humor, it is said, can dilute and trivialize; a joke can let the ignorant off the hook. This is nonsense. Humor is most necessary in days of overwhelming despair. And satire is inescapable when faced with the deluge of red ribbons." In Tony Kushner's extraordinary, powerful seriocomedy, *Angels in America* (1991), Prior, suffering from AIDS, peers into a mirror and grimly declares, "I look like a corpse." But suddenly he places a colorful turban on his head and, transformed, shouts, "A corpsette!" "You know you've hit rock bottom," he moans at one point, "when even drag is a drag." Throughout, the audience erupts into relieved laughter, distanced and embraced.[44]

Adding to the expanding repertoire on the public stages throughout the country were a small number of Latino, Native American, and Asian-American comics. Influenced by street argot and black style, they fractured stereotypes as they affirmed their own identities. "Hey, do you know me?" zinged a swaggering Paul Rodriguez in a gang-style headband and black leather jacket before a predominantly white audience, a sense of rage physically expressed. "I'm not here to be funny. I'm here to create racial tension." With that he whipped out a giant knife and, smiling broadly, "It's recognized and respected all over the world." Parodying an American Express commercial of the 1980s in which predominantly white male celebrities extolled the advantages of owning the card, he declared, "My name is Paul Rodriguez. But when I travel, people don't know who the hell I am. That's why I carry the Mexican Express Card." Exposing his background, he chided stereotyping: "I tell people that I'm Mexican, because there are so many Arabs in this neighborhood. And they look like Mexicans. They're short. We're short. They're brown. We're brown. They've got money. . . . We're brown." "If E.T. had landed in my yard, I would have brought him into the house and my father would have said, 'Hey, I told you, don't be bringing no Filipinos home.'" Countering jokes about Mexican-American culture, Rodriguez explained that a low-rider cruises at 35 miles per hour in the fast lane because "he has 40 other Mexicans in the trunk." As to why there are so few divorces among Mexicans, "Who wants custody of 25 kids?"[45] In 1994 he coproduced a series of four stand-up HBO comedy specials, entitled *Loco Slam!*, that were taped in Los Angeles and presented nineteen Latino comedians.

At the same time came the comedy of Charlie Hill, a descendant of the Oneida tribe in Wisconsin. Deeply influenced by Dick Gregory, "the humanness of all of us," Hill was perhaps the sole Native American thriving on the circuit. Describing himself as an "observation comic" rather than an "ethnic comic"—the latter "always implies something inferior"—Hill had as his mission the dispelling of ignorance by getting "people to laugh with us instead of at us." "To this day, American people have a third-grade knowledge of Indian people and the image of native people in America is nothing short of slanderous. . . . They make fun of the way we laugh, the way we dance, the way we sing, what our names are, the very way we look."

Hill dissected countrywide practices of Native American customs; the whooping gym dances by schoolchildren, for example, were an affront to religious rites. "What if I got my kids together and said let's play Catholic?" he asked before seguing into a genuflection-shuffle and making the sign of the cross on one knee, chanting "1-2-3-4-1-2-3-4." Likewise, the logo of the Washington Redskins, a National Football League team that displays the profile of feather-headed male, was excoriated: "Why are we mascots? I'd like to see a team called the Kansas City Caucasians—with a white guy out in the field in a leisure suit." At the other end of the spectrum were self-referential gibes: "I married a Navajo woman. We had a traditional wedding—I gave her father three horses and a blender."[46]

"I try to get people to hear a story they refused to hear before," said Hill, expressing the thrust of multicultural humor. "I find when people are laughing, then we're connecting." This message found a highly receptive audience among young adults as cable television entered the embrace of humor in the mid-1980s and 1990s. HBO's *Young Comedian Specials, Def Comedy Jam,* and *Comedy Central;* A&E's *An Eve-*

ning at the Improv; and others, as well as the *Comic Relief* specials for the homeless organized by comedians Billy Crystal, Whoopi Goldberg, and Robin Williams, offered a panorama of ethnic and gender humor.

Yet to what extent retaliatory and self-reflective humor defused hostilities and nurtured compassion was not at all certain. Intense political and social hostilities in the later decades of the century more often than not overwhelmed enlarged, embracing comedy. Nonetheless, in its focus on cultural incongruities, minority humor substantially undercut pejorative ethnic, racial, and gender images. And, by defining and realizing their own identities, minorities achieved a degree of empowerment through rejoicing in and credentialing laughter.

12

The Tattered Dream

The 1980s and early 1990s, surely one of the most contradictory periods of the century, ended with the sounds of huzzahs. Bells were rung to herald the beginning of a new era of international peace and democratic dividends as the Cold War receded into history. Although many critics decried the Reagan administration's economic policies, its neglect of racial and gender issues, indifference to urban problems, and hostility toward social welfare, a substantial majority applauded the direction of events. As the phenomenally popular president had claimed over and again, his cheery face tilted upward, the glowing future was open to all self-sufficient citizens. His emphasis on optimism and grit, activism and success, military power and triumph was the embodiment of American bullishness. At the very least, the cheeringly snide appellation "Yuppie Generation" was apt. Yet not only did a significant joke war erupt during Reagan's and his successor's reign, there also appeared in people's joking the antithesis of their American Dream. Long before Reagan, in retirement, was perched atop a bluff overlooking the Santa Ynez Valley, the ebullient bells were muted by an alarming comedic murmur. It was the queasy laughter emanating from a jarring joke script delivering a message of disaster.

Why so great a disparity between the leader and people's humor? Part of the answer lay in the persona of the president himself. Representative Pat Schroeder's catchy label, the "Teflon President," fittingly summed up Reagan's situation. Devoid of ambiguities, a brilliant practitioner of Dale Carnegie's advertising formula of winning friends and influencing people, Reagan assumed for himself a political purity lacking in other national leaders. Rarely was he the object of ridicule that so often plagued other politicians. His immunity to derision was also in part due to his astute recognition and adroit use of humor. "There was the moment," a *New York Times* editorial rued, "when we realized that all Reagan jokes were true." When President Jimmy Carter attempted to counterjoke during the 1980 campaign, his poor delivery produced audience boos.[1] Stories and anecdotes woven into Reagan's political repartee, his catchphrases and one-liners, spooked his opponents and deflected attention from his own shortcomings. When teased about his daily naps, Reagan rejoined, "It's true hard work never killed anyone, but I figure, why take the chance?"[2]

As a result, jokes directed at him were usually benign, if not almost embracing. Comedians and the public alike jived the president about his laziness, unchanged hair color, penchant for concocting facts and figures, and especially his forgetfulness—"What didn't he know and when did he forget it?"—but it was largely good-natured. There were, on occasion, sharper-edged quips: "What do you get when you cross James Dean with Ronald Reagan? *A rebel without a clue.*" And late into his second term, one touching on his recollection and health: "Did you hear that IBM has brought out a new typewriter called the President? *It has no memory and no colon.*"[3]

Consequently, frustrations during the period were taken out on others in the political firmament. Senator Gary Hart's extramarital activities engendered antagonistic feelings, as illustrated by a wisecrack following the Donna Rice episode: *"Win one for the Zipper!"* a wry takeoff on Reagan's classic football movie one-liner, "Win one for the Gipper." Toward others there was blunt criticism, as illustrated by a story during the 1987–88 presidential primaries:

> Jimmy Carter, Richard Nixon, Gary Hart, Joe Biden, and Michael Dukakis were on a ship that began to sink. Carter yelled, "Women and children first."
> Nixon shouted, "Fuck them."
> Hart asked, "Is there time?"
> Biden responded, "Is there time?"
> Dukakis exclaimed, "Did you hear what Biden said!"[4]

It was instructive that Reagan's aura did not carry over to his successor. Not only did Bush's difficulty with language lead to mocking, he also laid the groundwork for one of the most vilifying assaults in American political history. J. Danforth Quayle, his running mate in 1988, evoked a comedic response that grew exponentially over the course of their administration. Indeed, no sooner had Bush announced his selection of Quayle as his running mate before the Republican National Convention than the joke-telling began: *In case of Bush's assassination, the Secret Service is under orders to shoot Quayle!* There was the *Quayle Quarterly,* a newsletter devoted exclusively to the vice president's seemingly endless historical gaffes and grammatical errors. Among the innumerable quips that addressed Quayle's intellectual range was one that summed up his public image, "What were Dan Quayle's two toughest years? *Third grade.*"[5]

On the other hand, there was Reagan, his charisma intact during his two terms despite the plunge of the stock market, the Iran-Contra scandal, the savings and loan boondoggle, manufacturing challenges from the Japanese and Germans, the deaths of 260 Marines in Lebanon, and growing numbers of homeless individuals and families, among other major social problems. His obsessive anticommunism and antiliberalism—to his mind and that of many of his followers, one and the same—diverted the media's and the public's attention from the wrenching social, racial, and class issues that built during the 1980s and exploded in the following decade.

Assuredly, Reagan's craft and aura deflected attention from the fissures appearing within society, but at the same time he generated a powerful desire to believe in his uplifting vision of a limitless destiny, the notion that Americans can overcome any obstacle. Nonetheless, the majority had not been paying attention to their own chorus of jokes that begun late in the 1970s and amplified to the end of the century. Within the various levels of the nation's cultural cubicles was a joking cynicism conveying a disenchantment about the nation's technological and economic systems. Not only did Reagan's optimism go unreflected in people's humor, but their laughter expressed an opposite sentiment. Rather than headiness, there was a sense of profound anxiety and disillusionment that emanated from a series of technological disasters coupled with feelings of personal and economic vulnerability.

One root of the anxiety reached back to the powerful social changes of the post–World War II years that produced the sick or cruel cycle, a middle-class response to the wrenching rearrangements in familial and religious institutions. The 1950s cycle occurred at a time of economic

expansion, when prosperity had produced millions of jobs for the unskilled lower classes against the backdrop of a sense of historic continuity, a belief in the political system's perpetual soundness.

Then in the early 1970s occurred a frightening scandal, a near
meltdown in constitutional government. President Richard M. Nixon's
involvement in the Watergate affair, his palpable lying and deceiving,
seriously impaired the trust in government that had been fostered by
Franklin D. Roosevelt's New Deal programs and further ennobled by
America's moral posture in World War II. With Watergate, the social
compact was clearly damaged, especially by its ambiguous resolution.

Compounding the situation shortly thereafter, and continuing until the close of the century, the roseate years of expansion collided
with scientific and technological failures magnified by the increasing
knowledge of planetary environmental contamination. The list of disasters unfolded like chapters in a gothic novel: the near meltdown at
Three Mile Island nuclear plant in Pennsylvania; the radioactive explosion at the Chernobyl complex in the Soviet Union; the waste-dis-
posal destruction of an entire community at Love Canal, New York;
the explosion of the spaceship *Challenger* and subsequent failures of
NASA space launches; Union Carbide's chemical leak at Bhopal, India, and the death of thousands; innumerable oil spills in oceans
throughout the world, symbolized by the massive spill in Prince William Sound in Alaska from the tanker *Exxon Valdez*; the devastating
famine in Ethiopia and other parts of the globe; the erosion of the
ozone layer over the Earth's poles; the increasing level of toxic substance in drinking water and foods; the dangers of asbestos-contami-
nated classrooms; the collapse of rusting bridges and the crash of
airliners; the deterioration of the inner cities; and the appearance of
the dreaded disease AIDS.

Understandably, these disasters produced a joke cycle of similar
proportion. William F. Honan discerningly observed:

> The Greeks invented tragedy as a form of mass entertainment.
> We moderns have perfected a related genre—the disaster story—
> that is perhaps as expressive of our preoccupations as tragedy was
> of theirs. While tragedy deals with the downfall of a great individ-
> ual, the disaster story concentrates on the destruction of a magnifi-
> cent machine . . . or an institution or political structure.
>
> These stories grip us because, although we pride ourselves on
> being individualists, what chiefly seems to fascinate us about the

world is our technology and our complex social and political organizations. When these become unhinged, the suffering of individuals figures into the drama but usually as an embellishment, not the central element.[6]

Further exacerbating the national drama was an enlarging concern about personal vulnerability. As the number of deaths caused by issueless violence and terrorist acts mounted, as the ethos of victimization permeated the culture, people perceived existence as anything but secure. What was evoked was not an entropic comedy—a fascinating fixture in American humor has always been a bemused anxiety arising from the possibility of disorder and disarray undermining the rational universe created by science and technology, as in the sign *THINk*—but an image of an American Frankenstein's monster. This was not the first time that the idea of a technological creation destroying its creator had been imagined. The 1930s film *Frankenstein* portrayed scientific technology miscalculating by begetting not the perfect being but a stalking monster.

By the 1950s the stalking monster had become the stalking Bomb—the awesome flip side of nuclear power. Like the omnipresent elephant in the joke cycle, there was no escaping this monster's propinquity. Thus disaster became, in the apt observation of William F. Fry, Jr., at the International Conference on Humor in 1984, "the touchstone of contemporary attention and communication."[7] Indeed, just a year earlier a graphic portrayal of the thermonuclear obliteration of Lawrence, Kansas, and the agonizing demise of surrounding communities caused by radiation was the subject of a prime-time television film, *The Day After*.

Catastrophic events overwhelmed sensibilities from the late 1970s into the 1990s, spawning a joke cycle that matched its technological proportions "as a mental balm to relieve the agony and anxiety of the unresolvable."[8] Each episode led to a format of riddles and conundrums, in effect, "current event jokes,"[9] that cast a ghastly shadow over existence.

1. The leaking of poisonous gas at the Union Carbide plant in Bhopal, India, killing 2,500, in 1984:

What's the new theme song of Union Carbide?
   Ten little, nine little, eight little, . . . Indians.[10]

2. The Ethiopian famine, 1985:

How many Ethiopians can you stuff into a phone booth?
All of them.

What's the fastest bird on Earth?
An Ethiopian chicken.

What does an Ethiopian call his dog?
Dinner.

How do you start a fire?
Rub two Ethiopians together.

What do you call an Ethiopian in a dinner jacket?
Optimistic.

What's the difference between an elevator in Boston and in Ethiopia?
One carries five people for 600 pounds; the other carries 600 people at five pounds.

What do Ethiopians use venetian blinds for?
Bunk beds.

How do Ethiopians wear their Rolex watches?
Around their waists.[11]

3. The radioactive explosion at the Soviet Union's Chernobyl plant in 1986:

What is the name of the new Russian coin?
The rubble.

What is the weather forecast in Kiev?
Overcast and 7000 degrees.

What has feathers and glows?
Chicken Kiev.

What do you get when you order a White Russian in Kiev?
A Black Russian.

What did the fallout do in Scandinavia?
Turned the people blue-haired and blonde-eyed.[12]

4. Crashes of PSA and Delta airliners in 1986–87:

What does Delta stand for?
Don't Ever Leave The Airport.

What does PSA stand for?
People Scattered All Over.[13]

5. The grounding of the *Exxon Valdez* oil tanker on a reef in Alaska's Prince William Sound, spilling 11 million gallons of oil, in 1989:

What's an Exxon cocktail?
10 million gallons on the rocks.

Do you know what Exxon executives are drinking these days?
Tanqueray on the rocks.

Do you know what Alaskan yuppies are watching?
10-W-Thirtysomething.[14]

6. Water pollution:

Did you hear the good news/bad news about drinking water in the year 2000?
The bad news is that in the year 2000 the only drinking water will be recycled sewage. The good news is that there won't be enough to go around.[15]

7. Hospital syringes and other medical waste washed onto beaches:

Hospitals are reporting seashells washing up at their doorsteps.[16]

8. The garbage saga of 1987 in which 3,100 tons of garbage loaded aboard a barge from Islip, New York, was turned away at ports from North Carolina to Louisiana, and also by the Mexican navy, before returning to the mainland:

The Garbage Without a Country.[17]

The nadir of dejection regarding technology came with the fiery explosion of the spaceship *Challenger* on January 28, 1986. Apart from its numbing impact, what both amazed and fazed the country was the immediacy and intensity of the response. *Challenger* jokes virtually erupted across the landscape and were swiftly disseminated by all available means. Ironically, both catastrophe and response were intensified by the latest technological developments: the explosion and crash by constant television replays, and the jokes via fax machines and the Internet.

As folklorist Elizabeth Radin Simons noted at the time, this catalyst produced a people's script aimed at several targets. One was the National Aeronautics and Space Administration (NASA), and the other was astronaut Christa McAuliffe, a schoolteacher.

To a considerable extent, the intensity of joking was related to NASA's own media-sculpted image. Despite the previous catastrophes, the deterioration of consumer products, and the spoilage of the environment, the national space program had been portrayed as a bastion of technological purity. By the constant trumpeting of engineering marvels—the touchdown on the moon was indeed a mind-boggling achievement—the NASA managers were engineering an equally adverse reaction should anything go awry. Hence the unthinkable explosion of *Challenger*, replayed over and again on television—in case anyone had missed the tragic occasion—produced a sense of betrayal.

"Being had" partly accounts for the assault on NASA. Ridiculing the agency was a type of compelling retaliation that complemented the nationwide need for coping with a disaster of unthinkable, elephantine proportions:

What does NASA stand for?
Need Another Seven Astronauts.
Need Another Seven Assholes.
Now Accepting Suicide Applications.

Did you hear that NASA is starting a new amusement park in Florida?
It's in a submarine.

Did you hear that Tang is no longer the official drink of the space program?
Yes, now it's Ocean Spray.

What do the New England Patriots [who were badly defeated in the Super Bowl] and the space shuttle have in common?
They both looked good for the first 73 seconds.

Why did the astronauts have Coke at their prelaunch party?
Because they couldn't get Seven-Up.

What was the last thing the commander said before the spaceship plunged into the ocean?
I said I wanted a Bud Lite.

Where did the *Challenger* crew take their vacation?
All over Florida.

Why is there no dandruff in Florida since the space shuttle blew up?
Because it's raining Head & Shoulders.

How many astronauts can fit in a Volkswagen?
Eleven: two in the front seat, two in the backseat, and seven in the ashtray.

When is the next space shuttle launch?
The Fourth of July.

Jeering NASA continued well after the *Challenger* crash. When the space agency had to postpone its Astro-1 mission on four occasions came the quip:

What do NASA and the cartoon family the Jetsons have in common?
They both have a dog named Astro.

Anthropologist Elliott Oring noted one particular element in the *Challenger* format, the large number of familiar commercial products: Tang, Coke, Seven-Up, Bud Lite, and Head & Shoulders. "This linking of the *Challenger* disaster with television commercials does not seem entirely coincidental. The juxtaposition of commercial products with images of disaster seems a particularly apt commentary on the television medium and the images it presents to viewers at home. Television news programs regularly conjoin images and stories of death, disease, and destruction with images of commercial products." By contrast, "the concatenation of brand name products and images of disaster achieved in the jokes is really no more incongruous than that achieved several times each evening by national and local television news programs."[18] In effect, the space program was downgraded to but another commercial enterprise.

While deriding of NASA resulted from its hubris, the spotlighting of Christa McAuliffe was puzzling. Simons noted that NASA's incompetence was linked with the nation's public school system, under attack at the time for "failing everywhere from the cities to the suburbs and everyone from the slow learner to the gifted, from the majority to the minority students." And with the sudden death of the first, and only, teacher-astronaut, the sallies "seem to confirm America's low opinion of teachers. In the jokes Christa McAuliffe is portrayed as dumb. Her thinking is illogical, nonsensical, reminiscent actually of moron jokes." It was not at all surprising, therefore, that the jokes circulated widely among students.[19]

At the same time, it can be argued that Christa McAuliffe was singled out because of her unusual status. As the sole unauthentic astronaut, she was the crew's most highly publicized member. On board was another female astronaut dressed in the same unisex space uniform that made the women indistinguishable from their male counterparts. What if the teacher-astronaut had been a male? Would *he* have been mocked as McAuliffe was? Many of the McAuliffe jokes were in the then highly prominent backlash mode. And here, instructively, the backlash quips were not limited to women but encompassed blacks as well. Consider a wisecrack about the sole black astronaut: "Why was there only *one* black astronaut on the *Challenger? Because they didn't know it was going to blow up."* There was, in addition, press speculation that President Reagan had been planning to contact McAuliffe in flight while he was addressing the Congress, a spectacular political coup if it had occurred. McAuliffe, then, stood out in a variety of ways, and the jokes about her extended to women's place and capabilities:

What's the space shuttle cocktail?
  Seven-Up, and a splash of teachers.

What does Christa McAuliffe teach?
  English, but she's history now.

What were the last words of Christa McAuliffe?
What's this little red button for?

What's the last thing that went through Christa McAuliffe's head?
The control panel.

Did you hear that Christa McAuliffe was nominated for Mother of the Year award?
Yeah, she only blew up once in front of the kids.

What color were Christa McAuliffe's eyes?
Blue—one blew this way, and one blew that way.

What were Christa McAuliffe's last words to her husband?
You feed the dogs, and I'll feed the fish.

What did the teacher become after her flight?
A beachcomber.[20]

As the jokes swiftly wended their way through the various levels of society, there were protests about their "tastelessness." Resistance to the jokes appeared as quickly as their transmission. "Pretty revolting, aren't they?" angrily wrote columnist Bob Marcotte in the *Rochester Times-Union*. "Pretty stupid, too. And grossly insensitive. . . . I didn't feel like laughing the day I watched the *Challenger* disintegrate in the sky. And I don't want to be tricked into laughing about it now." Immediately after a radio announcer in Los Angeles recounted a one-liner, "The rocketship *Challenger* blew up because the crew was free-basing on Tang," he was terminated. Another in San Francisco was suspended without pay for relating two shuttle jokes.[21] A microbiologist in Ohio, offended by an Internet user who printed a joke about the last words of the space shuttle crew, devised a program that automatically eliminated such messages on the nation's largest on-line network. *New York Times* television critic Walter Goodman responded to such criticism by reminding his readers that "tastelessness has a firm place in the history of American humor, from the frontier to the big city."[22] Questions of taste aside, represented were the unmistakable signs of articulated disenchantment and a growing unwillingness to believe that the conditions might quickly be reversed. A joke spoke to the illusion of a quick fix:

A man went to his doctor for a checkup. A series of tests were taken and the doctor instructed him: no red meat, no milk, no liquor, no smoking, and no sex. The man was aghast at all these prohibitions and asked the doctor: "Will I live longer if I follow your advice?"

"No," replied the doctor, "but it will seem that way."[23]

"To become disillusioned," wrote Paul Fussell, "you must earlier have been illusioned."[24] At what point did this earlier envisioning of social organization and technology combining to fulfill the expectations of democratic capitalism arise? It occurred at the intersection of two largely antithetical, historically competing currents: first, the powerful conviction that corporate capitalism was the unswerving path to the good bourgeois life; and the visionary idealism of the counterculture, which sought a vast political and ethical restructuring of American society.

These lofty dreams of creating political and socioeconomic arrangements to match values were severely wrenched in the unfolding decades of the century. On the one side were the declining quality of goods, the blatant fraudulence of the energy crisis, the scandalous corruption of savings and loan executives, the loss of jobs through downsizing juxtaposed to escalating CEO and organizational profits, and crass indifference toward minorities and the working and lower classes. On the other side was the inability to institutionalize a "counterculture," assassinations of political and civil rights leaders, undermining actions of state and federal justice departments, and exhausting opposition to the Vietnam War.

Economic constrictions undergirded by a renewed social Darwinism added to the fears of an uncertain future. Polls in the 1990s detailed that possibly for the first time the majority doubted the viability of the American Dream, convinced that it would be much harder to achieve than in the past. As Kevin Phillips observed, "More and more people have a feeling they're on the 'Down' escalator as opposed to the 'Up' escalator."[25] Said Yogi Berra, the onetime New York Yankees catcher and coach, "The future isn't what it used to be."[26]

Joke and reality entwined as political and economic configurations impacted on daily behavior. Increasing tensions led to a civic nastiness symbolized by the upthrust third finger. Forthright "in your face" graffiti appeared everywhere. Handwritten signs: "Park your car in this space and I'll break both your legs" and "Shoplifters will be stomped on, kicked, beaten, bounced off the walls. Survivors will then be prosecuted." On a house fence, a picture of a gun pointed at an intruder: "Beware of Owner." An automobile bumper sticker: "If You Don't Like the Way I'm Driving Dial 1 800 EAT SHIT." Office graphics: "If you love someone, set them free, but if they don't come back—hunt them down and kill them." A sign on a barrel protecting a parking space, "Hazardous Waste." A statement on a bathroom stall: "Yank me off this fuckin' Earth. Yank me off this Joke." An office graffito: "Some People Are Still Alive Simply Because It Is Illegal To Kill Them."[27]

The *Wall Street Journal* assayed the prevailing "hard-edged" atmosphere and proffered an example, a one-upmanship story:[28]

> After a considerable waiting period, Pat finally got a phone in his car. He couldn't wait to call Mike. "I'm calling you from my car," he told Mike.
>
> Mike was enraged with envy. He ordered, and finally got, a phone for his car. He immediately called Pat. "Pat," he said, "I'm calling you from my car."
>
> Replied Pat, "Excuse me a moment, Mike, my other phone is ringing."[29]

Into this milieu came humor reminiscent of the late 1950s and 1960s, the cruel cycle but with a purposeful viciousness, "created as much by the common folk as by the intelligentsia."[30] To the question "What do you call . . . ?"

a guy with no arms and legs who's in a ditch?
Phil.

a guy with no arms or legs who water skis?
Bob.

a woman with one leg?
Peg or
Ilene.

a man with no arms and legs on your doorstep?
Matt.

a leper in a hot tub?
  Stu.

a guy whose legs are missing halfway down?
  Neal.

a man with no arms or legs on a wall?
  Art.[31]

Viciousness for its own sake:

What's the hardest thing about feeding a vegetable?
  Getting him out of the chair.

How did the chicken cross the road?
  Stapled to the back of another chicken.

How many mice does it take to screw in a lightbulb?
  Two—that's all that can fit.[32]

These examples not only confirmed the nastiness of contemporary existence but also, combining with disasters, offered the specter of a totally irrational universe, one in which the incongruous made sense. "The most profound jokes invoke paradox, the ultimate incongruity," wrote Timothy Ferris. "Their subject is the inadequacy, not just of a particular model of reality, but of *all* models."[33]

When it was applied to society's role models, people's distrust of celebrities and professionals was palpable. It was during this period that two of the most powerful and revered groups came under withering attack. Lawyers and doctors were disparaged in a barrage of jokes. Ironically, the sharp increase in malpractice suits at once suggested a litigious society in need of lawyers' talents, but one also reflecting a loss of faith in legal and medical practitioners. Jokes abounded about greed; unnecessary or, worse, botched operations; and the absence of ethical standards:

1. Incompetence:

Why does a surgeon wear rubber gloves and a mask?
  So he won't leave fingerprints and can't be identified.

2. Costs:

> What's the difference between an itch and an allergy?
> *About $175 a visit.*

3. Greed:

> A woman standing on line at a cinema complains to her husband about a pain in her neck. Immediately a strange man standing behind them reaches over and begins to massage her neck. The woman is startled, and asks him what he's doing. "Oh," he explains, "I'm a chiropractor. I overheard your complaint and I think I can help."
>
> The woman replies, "Listen, my husband is a lawyer. Do you think that if he overheard people complaining about their legal problems, he would immediately fuck them?"[34]

> A man goes to his doctor for a checkup and the doctor tells him, "I'm afraid I must operate immediately."
>
> "But," says the man, "I feel fine!"
>
> "I'm sorry," says the doctor, "but I just checked you and you *must* have this operation. It will be difficult to perform, and it will cost you five thousand dollars."
>
> "But I don't have that much money," says the man.
>
> "That's all right," answers the doctor, "you don't have to pay it all at once. You can pay it in installments, paying a little every month."
>
> "Oh," replies the man, "like you're buying a car."
>
> "Yeah, I am," says the doctor.[35]

Popular culture icons suffered diminution as well. Superman, whose arrival from the planet Krypton in 1938 juxtaposed with John Wayne's rugged entrance barely a year afterward in John Ford's film *Stagecoach*, was the subject of a disparaging joke early in the 1980s:

> Two men were drinking at a bar located atop a hotel and got on the subject of unusual feats. Said one, "You know, in this hotel, you can jump from the top floor, travel down from the 60th to the 10th and then bounce all the way up."
>
> The other guy expressed surprise. "Quit bullshitting."
>
> The first replied, "In this hotel, you can actually do it."
>
> "Oh, yeah," exclaimed the skeptic.
>
> "Watch," and the first man jumped out the window, went past

the 50th, 40th, 30th, 20th, then at the 10th floor bounced all the way back to the 60th.

The other guy was astonished. "I told you," the first man repeated, "you can do it also." Still the guy demurred. So they made a bet. The guy then took a deep breath, jumped out the window, and passed the 50th, 40th, 30th, 20th, 10th, and slammed into the pavement.

The first guy smiled, walked over to the bartender, and ordered another drink. The bartender exclaimed, "You know, Superman, you sure are a son of a bitch when you're drunk."[36]

By late in the decade, a medical joke symbolized the nation's outlook:

A very ill man goes to see his doctor for a series of tests. The doctor reviews the results and tells him he is suffering from AIDS, syphilis, tuberculosis, shingles, and an undiagnosed disease. "Nurse," yells the doctor, "place this man in isolation room number one. And feed this man a diet of pancakes and flounder."

With eyes half open, the man asks, "Doctor, will that cure my illnesses?"

"Fuck, no," answers the doctor, "they're the only things we can slide under the door."[37]

Expectedly, the plummeting of the stock market on October 19, 1987, figured in the disaster mode. No sooner had the Dow-Jones plunged, ending the Yuppie bull market, than the investment community responded with bully gallows jokes. One broker noted some "twenty-seven one-liners in ten minutes," their overall tone attesting to a diminished American Dream: *There are a lot of good buys on Wall Street . . . good-bye house, good-bye car, good-bye American Express platinum card.* Resurrected was a sturdy jest: "What's the best way to make a million in the stock market? *Start with $2 million.*" Several recalled the jokes told during the crash of 1929: "I used to have an uncle working on Wall Street. He used to have a corner on the market. *Now he has a market on the corner;*" "Get my broker, Miss Jones. *Yes sir. Stock or pawn?*"; "Have you heard the new Smith Barney slogan? *We make money the old-fashioned way . . . We sell apples*"; "Why haven't more brokers taken the plunge? *You can't open the windows;*" a reception clerk to a broker at the Hyatt, "*For sleeping or jumping, sir?*"

Investment firms and investors were natural targets. A sign above a trading post at the American Stock Exchange summed up the mordant tone: *Lost: Three-legged dog, blind in one eye, recently castrated. Answers to the name of Lucky.*[38] A rumor on Wall Street was that the two largest securities firms, Shearson Lehman Brothers and Paine Webber, planned to merge under the new name *Shear Paine*. Individual brokers derogated their own agencies: "Why are E. F. Hutton employees like mushrooms? *Because they're always kept in the dark, shit on, and canned.*"[39] The most widely circulated quip centered on the Harvard Business School: "What do you call a Harvard M.B.A.? *Waiter!*" Others lamented the general plight of brokers: "What's the difference between a stockbroker and a pigeon? *The pigeon can still leave a deposit*"; "How many stockbrokers can you fit into the back of pickup truck? *Two—with their lawn mowers.*" A connection to the backlash: A man comes home to his penthouse, tells his wife they've lost it all— their savings in the market, their home, car, everything. She opens the window and jumps. As she plummets earthward, the man sighs, "Thank you, Paine Webber." Finally, the Yuppie lifestyle was scorned: "Did you hear about the Yuppie broker who wanted to kill himself? *He couldn't decide whether to jump out of the Trump Tower or the Eastern Shuttle*"; "What is the new disease that attacks only Yuppies? *RAIDS: Reduced Annual Income Decline Syndrome.*"[40]

Not just the stock market but also the financial misfortunes of others became part of the equation. "Failure's in this year," was the opening line of a flyer disseminated by the public affairs department of the Continental Illinois Corporation prior to its annual Christmas party in 1984.[41] Just as the spurt in oil prices in the 1970s swelled profits, so the drop in prices produced a gusher of despair jokes. Financial power in Texas had often been trumpeted in jokes, such as: An oil man has a heart attack in his office, falls on the floor, and yells to his secretary, *"Don't just stand there! Go out and buy me a hospital!"*[42] An adverse tone accompanied the plunge in prices:

What's the difference between a pigeon and a Texas oil driller?
    A pigeon can still make a deposit on a Mercedes.

What do you call it when a West Texas oilman gives his son ten stripper wells?
    Child abuse!

How do you get a Texan down from a tree?
Cut the rope.

In Odessa, they're selling Mercedes without seats.
Don't worry. Everyone out there's lost their fannies anyhow.[43]

At the other end of the spectrum was the plight of hundreds of thousands of homeless across the land: "Why can't they take photos of the homeless? *Because every time they say 'cheese,' they stand in line."* The economic difficulties in the northeastern states: *Times are so tough in Rhode Island that the Mafia had to lay off five judges.*[44]

Beyond the metaphor was event, and people seized on any misfortune, weaving one joking riddle after another in giddy conceit. Immunity applied to no one. The drowning of actress Natalie Wood in 1981 appears to have initiated the pattern:

What's the only wood that doesn't float?
Natalie.

[Husband] Robert Wagner asks his wife if she's going to bathe on the boat.
No, I'll wash up on shore.

Natalie Wood greeting her guests:
Have a drink, eat, but don't go overboard.

What's 2, 2½, and 4?
Natalie Wood's final diving scores.[45]

The wounding of President Ronald Reagan and Press Secretary James Brady in an assassination attempt in 1981:

What did James Brady say to Ronald Reagan?
If I had half a brain, I'd quit this job.[46]

Len Bias, University of Maryland basketball player selected by the Boston Celtics, who overdosed on cocaine in 1986:

Why didn't Len Bias make it into the NBA?
His heart wasn't in it.

What did Len Bias and Rock Hudson have in common?
  Both died of bad crack.[47]

The indictment and conviction of Marion Barry, mayor of Washington, D.C., on drug charges in 1990:

What do Marilyn Quayle and Marion Barry have in common?
  They both blow a little dope on occasion.

What did Marion Barry tell the press?
  Just say Yo!

What is white on the inside and black on the outside?
  Marion Barry's nose.[48]

The seizure of the cruise ship *Achille Lauro* by Palestine Liberation Organization terrorists who shot passenger Leon Klinghoffer, who was confined to a wheelchair, then pushed him overboard:

What does PLO stands for?
  Push Leon Overboard.

What did the fish call Klinghoffer?
  Meals on Wheels.

Why didn't Leon shower on board ship?
  Because he washed up on shore.[49]

The holdup and killing of patrons at a McDonald's in San Ysidro, California, in 1986:

A new sign at McDonald's:
  16 billion served, 21 injured, 5 killed.

What's the new item on a McDonald's menu?
  Duck.[50]

The *fatwa* issued by Ayatollah Ruhollah Khomeini in 1989, and continued by the Iranian government, to any Muslim for dispatching Salman Rushdie, author of *The Satanic Verses*, who immediately went into hiding in England:

What's the difference between Salman Rushdie and Elvis Presley?
Rushdie is a dead man.

What do you call someone with big boobs, blonde, and Swedish?
Salman Rushdie.[51]

The 1989 killing in Boston of Carol Stewart, pregnant wife of Charles Stewart, who claimed they both had been assaulted and both shot by a black assailant (the husband committed suicide soon thereafter, by jumping off a bridge, when it was uncovered that he had planned the entire operation):

What's the Charles Stewart drink?
Two shots, a splash, with a twist.

What's the difference between Charles Stewart and Larry Bird?
Bird jumps before he shoots.

What were Charles Stewart's last words?
A black man pushed me.[52]

Children's entertainer Pee-wee Herman, arrested in 1991 for masturbating in an X-rated movie theater in Sarasota, Florida:

Did you hear Pee Wee Herman's lawyers offered to defend him for free?
He said no because he couldn't get himself off.

Pee-wee Herman ruined his career single-handedly.

When CBS got wind of it, they jerked his show right away.[53]

The capture in 1991 of Jeffrey Dahmer, serial killer in Milwaukee, who had cannibalized his victims:

Did you hear Jeffrey Dahmer called Pee-wee Herman?
He asked him to quit playing with his food.
To which Pee-wee replied, *"I'll show you mine if you show me theirs."*

I hear Dahmer's lawyers are charging him an arm and a leg.

Dahmer has guts!

How does Jeffrey Dahmer stack up against other serial killers?
He's head and shoulders above the rest!

Heard about the new Jeffrey Dahmer refrigerator?
Seats six.

Did you hear that the Israelis are investigating Jeffrey Dahmer?
They suspect he's exporting arms to the Arabs.[54]

The U.S. Senate Judiciary Committee hearings on the nomination of Clarence Thomas to the U.S. Supreme Court in 1991, during which he was charged with sexual harassment by Anita Hill, a lawyer and former aide to Thomas:

Senator to Judge Thomas: Could you please explain to us your opinion on *Roe* v. *Wade?*
Thomas: *Senator, I haven't seen that one, but I loved* Debbie Does Dallas.

Have you heard about the Anita Hill doll?
You pull the string and ten years later it talks.

What is this?: "Hello, Hello, Hello, Hello, Nice Tits, Hello, Hello, Hello"?
Clarence Thomas's first day at the Supreme Court.[55]

The 1993 siege and destruction of the compound of the Branch Davidians, a religious cult, in Waco, Texas, with the loss of more than eighty lives, including that of its leader, David Koresh:

What does Waco stand for?
Wicked, Awesome, Cookout or
Washington Approved Cookout.

You hear what they're renaming Waco?
Corpus Crispy.

What do Rodney King and David Koresh have in common?
They're both black.

Why did the Branch Davidians do it in Waco?
  To keep up with the Joneses.

Who's doing the cleanup at the Waco cookout?
  Jeffrey Dahmer, with a bottle of barbecue sauce![56]

A suit by a fourteen-year-old boy against superstar Michael Jackson in 1993, charging him with sexual molestation, which was settled out of court in 1994:

Did you hear that Michael Jackson plans to write a book?
  It's called Child Rearing.

A cablegram from the pope to Michael Jackson:
  Cease Your Activities; You Are Not Yet Ordained.

What do K Mart and Michael Jackson have in common?
  Boys' underwear, one-half off.[57]

The dramatic trial of O. J. Simpson in 1995, in which the former football star and commercial icon was prosecuted for the murders of his former wife and her male friend:

Which is healthier, Tang or OJ?
  Tang. OJ can really kill you.

Why do they call O. J. Simpson "The Juice"?
  Because he beat his wife to a pulp.

What does O.J. like best about Thanksgiving?
  Carving the white meat.

Did you hear that O.J. got three phone calls when he first went to jail?
  First, Michael Jackson called, offering to take care of the kids. Second was Mike Tyson, offering to room with him in exchange for some fresh-squeezed OJ in the morning. Last, Jeff Dahmer called to complain that O.J. was throwing away the best parts![58]

A "hellish laughter," in Günter Grass's telling phrase, engulfed American culture at century's close.[59] Comedy had by then become a national quest, voiced in hundreds of comedy clubs, television sitcoms, and films, as the nation sought meaning and clarity in the routines of the stand-up comics and in their own joking. The disaster scripts were a stark yet spirited endeavor to celebrate existence and purpose. The rebellious laughter, however, yielded no communal connection but illuminated a society coping with malaise and disillusionment. Paul Lewis observed that "it may not be too fanciful to see the dark humor released by the [*Challenger*] event as a response to our national immune system."[60]

Opposing comedic strains prevailed across the country, one expressing the decade's disenchantment, the other espousing traditional cheerfulness. A graphic flyer showed a clown tipping his hat and caustically exclaiming:

> THIS LIFE IS A TEST.
> IT IS ONLY A TEST.
> HAD THIS BEEN AN ACTUAL LIFE,
> YOU WOULD HAVE BEEN GIVEN FURTHER
> INSTRUCTIONS ON WHERE TO GO
> AND WHAT TO DO.[61]

At the same time, despite its gallows mode, a graffito imparted an optimistic note:

> What do you call a guy who has syphilis, herpes, AIDS, and gonorrhea?
> *A hopeless romantic!*[62]

13

Postlude: How Many Jokes Does It Take to Change a Zeitgeist?

If one wishes to know, wrote Alan Dundes in *Cracking Jokes* (1987), "what is really on a people's collective mind, there is no more direct and accurate way of finding out than by paying attention to precisely what is making the people laugh."[1] Anthropologist Edward T. Hall offered further insight when he maintained that "people laugh and tell jokes, and if you learn the humor of a people and really control it you know that you are also in control of nearly everything else."[2] And in "The Place of Laughter in Tudor and Stuart England," Keith Thomas argued that "jokes are a pointer to . . . areas of structural ambiguity in society itself; and their subject matter can be a revealing guide to past tensions and anxieties."[3]

Comprehending the societal meaning of humor requires ascertaining the culture code in which it operates.[4] Evolving from historic patterns and buttressed by assumptions of time and place, the code is "a system of rules and expectations that every human being acquires simply by being a member of a particular sociocultural system."[5] Humor's most determining attribute lies in its fostering of communal solidarity, a sense of belonging to a collective unit. "How often has the remark been made," Henri Bergson wrote in *Laughter* (1900), "that many comic effects are incapable of translation from one language to another, because they refer to the customs and ideas of a particular social group."[6] Thus does humor conserve and recapitulate the symbols, experiences, and the attentiveness of the folk. And it is precisely within the clan that humor's social signification is defined.

Seminal works on humor's properties are in substantial agreement regarding its social cohesiveness. In his pathbreaking *Wit and Its Relation to the Unconscious* (1905), Sigmund Freud maintained that humor is wholly a social process wherein the shared actions of the participants allow them to aggress and/or regress together. Bergson emphasized the complicity involved in communal laughter: "Our laughter is always the laughter of a group. You would hardly appreciate the comic if you felt yourself isolated from others. Laughter appears in need of an echo." An illustration was offered: "A man was asked why he did not weep at a sermon when everyone else was shedding tears. He replied: 'I don't belong to the parish.'" Likewise, in *On Aggression* (1963), ethologist Konrad Lorenz observed that "laughter forms a bond" but simultaneously "draws a line," producing "a strong fellow feeling among the participants and joint aggressiveness against outsiders." Finally, there was theater critic Max Beerbohm's delicious laconic statement: "Laughter rejoices in bonds."[7]

Sociologist Karl Mannheim, in *Essays on the Sociology of Knowledge* (1952), expounded how belonging to a particular group at a particular period produces generational binding:

> The fact of belonging to the same class, and that of belonging to the same generation or age group, have this in common, that both endow the individuals sharing in them a common location in the social and historical process, and thereby limit them to a specific range of potential experiences, predisposing them for a certain characteristic mode of thought and experience, and a characteristic type of historically relevant action.[8]

Mannheim's construct of generational cohesion relates to historian Carl Becker's constellation of ideas and events, a "climate of opinion," as he described it. Becker maintained that in response to powerful changing conditions, societies create a distinctive intellectual flavor or style.[9] Although he himself was unconcerned with humor, he stated that every age generates its own idiosyncratic "comedic climate," which in turn fastens group and moment together.

Deciphering the relation between communal laughter and social vicissitudes that generates a particular comedic climate is tricky, and rests on juxtaposing empirical data with historical inferences. "I now understand why so few historians have written about humor," Mary Lee Townsend wrote in *Forbidden Laughter: Popular Humor and the*

Limits of Repression in Nineteenth-Century Prussia (1992). "The theoretical issues are endless, and reaching final judgment about something as slippery as humor often seems impossible." Nonetheless as Townsend "dug into humor," she quickly "discovered that it opened up a window onto the world of the 'average' German."[10]

But how to locate the elements that comprise a comedic zeitgeist? The answer was partly supplied by anthropologist Clifford Geertz in his artful phrase "thick description." The notion refers, though not exclusively, to a dense accumulation of ordinary anecdotal information about a culture, in contrast with its abstract or theoretical underpinnings. This approach to interpretation rests on the collection and collation of the details of social life, and an extrapolation of their patterns. Of all the informing details, few more readily offer insight into societal affairs than people's laughter. Like Dundes, Townsend argued that "jokes often capture an immediateness that more labored texts such as memoirs cannot provide."[11] Taken together, the jokes, conundrums, graffiti, tales, quips, graphics, and impromptu humor constitute a vast body of social data. And although some of these "voices" vanish, a substantial portion wends its way into folk memory and into print and other media. "Survivals in the popular culture" was Garry Wills's description of such ephemera.[12]

Certain slants of people's humor—graffiti, for instance—illumine complex social relationships. "Since graffiti are artifacts of anonymous behavior fixed in time and space," wrote C. Fred Blake in his study of Hawaiian ethnic relations and racial insults, "I find it useful to treat them as an archaeologist treats potsherds from the shell middens of an archaeological community."[13] Poet John Ciardi acknowledged graffiti's authenticity: "Intellectual or folk, there is something about the humbleness, honesty, playfulness, and anonymity of graffiti that can catch the attention and kindle a response as more formal writing cannot."[14]

Comedic artifacts range from the mundane to the cosmic. "People's" humor, it must be reiterated, is not monolithic, despite the national joke cycles or wide-ranging jokes signifying major communal concerns and protest. It is many-clustered, illuminating class, ethnic, political, and gender differences and interests. In a pluralistic society there are subcultural texts that often transcend the national.[15]

Nonetheless, whether national or subcultural, the various types of people's humor provide a cultural seismograph that registers the slightest tremors of daily existence. Decoding its shifts can be trouble-some, yet Dundes posited a critical assumption: "I have come to be-lieve that no piece of folklore continues to be transmitted *unless* it means something—even if neither the speaker nor the audience can articulate what that meaning might be."[16]

What of the character of humor itself? There was for many de-cades a striking consensus regarding the basis of humor's thrust. Echoing the complex psychoanalytic tenets of Freud, analysts focused on the aggressive and hostile character of laughter. Scholars like Con-stance Rourke in *American Humor: A Study of the National Character* (1931) insisted that the American mode had been "swift and coarse and ruthless, beyond art and against the established heritage, against the bonds of pioneer existence."[17]

More recently, other thinkers have emphasized contradiction and in-congruity as the wellsprings of humor. Laughter, Elliott Oring has argued, "depends upon the perception of an *appropriate incongruity*—that is, the perception of an appropriate interrelationship of elements from domains that are generally regarded as incongruous."[18] This premise forms the basis of the most edifying piece on the paradigm of American humor, Louis D. Rubin, Jr.'s, "The Great American Joke." In Rubin's view, incongruity is "emblematic of the nature and problem of democracy":

> On the one hand there are the ideals of freedom, equality, self-government, the conviction that ordinary people can evince the wis-dom to vote wisely, and demonstrate the capacity for understanding and cherishing the highest human values through embodying them in their political and social institutions. On the other hand there is the *Congressional Record*—the daily exemplary reality of the fact that the individual citizens of a democracy are indeed ordinary people, who speak, think and act in ordinary terms, with a suspicion of ab-stract ideas and values.[19]

Emanating from the incongruous are the motifs of entropy and the good news/bad news jokes. Classic American cartoons—a man painting himself into a corner, pruning a tree limb while perched at its end, alone on a desert island with a copy of Bartlett's *Famous Quo-tations for the Listening Audience*, the signs PLAN AHEAd or THINk—

provide the code message. Its popular axiom is Murphy's Law: "Things that can go wrong, will." Arlen J. Hansen contended that because it is an extension of the spirit of democracy, this type of humor "presupposes an innate attraction to anarchy, iconoclasm, and—to an extent—chaos. It feeds the hunger for chase and activity, and its usual effect is the breaking down of an established *normal* system, causing both the matter and the structure of that system to deteriorate."[20]

For these reasons, people's humor frequently serves as a warning system of emerging social issues. "American problems," shrewdly observed Naomi Bliven, "often make their debut as jokes expressing shared resentment: e.g., the physician pleading with the plumber to make a house call. Our problems seem to need to ripen before they appear as public or political issues."[21]

"Shared resentment" sums up the prevailing social milieu of the past half-century, the comedic climate reflecting and capturing an increasing sense of alienation. In one way or another the plethora of scripted cycles and joke wars denoted a rebellious clamor arising from the gap between America's lofty expectations and events and episodes, disappointing, disruptive, and disillusioning.

In his trenchant essay "The Meaning of Comedy," Wylie Sypher observed that "We have lived amid the 'dust and crashes' of the twentieth century and have learned how the direct calamities that befall man seem to prove that human life at its depths is inherently absurd. The comic view and tragic view of life no longer exclude each other."[22] Not in a subuded fashion, therefore, has the presence of such massive humor furthered a reconciling, salving element in American culture.

People's humor thrives despite the encompassing range of the media that tend to overwhelm. Society is vastly informed and enlivened by its prodding presence, spontaneous refraction of events and issues, crisscrossing within and between classes and ethnic groups, and its notable resilience. People's voices have been, always will be, with and of us.

Notes

Index

Notes

1. Introduction

1. Constance Rourke, *American Humor: A Study of the National Character* (New York: Harcourt, Brace, 1931), 297.

2. Max Eastman, *Enjoyment of Laughter* (New York: Simon and Schuster, 1936), 171.

3. E. B. White, *Essays of E. B. White* (New York: Harper & Row, 1977), 245.

4. Mahadev L. Apte, "Ethnic Humor Versus 'Sense of Humor,'" *American Behavioral Scientist* 30 (Jan./Feb. 1987): 29.

5. Jesse Bier, *The Rise and Fall of American Humor* (New York: Holt, Rinehart & Winston, 1968), 293–308.

6. Robert Hatch, "Laugh Now, Pay Later," *Horizon* 5 (Mar. 1963): 107.

7. Joseph P. Kahn, "Can't We Take a Joke, Anymore?" *Boston Sunday Globe*, Oct. 24, 1993, 1, 26.

8. Preston Lerner, "The Boom in American Humor," *Dallas Morning News*, May 8, 1988, 1F.

9. Stephanie Koziski, "The Standup Comedian as Anthropologist: Intentional Culture Critic," *Journal of Popular Culture* 18 (Fall 1984): 57.

10. Chet Raymo, "Not with a Bang but a Laugh," *Boston Globe*, Mar. 26, 1984, 40.

11. Tony Hendra, *Going Too Far* (New York: Doubleday, 1987), 1.

12. Maurice Charney, *Comedy High and Low: An Introduction to the Experience of Comedy* (New York: Oxford Univ. Press, 1978), viii.

13. Alan Dundes, "At Ease, Disease—AIDS Jokes as Sick Humor," *American Behavioral Scientist* 30 (Jan./Feb. 1987): 73.

14. Louis D. Rubin, Jr., "The Great American Joke," *South Atlantic Quarterly* 72 (Winter 1973): 84.

15. Author's notes. Dartmouth College Student Union, May 5, 1982.

16. Author's notes. Woods Hole ferry terminal, Aug. 23, 1978.

17. Paul Weiss, *History: Written and Lived* (Carbondale: Southern Illinois Univ. Press, 1962), 45.

18. Sigmund Freud, *Collected Papers*, vol. V, James Strachey, ed., (New York: Basic Books, 1966), 216–17. Freud's emphasis.

2. American Dream/American Laugh

1. Louis D. Rubin, Jr., "The Great American Joke," in *Humor in America: An Anthology,* Enid Veron, ed. (New York: Harcourt Brace Jovanovich, 1976), 262.

2. Paul Fussell, *The Boy Scout Handbook and Other Observations* (New York: Oxford Univ. Press, 1982), 259.

3. Author's notes. Boston, Mar. 1992. Recounted by Richard Landes, historian; several doctors, Boston, Oct. 1988. See also Jim Pietsch, *The New York City Cab Driver's Joke Book* (Warner Books, 1986), 74.

4. Author's notes. Boston, Aug.–Oct. 1988. Recounted by Drs. Mark Friedman and Larry Roth. See also Pietsch, *The New York City Cab Driver's Joke Book,* 11.

5. Moses Rischin, *The American Gospel of Success* (Chicago: Quadrangle, 1965), 3.

6. John Lahr, *Automatic Vaudeville* (New York: Alfred A. Knopf, 1984), 224.

7. *Phoenix: The Posthumous Papers of D. H. Lawrence, 1938* (New York: Viking Press, 1972), 267.

8. Lahr, *Automatic Vaudeville,* 221.

9. Alan Dundes and Carl R. Pagter, *Work Hard and You Shall Be Rewarded: Urban Folklore from the Paperwork Empire* (American Folklore Society, 1975; Bloomington: Indiana Univ. Press, 1978), xi.

10. Author's notes. Boston, Oct. 1986. Warner was referring to Boston University, but his assessment applies to much of corporate society.

11. Dundes and Pagter, *Work Hard and You Shall be Rewarded,* 147–53.

12. Author's notes. Boston, Oct. 1985.

13. Author's notes. Los Angeles, Oct. 1977. Heard as a young teenager in Brooklyn, N.Y., and recounted by Dr. Sheldon Benjamin when he was a teenager in the Bronx, N.Y., in the 1930s.

14. Author's notes. Boston, Dec. 1983. An earlier English version is noted in Mark Barker, *The Writing on the Wall: A Collection of Good Old British Graffiti* (London: John Clare Books, 1979), 83: Life is like a crap sandwich: / the more bread you've got, the / less shit you eat.

15. Author's notes. Sung by teenagers in New York, Philadelphia, and Chicago in the 1930s and 1940s. French scholar Dorothy Kaufmann remembers it as a song at Camp Lowy, N.Y., in the 1940s and 1950s.

16. Sigmund Freud, *Collected Papers,* vol. V, James Strachey, ed. (New York: Basic Books, 1966), 217.

17. Alexis de Tocqueville, *Democracy in America,* vol. 2 (New York: Vintage Books, 1945), 270.

18. "A fool and his money are soon parted" was originally an English proverb dating back to 1699; see Bartlett Jere Whiting, *Early American Proverbs and Proverbial Phrases* (Cambridge, Mass.: Belknap Press of Harvard Univ. Press, 1977), 160; Wolfgang Mieder in *The Prentice-Hall Encyclopedia of World Proverbs* (Englewood Cliffs, N.J.: Prentice-Hall, 1986) provides a Russian parallel: "A fool and his goods are soon parted; a wise man and his poverty always remain united" (168). In this regard, Alan Dundes notes that the proverb does not seem to be English and "may well be an American invention. If so, it would dovetail with the image of America as a land where gold can

be picked up on the streets—it is in such abundance" letter from Professor Alan Dundes to Dr. Robert Mandel (July 5, 1996), 5.

19. Michael Knight, "Untermeyer at 90: An Anthology of Living," *New York Times,* Sept. 30, 1975, 32.

20. Louis Kronenberger, "The American Sense of Humor," in *Humor in America: An Anthology,* Enid Veron, ed. (New York: Harcourt Brace Jovanovich, 1976), 266.

21. Author's notes. Los Angeles, early 1960s. A similar version is in Alan Dundes and Carl R. Pagter, *Never Try to Teach a Pig to Sing* (Detroit: Wayne State Univ. Press, 1991), 116–17.

22. Charles Dickens, *American Notes and Pictures from Italy* (New York: Oxford Univ. Press, 1966), 245–46.

23. Author's notes. Los Angeles, Mar. 1963. Recounted by a *Los Angeles Times* journalist and several political figures.

24. Robert L. Heilbroner, *The Future as History* (New York: Harper and Bros., 1959), 16–17.

25. Author's notes. Los Angeles, Oct. 1977. Recounted by psychiatrist Roger Gould from a scriptwriter. Although the tale had been making the rounds in the United States since the early 1950s, its origin is European. See Norman Lockridge, ed., *Waggish Tales of the Czechs* (Candide Press, 1947), 260–63.

3. Urban Fulcrum

1. Richard Hofstadter, *The Age of Reform* (New York: Alfred A. Knopf, 1955), 23: "The United States was born in the country and has moved to the city."

2. Author's notes, Feb. 1993. The observation is from an anonymous reader who critically evaluated and subsequently rejected the author's chapter submitted to the *Journal of Urban History.*

3. Mark Twain, "How to Tell a Story" (1895), in *American Literature: The Makers and the Making,* Cleanth Brooks, R. W. B. Lewis, and Robert Penn Warren, eds. (New York: St. Martin's Press, 1973), 1292.

4. Bernard De Voto, ed., *Mark Twain in Eruption* (New York: Harper & Row, 1940), 252–53.

5. Robert K. Dodge, ed., *Early American Almanac Humor* (Bowling Green, Ohio: Bowling Green State University Popular Press, 1987), 91.

6. Ibid., 124.

7. Marshall P. Wilder, ed., *The Wit and Humor of America,* vol. 7 (New York: Funk & Wagnalls, 1907), 1250, 1296.

8. Scott Alarik, "A Festival of Storytelling," *Boston Globe Calendar,* Sept. 2, 1991, 11.

9. "Quote—Unquote," *Boston Globe,* May 7, 1992, 82.

10. *The Best of Lenny Bruce,* Fantasy Records, LP7012, 1963.

11. Sanford Pinsker, "The Urban Tall Tale: Frontier Humor in a Contemporary Key," in Sarah Blacher Cohen, ed., *Comic Relief: Humor in Contemporary American Literature* (Urbana: Univ. of Illinois Press, 1978), 251.

12. Stephen Leacock, ed., *The Greatest Pages of American Humor* (Garden City, N.Y.: Sun Dial Press, 1936), 271.

13. The phrase "city as event" appeared in the notes of a photographic exhibit, *Visions of the American City,* at the Art Gallery, Boston University, October 1991, by Susan Faxon, associate director and curator of painting, prints, and drawings at the Addison Gallery of American Art, Phillips Academy, Andover, Mass.

14. Twain, "How to Tell a Story," 1292.

15. Sanford Pinsker, "The Instruments of American-Jewish Humor: Henny Young-man on Violin, Mel Brooks on Drums, Woody Allen on Clarinet," *Massachusetts Review* 22 (Winter 1981): 740.

16. *Henny Youngman's Pocket JESTER* (Hoechst/Mass: West-Germany) (measuring tape copyrighted in France, United States, Japan, Brazil), n.d.

17. Steven Wright, *I Have a Pony,* Warner Bros. Records,

18. Leacock, *The Greatest Pages of American Humor,* 271.

19. Lewis Mumford, *Technics and Civilization* (New York: Harcourt, Brace, 1934), 14.

20. Herbert G. Gutman, *Work, Culture and Society in Industrializing America* (New York: Vintage Books, 1977), 23.

21. Gunther Barth, *City People: The Rise of Modern City Culture in Nineteenth-Century America* (New York: Oxford Univ. Press, 1980), 224.

22. Ibid., 217.

23. Abel Green and Joe Laurie, Jr., *Showbiz: From Vaudeville to Video* (New York: Henry Holt, 1951), 7.

24. Robert W. Snyder, *The Voice of the City* (New York: Oxford Univ. Press, 1989), 111.

25. John Lowe, "Theories of Ethnic Humor: How to Enter, Laughing," *American Quarterly* 38 (Jan. 1986): 442.

26. Barth, *City People,* 216.

27. Larry Mintz, "Standup Comedy as Social and Cultural Mediation," in Arthur P. Dudden, ed., *American Humor* (New York: Oxford Univ. Press, 1987), 92.

28. Mary Jo Neitz, "Humor, Hierarchy, and the Changing Status of Women," *Psychiatry* 43 (Aug. 1980): 222.

29. Lowe, "Theories of Ethnic Humor," 441–42.

4. Outsiders/Insiders

1. Daniel Royot, "Humor in Transit: Aspects of a Common Language," in Yves Carlet and Michelle Granges, eds., *Confluences Americaines* (Nancy, France: Presses Universitaires, 1990), 183.

2. Eric Bentley, *The Life of the Drama* (New York: Atheneum, 1970), 306.

3. Larry Mintz, "Standup Comedy as Social and Cultural Mediation," in Arthur P. Dudden, ed., *American Humor* (New York: Oxford Univ. Press, 1987), 92–93.

4. Henri Bergson, "Laughter," in Wylie Sypher, ed., *Comedy* (New York: Doubleday, 1956), 187.

5. Issac Deutscher, *The Non-Jewish Jew and Other Essays* (New York: Oxford Univ. Press, 1969), 27.

6. Mark Shechner, "Jewish Comics: Stage & Screen," unpublished MS, 1.

7. Mel Watkins, *On the Real Side* (New York: Simon and Schuster, 1994), 23.

8. Author's notes. Recounted by Solomon Jones, UCLA graduate student, Apr. 1970. "Laughing box" is sometimes a "laughing barrel."

9. John A. Williams and Dennis A. Williams, *If I Stop I'll Die: The Comedy and Tragedy of Richard Pryor* (New York: Thunder's Mouth Press, 1991), 90.

10. Jessie Fauset, "The Gift of Laughter," in Alain Locke, ed., *The New Negro* (New York: Albert and Charles Boni, 1925), 166.

11. Victor E. Frankl, *Man's Search for Meaning: An Introduction to Logotherapy* (New York: Pocket Books, 1963), 68–69.

12. S. Felix Mendelsohn, *Let Laughter Ring* (Philadelphia: Jewish Publication Society of America, 1941), 109; author's notes, Sept. 1966; Touré, "Snoop Dogg's Gentle Hip-Hop Growl," *New York Times*, Nov. 21, 1993, H32.

13. Richard Raskin, *Life Is like a glass of Tea: Studies of Classic Jewish Jokes* (Aarhus, Denmark: Aarhus Unver. Press, 1992), 186–89), cites no fewer than ten versions of the joke and provides the texts. See also Harvey Mindess, *Laughter and Liberation* (Los Angeles: Nash Publishing, 1971), 238.

14. Author's notes. Los Angeles, Apr. 1968.

15. Author's notes. Los Angeles, Oct. 1971.

16. Morton D. Zabel II, ed., *Literary Opinion in America* (New York: Harper Torchbooks, 1962), 401.

17. Miguel de Unamuno, *The Tragic Sense of Life* (1921; repr. Dover Books, 1954), 315.

18. Author's notes. Boston, 1980s.

19. Author's notes. Los Angeles, Aug. 1972.

20. Germaine Greer, *The Female Eunuch* (New York: McGraw-Hill, 1971), 52.

21. Ann Beatts, "Can a Woman Get a Laugh and a Man Too?" *Mademoiselle*, Nov.–Dec. 1975), 140, 182–86.

22. Nancy A. Walker, *A Very Serious Thing: Women's Humor and American Culture* (Minneapolis: Univ. of Minnesota Press, 1988), ix.

23. Lisa Sulewski, "Feminist Humor: A Call for a Women's Ghetto," unpublished MS, Jan. 1992, 3.

24. Walker, *A Very Serious Thing*, 35.

25. Carol Mitchell, "Hostility and Aggression Toward Males in Female Joke Telling," *Frontiers* 3 (Fall 1978): 19–21. A similar version from Bradford, England, is reported in Nigel Rees, *Graffiti 4* (London: Unwin Paperbacks, 1982), 121: "Sex is like a snowstorm—you never know how many inches you'll get or how long it will last."

26. "Sex Roles & Humor," *Cultural Correspondence* 9 (Spring 1979): 6.

27. Nancy A. Walker and Zita Dresner, *Redressing the Balance: American Women's Literary Humor from Colonial Times to the Present* (Jackson: Univ. Press of Mississippi, 1988), xxxi–xxxii.

28. Author's notes. Oct. 1983.

29. Ibid.

30. Gloria Kaufman and Mary Kay Blakely, *Pulling Our Own Strings: Feminist Humor and Satire* (Bloomington: Indiana Univ. Press, 1980), 13.

31. Author's notes. From William Zehv, Oct. 1983.

32. Katherine Bishop, "With a Résumé in Hand and a Ring in the Nose," *New York Times*, Feb. 13, 1992, A18.

33. Walker, *A Very Serious Thing*, 71.

5. The Child and the Giant

1. Eric Goldman, "Good Riddance to the Fifties," *Harper's,* Jan. 1960, 22–27.

2. James Thurber, "The Future, if Any, of Comedy," *Harper's,* Dec. 1961, 40; Walt Kelly, "A Crying Need for the Cleansing Lash of Laughter," *New York Times Book Review,* Aug. 10, 1952, 5; Robert Hatch, "Laugh Now, Pay Later," *Horizon* 5 (Mar. 1963): 107; Jack Smith, "As Cartoonist Feiffer Sees Us: Issues Hushed by 'Big Daddy' Image," *Los Angeles Times,* June 23, 1965, sec. 2, 1.

3. Thornton Wilder, "The Silent Generation," *Harper's,* Apr. 1953, 34–36.

4. Adam Gopnik, "Kurtzman's Mad World," *The New Yorker,* Mar. 29, 1993, 75.

5. Alan Dundes, "The Dead Baby Joke Cycle," *Western Folklore* 38 (July 1979): 147–49.

6. Kenneth Allsop, "Those American Sickniks," *The Twentieth Century* 170 (July 1961): 98.

7. Thurber, "The Future . . . of Comedy," 40; Kingsley Amis, "My Kind of Comedy," *The Twentieth Century* 170 (July 1961): 49; Allsop, "Those American Sickniks," 97, 105–6; Benjamin DeMott, "An Unprofessional Eye: The New Irony: Sickniks and Others," *American Scholar* 31 (Winter 1961–62): 110.

8. Tony Hendra, *Going Too Far: The Rise and Demise of Sick, Gross, Black, Sophomoric, Weirdo, Pinko, Anarchist, Underground, Anti-Establishment Humor* (New York: Doubleday, 1987), 10.

9. Brian Sutton-Smith, " 'Shut Up and Keep Digging': The Cruel Joke Series," *Midwest Folklore* 10 (Spring 1960): 12.

10. Ibid., 11–22; Roger Abrahams, "Ghastly Commands: The Cruel Joke Revisited," *Midwest Folklore* 11 (Winter 1961–62) 235–46; Alan Dundes, "The Dead Baby Joke Cycle," 145–57.

11. Sutton-Smith, " 'Shut Up and Keep Digging,' " 11–12; Abrahams, "Ghastly Commands," 235–46.

12. Maurice D. Schmaier, "The Doll Joke Pattern in Contemporary American Oral Humor," *Midwest Folklore* 13 (Winter 1963–64): 205–6.

13. Ibid.

14. Roger D. Abrahams and Alan Dundes, "On Elephantasy and Elephanticide," *Psychoanalytic Review* 56 (1969): 225–41. See also Abrahams, "The Bigger They Are the Harder They Fall," *Tennessee Folklore Society Bulletin* 29 (1963): 94–102.

15. Mac E. Barrick, "The Shaggy Elephant Riddle," *Southern Folklore Quarterly* 28 (1964): 268.

16. Mary McDougall Gordon, ed., *Overland to California with the Pioneer Line: The Gold Rush Diary of Bernard J. Reid* (Stanford, Calif.: Stanford Univ. Press, 1983), 31; Elisabeth L. Egenhoff, ed., *The Elephant as They Saw It* 45 (*California Journal of Mines and Geology,* October 1949), 62. I am indebted to William F. Fry, Jr., for bringing this early history of elephant folk usage to my attention.

17. Bruno Bettelheim, *The Uses of Enchantment: The Meaning and Importance of Fairy Tales* (New York: Alfred A. Knopf, 1976), 3–19.

18. Abrahams and Dundes, "On Elephantasy and Elephanticide"; Barrick, "The Shaggy Elephant Riddle," 266–90; Alvin Schwartz, *Witcracks* (Philadelphia: Lippincott, 1973).

19. Sutton-Smith, " 'Shut Up and Keep Digging,' " 21.

6. Repression and Riposte

1. Malcolm Muggeridge, "America Needs a *Punch*," *Esquire* 49, Apr. 1958, 60.

2. Cited in a column by Jack Smith, *Los Angeles Times*, Mar. 19, 1987, sec. IV, 1.

3. Paul Krassner, *Confessions of a Raving, Unconfined Nut* (New York: Simon and Schuster, 1993), 43.

4. Corey Ford, "Are You Afraid to Laugh?" *Saturday Evening Post*, Sept. 20, 1958, 30–31.

5. "The Shmoo's Return," *The New Yorker*, Oct. 26, 1963, 40.

6. *Conversations with James Thurber*, Thomas Fensch, ed. (Jackson: Univ. Press of Mississippi, 1989), 104.

7. Krassner, *Confessions*, 42.

8. Margo Jefferson, "Experts in the Comedy of Self-love," *New York Times*, Nov. 24, 1993, C24.

9. Jesse Bier, *The Rise and Fall of American Humor* (New York: Holt, Rinehart and Winston, 1968), 293–308.

10. Susan Sontag, *Against Interpretation and Other Essays* (New York: Farrar, Straus and Giroux, 1965), 225.

11. Richard Hofstadter, *Anti-Intellectualism in American Life* (New York: Alfred A. Knopf, 1969), 3.

12. *Time*, Jan. 5, 1948, 71.

13. Bosley Crowther, "The New York Times Film Reviews," *New York Times*, Dec. 27, 1947, sec. 9, 2.

14. Nora Sayre, *Running Time: Films of the Cold War* (New York: Dial Press, 1982), 54–55.

15. Ibid., 22.

16. Timothy Lyons, "The U.S. vs. Charlie Chaplin," *American Film* 9 (Sept. 1984): 29; Charles J. Maland, *Chaplin and American Culture* (Princeton: Princeton Univ. Press, 1989), 279–313.

17. Stephen J. Whitfield, *The Culture of the Cold War* (Baltimore: Johns Hopkins Univ. Press, 1991), 189.

18. See Roger Manvell, *Chaplin* (Boston: Little, Brown, 1974), 213; Phil Kirby, "The Legion Blacklist," *The New Republic*, June 16, 1952, 14–15; *Nation*, Jan. 31, 1953, 90.

19. Speech, Nov. 5, 1952. Quoted in Clifton Fadiman, ed., *The American Treasury, 1455–1955* (New York: Harper and Row, 1955), 350.

20. Jack Smith, "As Cartoonist Feiffer Sees Us: Issues Hushed by 'Big Daddy' Image," *Los Angeles Times*, June 23, 1965, sec. 2, 1.

21. Tony Hendra, *Going Too Far* (New York: Doubleday, 1987), 92.

22. Walt Kelly, "A Crying Need for the Cleansing Lash of Laughter," *New York Times Book Review*, Aug. 10, 1952, 5.

23. Nat Hentoff, "The Humorist as Grand Inquisitor," in *Seeds of Liberation*, Paul Goodman, ed. (New York: George Braziller, 1964), 388–89.

24. John Cohen, ed. *The Essential Lenny Bruce* (New York: Ballantine, 1967), 70.

25. Hendra, *Going Too Far*, 35.

26. Ibid., 31–32.

27. Reuben Ship, *The Investigator: A Political Satire in Documentary Form,* Dis-curiosities, LP6834, 1954 reissued by Broadside Records LP451, 1966.

28. Hendra, *Going Too Far,* 167–68, note.

29. Author's notes. Univ. of Southern California, Apr. 1963.

7. Guerrilla Satirists

1. Edward Zuckerman, *The Day After World War III* (New York: Viking Press, 1979), 138.

2. Paul Boyer, *By the Bomb's Early Light: American Thought and Culture at the Dawn of the Atomic Age* (New York: Pantheon Books, 1985), 352–56.

3. Jack Kerouac, *On the Road* (New York: Viking Press, 1957), 128.

4. Richard Feynman, panel, Kresge Auditorium, Massachusetts Institute of Technology, Cambridge, Apr. 8, 1961. I am grateful to MIT physicist John King for bringing the conference to my attention.

5. Kerouac, *On the Road,* 128; letter, David Broome, Jan. 7, 1987, who copied it at the library of Pima Community College, Tucson, Ariz.

6. Douglas T. Miller and Marion Nowak, *The Fifties: The Way We Really Were* (New York: Doubleday, 1977), 47–48.

7. Robert L. Heilbroner, *The Future as History* (New York: Grove Press, 1961), 62.

8. Lenny Bruce, *How to Talk Dirty and Influence People* (Chicago: Playboy Press, 1972), 233.

9. Bruce Jay Friedman, *Black Humor* (New York: Bantam Books, 1965), ix.

10. Thomas LeClaire, "Death and Black Humor," *Critique* 17 (1975–76): 6, 33–34.

11. Morris Dickstein, "Black Humor and History," *Partisan Review* 43 (1976): 188.

12. Michael Wharton, "Beyond a Joke," *Twentieth Century,* July 1961, 10.

13. Max Schultz, *Black Humor Fiction of the Sixties* (Athens: Ohio Univ. Press, 1973), 8.

14. Jesse Bier, *The Rise and Fall of American Humor* (New York: Holt, Rinehart and Winston, 1968), 294.

15. "American Humor: Hardly a Laughing Matter," *Time,* Mar. 4, 1966, 46–47.

16. Louis Hasley, "Black Humor and Gray," *Arizona Quarterly* 30 (Winter 1974): 318.

17. Hamlin Hill, "Black Humor: Its Cause and Cure," *Colorado Quarterly* 17 (Summer 1968): 58–59.

18. Bier, *The Rise and Fall of American Humor,* 294–95, 300–1, 305.

19. Kenneth Rexroth, "San Francisco Letter," *Evergreen* 1 (1957): 11.

20. Students for a Democratic Society, *The Port Huron Statement* (Chicago, 1966), 4, 6.

21. Author's notes. Univ. of California, Irvine, Oct. 1970.

22. "Washroom Wit," *Newsweek,* Oct. 10, 1966, 110–11.

23. Author's notes. From many sources around the country during the 1960s and 1970s.

24. Ray Ginger, *Ray Ginger's Jokebook About American History* (New York: New Viewpoints, 1974), 135.

25. "Washroom Wit," 112; Gerald Gardner, *The Mocking of the President* (Detroit: Wayne State Univ. Press, 1988), 173; Robert Reisner, *Graffiti: Selected Scrawls from Bath-*

room Walls (New York: Parallax, 1967), 28–29; Robert Reisner and Lorraine Wechsler, *Encyclopedia of Graffiti* (New York: Macmillan, 1974), 5–6; author's notes. Los Angeles, Boston, San Francisco, Minneapolis, and New York, 1964–70.

26. Author's notes.

27. Author's notes. "Washroom Wit," 112; *Reader's Digest*, Oct. 1967, 182; Reisner, *Graffiti*, 44, 48.

28. Author's notes; Reisner, *Graffiti*, 48.

29. Author's notes; Ronald G. Webb, "Political Uses of Humor," *ETC* 38 (Spring 1981): 45.

30. Author's notes. Boston, May 1977. See also Alan Dundes and Carl R. Pagter, *Never Try to Teach a Pig to Sing* (Detroit: Wayne State Univ. Press, 1991), 348–49.

31. Author's notes. Los Angeles, Berkeley, Chicago, 1967–72; Robert Reisner, *Graffiti: Two-Thousand Years of Wall Writing* (New York: Cowles, 1971), 184–85.

32. Barbara Goldman, *"On the Road* and *Tales of Power:* The Search for Spiritual Peace in Mid-Twentieth-Century American Life," unpublished MS (1974), 1–2.

33. "Science and Faith, Debate and Graffiti," *Boston Sunday Globe*, July 22, 1979, 6.

34. "God's Place in Politics," *Boston Globe*, June 21, 1990, 77.

35. Author's notes. Los Angeles, Boston, Minneapolis, Berkeley; Reisner, *Graffiti: Two Thousand Years*, 170–73; Jim Hougan, "Kilroy's New Message," *Harper's*, Nov. 1972, 24.

36. Stephen J. Whitfield, "The Stunt Man: Abbie Hoffman (1936–1989)," *Virginia Quarterly Review* 66 (Autumn 1990): 567.

37. Jerry Rubin, *Do It!* (New York: Simon and Schuster, 1970), 132.

38. Abbie Hoffman ("Free"), *Revolution for the Hell of It* (New York: Dial Press, 1968), 80, 67, 187.

39. Jerry Rubin, *We Are Everywhere* (New York: Harper and Row, 1971), 36.

40. Hoffman, *Revolution for the Hell of It*, 32.

41. Abbie Hoffman, *Square Dancing in the Ice Age* (New York: G. P. Putnam's Sons, 1982), 43.

42. Hoffman, *Revolution for the Hell of It*, 115.

43. Whitfield, "The Stunt Man," 566–67.

44. Tony Hendra, *Going Too Far* (New York: Doubleday, 1987), 44.

45. Robert Brustein, "Village Idiots," *New Republic*, Jan. 31, 1994, 38.

46. Robert C. Elliott, *The Power of Satire: Magic, Ritual, Art* (Princeton: Princeton Univ. Press, 1960), 275.

8. "Is There Life Before Death?"

1. Author's notes. Boston, July 1970.

2. "Navy Issues Rules on Hair," *Boston Globe*, June 24, 1976, 62.

3. Author's notes. New York, May 1972; Boston, Oct. 1976.

4. Richard J. Barnet, *The Lean Years: Politics in the Age of Scarcity* (New York: Simon and Schuster, 1980), 15–16. Barnet's emphasis.

5. Tonnie Katz, "What Can You Buy for Less Than a Dollar? The List Is Dwindling," *Boston Globe*, Sept. 2, 1976, 1.

6. Quoted in *Consumer Reports*, Jan. 1961, 6.

7. Author's collection. See also Alan Dundes and Carl R. Pagter, *Urban Folklore*

from the Paperwork Empire (Bloomington: Indiana Univ. Press, 1975), reissued as *Work Hard and You Shall Be Rewarded* (1978).

8. Author's notes. Cambridge, Oct. 1976.

9. Author's notes. From Helen MacLam, graduate student, Boston Univ., Nov. 1977. The joke was widely printed as well.

10. Columnist Jack Anderson divulged the information at the 1972 meeting of the American Bar Association in Montreal and also wrote several columns on the affair. See his syndicated "Washington Merry-Go-Round," May 22, 1972.

11. Richard Hofstadter and Michael Wallace, eds., *American Violence: A Documentary History* (New York: Knopf, 1970), 3.

12. "Living with Crime, U.S.A.," *Newsweek*, Dec. 18, 1972, 31.

13. Neil Postman, *Amusing Ourselves to Death: Public Discourse in the Age of Show Business* (New York: Viking Penguin, 1985), 107–8.

14. George F. Will, "Swing Low, Looming Plum," *Boston Globe*, Aug. 31, 1976, 18.

15. J. F. ter Horst, "Today's Trendy Textbooks: Lessons in Double Speak," *Los Angeles Times*, Dec. 6, 1976.

16. Postman, *Amusing Ourselves to Death*, 100.

17. "T.V.'s Cole Suspended," *Boston Globe*, Dec. 13, 1975, 32.

18. E. B. White, *Essays of E. B. White* (New York: Harper and Row, 1977), 79.

19. Author's notes. From many sources in the 1970s and early 1980s.

20. Author's notes. Boston, Nov. 1979.

21. Milan Kundera, *Immortality* (New York: Grove Press, 1991), 332.

22. Author's notes. Boston, 1976; also seen in other parts of the country.

23. *New York Times*, May 28, 1974, 41, and Apr. 20, 1976, 39.

24. Melvin Maddocks, "We Are Not Amused—and Why," *Time*, July 20, 1970, 30–31.

25. Ben Fong-Torres, "Steve Martin Sings," *Rolling Stone*, Feb. 18, 1982, 11.

26. Tony Schwartz, "Comedy's New Face," *Newsweek*, Apr. 3, 1978, 60; author's notes. Boston, Oct. 1978.

27. Schwartz, "Comedy's New Face," 62. Slightly differing versions of the routine exist elsewhere.

28. Steve Martin, *A Wild and Crazy Guy*, Warner Bros., HS3238, 1978.

29. Denise L. Lawrence, "A Rose by Any Other Name . . . The Occasional Doo-Dah Parade," *Urban Resources* 4 (Spring 1987): 37–42; Hal Lancaster, "Doo Dah, Doo, Dah: Parody Parade Irks Pasadena's Social Set," *Wall Street Journal*, Dec. 28, 1979, 1, 21.

30. Frank Trippett, "How to Raise the U.S. Mirth Rate," *Time*, Apr. 3, 1978, 94.

31. Judith B. Kerman, "The Light Bulb Jokes: Americans Look at Social Action Processes," *Journal of American Folklore* 93 (Oct.–Dec. 1980): 454–58. Kerman's emphasis.

32. Alan Dundes, "Many Hands Make Light Work or Caught in the Act of Screwing in Light Bulbs," *Journal of Western Folklore* 40 (Apr. 1981): 261–66.

33. Author's notes. From sources all over the country. See also Kerman, "The Light Bulb Jokes"; and Dundes, "Many Hands Make Light Work."

9. The Undeclared Joke Wars

1. "A Defense of Poetry," in *Shelley's Poetry and Prose*, Donald H. Reiman and Sharon B. Powers, eds. (New York: W. W. Norton, 1977), 491.

2. Author's notes. Boston, history professor, Nov. 1980; Los Angeles, decorator, Oct. 1982; Phoenix, Ariz., college student, late 1970s.

3. Author's notes. Feb. 1981; also printed in *Atlantic Monthly*, July 1982, 12.

4. Christopher Lasch, "Fraternalist Manifesto," *Harper's*, Apr. 1987, 17.

5. James A. Michener, "You Can Call the 1980s 'The Ugly Decade,'" *New York Times*, Jan. 1, 1987, 27.

6. "Notes and Comments," *The New Yorker*, Oct. 14, 1991, 47.

7. Author's notes. Boston, Dec. 31, 1983.

8. Irving Howe, "Clinton, Seen from the Left," *New York Times*, Jan. 20, 1993, A23.

9. Richard M. Stephenson, "Conflict and Control Functions of Humor," *American Journal of Sociology* 56 (1951): 559–60.

10. Author's notes. Oklahoma City and Atlanta, May and June 1985–86.

11. Jeffrey Salkin, "Shylock in Drag? On JAP Jokes and Other Modern Vulgarities," *Moment* 5 (Mar. 1982): 37.

12. Gary Spencer, "An Analysis of JAP-baiting Humor on the College Campus," *Humor: International Journal of Humor Research* 2–4 (1989): 329–48, esp. 344–46. A study reaching a similar conclusion regarding the relation between oppressive joking and physical violence directed at African-Americans is Joseph Boskin, *Sambo: The Rise and Demise of an American Jester* (New York: Oxford Univ. Press, 1986).

13. Bernard Saper, "The JAP Joke Controversy: An Excruciating Psychosocial Analysis," *Humor: International Journal of Humor Research* 4 (1991): 237. Saper's emphasis.

14. Jesse Bier, *The Rise and Fall of American Humor* (New York: Holt, Rinehart and Winston, 1968), 21.

15. Alan Dundes, "The J.A.P. and the J.A.M. in American Jokelore," *Journal of American Folklore* 98 (1985): 469–70.

16. Susan Faludi, *Backlash: The Undeclared War Against American Women* (New York: Crown, 1991), xxi.

17. Author's notes. From a doctor's wife, Long Island, N.Y., June 1986.

18. Author's notes. From a Salt Lake City policeman, State Police Academy, June 1982.

19. Author's notes. From a Cambridge, Mass., doctor, Sept. 1984.

20. Author's notes. From an investment broker, Feb. 1986.

21. Author's notes. From a variety of sources around the country, Aug. 1984.

22. Author's notes. From lawyers and students in Boston, New York, and Los Angeles, 1985–86.

23. Gerri Hirshey, "The Comedy of Hate," *GQ* 56 (Aug. 1989): 227.

24. Brett Milano, "Guerrilla Humor," *Boston Globe*, June 5, 1987, 73.

25. Jim Sullivan, "Shock Comedy's Harsh Mouthpiece," *Boston Sunday Globe*, Oct. 22, 1989, 81, 87–89; John O'Connor, "Taking a Pratfall on the Nastiness Threshold," *New York Times*, July 22, 1990, 25; Janet Maslin, "Andrew Dice Clay Essence: Misogyny, Insult and Sex," *New York Times*, May 18, 1991, 15.

26. Author's notes. From David Broome, Tucson, Ariz., Nov. 1986. Also heard from other sources.

27. Mary Lefkowitz, "Working Towards the Wedding," *Times Literary Supplement,* Dec. 24, 1982, 1429.

28. Kathryn Stechert, "Can't You Take a Joke?" *SAVVY,* June 1986, 36.

29. Author's notes. From students, friends, Intertel, newspaper and magazine articles that appeared throughout the country in 1990–91.

30. Faludi, *Backlash,* 61–64.

31. Anthony Astrachan, *How Men Feel: Their Response to Women's Demands for Equality and Power* (New York: Anchor Press/Doubleday, 1986), 384–85.

32. Author's notes. From sources in Boston, Washington, D.C., and Los Angeles, Feb.–May 1993. Also Nathan Cobb, "The Hillary Jokes—Not Everyone Is Laughing," *Boston Globe,* Apr. 6, 1993, 1, 14.

33. Cobb, "The Hillary Jokes," 14.

34. Reuters, "Rift Along Sexual Lines After Bobbitt Verdict," *New York Times,* Jan. 23, 1994, 20; Ellen Goodman, "Watch Out—The Straw Feminist Is Back, and They Say She's Mad," *Boston Globe,* Jan. 27, 1994, 11; Tom Mashberg, "Jury Acquits Wife in Sexual Mutilation," *Boston Globe,* Jan. 23, 1994, 1,6.

35. Author's notes. Los Angeles, Rochester, N.Y., and Boston, from many sources. For an extensive rundown of the script, see Alan Dundes and Carl R. Pagter, *Sometimes the Dragon Wins* (Syracuse, N.Y.: Syracuse Univ. Press, 1996), 206–12.

36. Mary Jo Neitz, "Humor, Hierarchy, and the Changing Status of Women," *Psychiatry* 43 (Aug. 1980): 222.

37. John Lowe, "Theories of Ethnic Humor: How to Enter, Laughing," *American Quarterly* 38 (Jan. 1986): 439. See also Howard L. Ehrlich, "Observations on Ethnic and Intergroup Humor," *Ethnicity* 6 (1979): 397.

38. Lydia Fish, "Is the Pope Polish? Some Notes on the Polack Joke in Transition," *Journal of American Folklore* 370 (Oct.–Dec. 1980): 452.

39. Alan Dundes, "A Study of Ethnic Slurs: The Jew and the Polack in the United States," *Journal of American Folklore* 84 (1971): 202. In this regard, see also the impressive work of Christie Davies, *Ethnic Humor Around the World: A Comparative Analysis* (Bloomington: Indiana Univ. Press, 1990).

40. Lowe, "Theories of Ethnic Humor," 447–48.

41. Author's notes. Los Angeles, several persons, July 1978.

42. Author's notes. From a New York investment broker, Feb. 1986.

43. Edwin McDowell, "Ethnic Jokebooks Flourish Despite Criticism," *New York Times,* July 30, 1983, 1, 9.

44. Mac E. Barrick, "The Helen Keller Joke Cycle," *Journal of American Folklore* 93 (Oct.–Dec. 1980): 441–49.

45. Joseph Epstein, *Familiar Territory: Observations on American Life* (New York: Oxford Univ. Press, 1979), 64.

46. Where did the admiral pick up these statements? Alan Dundes and Carl R. Pagter, in *Never Try to Teach a Pig to Sing* (Detroit: Wayne State Univ. Press, 1991), 408–9, note a photocopy graffito in 1987: "25 Good Reasons Why Beer Is Better Than Women."

47. Ronald Reagan: Arthur Spiegelman, Reuters, February 18, 1980, and *Washington Post,* May 1, 1980; Earl C. Butz: *NBC Weekend,* Nov. 7, 1977; David Beckwith: *Boston*

Globe, Nov. 23, 1991, 10; conservatives: Terrel H. Bell, *The Thirteenth Man: A Reagan Cabinet Memoir* (New York: Free Press, 1988), 103–4; John Chandler: *Boston Globe,* Sept. 4, 1987, 13, 15; Emory Folmar: *New York Times,* May 9, 1992, 9; conservatives: Bell, *The Thirteenth Man,* 104; Jerry O. Tuttle: *New York Times,* July 18, 1992, 1, 7; Hawley Atkinson: *Boston Globe,* Dec. 9, 1983, 18; Evan Meacham: "Ethnic Joke Backfires on Arizona Governor," *Chicago Tribune,* Jan. 13, 1988, C13; J. Peter Grace: "Businessman Issues Apology for Remarks," *New York Times* Oct. 8, 1992, B17, and *Boston Globe,* Oct. 10, 1992, 11; James G. Watt: *Boston Globe,* Sept. 23, 1983, 1, 12.

48. Author's notes. From Matthew Boskin, investment broker, New York, Apr. 1985, and Sheldon Benjamin, periodontist, Los Angeles, Mar. 1986.

49. Jesse Bier, "Derogatory American Humor—and the Polish Joke," unpublished MS, 1–8.

50. Irwin T. Sanders and Ewa T. Morawska, *Polish-American Community Life: A Survey of Research* (Boston: Community Sociology Training Program, Department of Sociology, Boston Univ. Polish Institute of Arts and Sciences in America, 1975), 71–72.

51. James Thurber, *My Life and Hard Times* (New York: Harper and Row, 1933), 115–20.

52. Dundes, "A Study of Ethnic Slurs," 200–202.

53. Margo Jefferson, "Experts in the Comedy of Self-Love," *New York Times,* Nov. 24, 1993, C24.

54. Author's notes. 1970s–90s. Lincoln: sweater manufacturer, Los Angeles, Jan. 1983; MARTA: stockbroker, Atlanta, May 1986; Williams and Derek: retired businessman, Century West Club, Los Angeles, Apr. 1983; second grade: investment broker, New York, Sept. 1987; physician, Boston, Aug. 1984; Harlem cheer: junior high school student, Newton, Mass., June 1984; scholar: academic, Boston/California, Apr. 1984; loafers: university student, Boston, and others, May 1982; jobs: high school student, Boston, and others, Aug. 1982; Washington: stockbroker, New York, Dec. 1987; sickle-cell anemia: state policeman, Police Academy, Tucson, Jan. 1983; university student, Vermont, and others, May 1985; impotent: dental assistant, Los Angeles, Mar. 1984; black women and toys: jewelry salesman, Boston, and others, Aug. 1987; Father's Day: lawyer, Atlanta, and others, Sept. 1983; pallbearers: state policeman, Police Academy, Salt Lake City, June 1982; names: comedy writer, Los Angeles, Sept. 1981; groundhog: beer executive, Cleveland, Feb. 1984; fairy tales: investment broker, New York, Feb. 1986; Beverly Hills: policeman, Tucson, and others, Feb. 1983; bicycle: high school student, Lincoln, Mass., Apr. 1985; rape: podiatrist, Los Angeles, Apr. 1982; white/black ratio: investment broker, New York, Nov. 1985.

55. Author's notes. Empire State: investment broker, New York, Apr. 1983, and others; social climber: policeman, San Antonio, Mar. 1982; Cadillac: clothing manufacturer, Los Angeles, Jan. 1983; welfare and car thief: periodontist, Los Angeles, Dec. 1980, and others; investment broker, Boston, Sept. 1983; Pole: state trooper, Salt Lake City, Feb. 1984; spray paint and genie: computer specialist, Lowell, Mass., Mar. 1982, ophthalmologist, Boston, May 1983, and others; jumper cables: policeman, Tucson, Apr. 1984; cars: periodontist, Los Angeles, Oct. 1981; insurance: policeman, Salt Lake City, June 1982, and others.

56. Author's notes. Recounted by Arnold Pasternak, airline captain, New York City, July 1966.

57. Alan Dundes, "At Ease, Disease—AIDS Jokes as Sick Humor," *American Behavioral Scientist* 30 (Jan./Feb. 1987): 79.

58. Author's notes. G.A.Y.: stockbroker, Atlanta, July 1983, and others; vegetable: stockbroker, Boston, Apr. 1983; AIDS: men's bathroom, Beverly Hills office building, Feb. 1988, and others; dolls: stockbroker, New York, Feb. 1986; turkeys: student, Univ. of California, Los Angeles, Oct. 1987; roller skates: student, Boston, Sept. 1987, and others; drug: diamond assessor, Boston, Aug. 1987; prevention: lawyer, Los Angeles, July 1986. See also Dundes, "At Ease, Disease," 76–79; and Casper G. Schmidt, "AIDS Jokes or, Schadenfreude Around an Epidemic," *Maledicta* 8 (1984–85): 69–70.

59. Historian, Univ. of Kansas, Oct. 4, 1988.

60. Author's notes. Liberace: law student, Tulsa, Okla., May 1987, and investment broker, New York, Mar. 1987; Rock Hudson: ophthalmologist, Boston, Sept. 1985, and students, Los Angeles and Boston, June 1986. See also the Hudson jokes cited in Dundes, "At Ease, Disease," and Mac E. Barrick, "Celebrity Sick Jokes," *Maledicta* 6 (Summer–Winter 1982): 57–62.

61. Author's notes. Financial adviser, Los Angeles, July 1983; language specialist, Stoneham, Mass., July 1983; bar customer, Boston, July 1983; jazz musician, Cambridge, Mass., Oct. 1983; lawyer, Boston, Sept. 1983.

62. Author's notes. University administrator, Boston, Nov. 1985; investment broker, New York, Oct. 1985. For a fuller text on the AIDS script, see Dundes and Pagter, *Sometimes the Dragon Wins,* 332–33.

10. Comedic Correctness

1. Sigmund Freud, *Jokes and Their Relation to the Unconscious,* VIII (Hogarth Press and the Institute of Psycho-Analysis, 1905), 105, 103.

2. Clifton Fadiman, *The American Treasury 1455–1955:* (New York: Harper and Row, 1955), 638.

3. *Ray Ginger's Jokebook About American History* (New York: New Viewpoints, 1974), 85.

4. William Safire, "On Language: Good-Deed Dungeon," *New York Times Magazine,* Jan. 9, 1994, 16.

5. Jim Pietsch, *The New York City Cab Driver's Joke Book* (New York: Warner Books, 1986), 44.

6. Author's notes. Boston, Los Angeles, New York, Rochester, N.Y., and Washington, 1972–82; Pietsch, *Cab Driver's Joke Book,* 44.

7. Mark Muro, "Blue Bloods Say Term Is Unfair and Amounts to Brahmin-Bashing; Does 'WASP' Sting?" *Boston Globe,* Nov. 15, 1990, Living sec., 101.

8. Ibid.

9. Edward Hoagland, "'WASP' Stings. It Isn't Amusing," *New York Times,* Sept. 16, 1988, A35; Muro, "Blue Bloods," 101, 104; Richard Bernstein, "'Just Kidding'—but at Whose Expense?" *New York Times,* Apr. 8, 1990, H34.

10. Mahadev L. Apte, "Ethnic Humor Versus 'Sense of Humor,'" *American Behavioral Scientist* 30 (Jan./Feb. 1987): 33.

11. Ibid., 32.

12. *Boston Globe,* June 16, 1975, 17.

13. Evelyn Nieves, "Protests Rise over Skit by Lawyer in Blackface," *New York Times,* Dec. 28, 1991, 25.

14. The National Federation of Temple Sisterhoods, 36th Biennial Assembly, Nov. 1987, 4–12; *Boston Globe,* Nov. 14, 1987, 19.

15. "Taking Offense," *Newsweek,* Dec. 24, 1990, 48.

16. "On Campus: Free Expression Debate Had Other Flash Points," *New York Times,* Dec. 29, 1993, B6.

17. Philip Van Munching, "No Dice for Saturday Night," *New York Times,* May 12, 1990, 23.

18. "Flip Ad on Famine Gets the Heave-ho," *Boston Globe,* Sept. 22, 1993, 2.

19. Karen Grigsby Bates, "Whoopi, Ted: We Are Not Amused," *Los Angeles Times,* Oct. 13, 1993, B7.

20. Diane White, "In Short, It's Only a Tune," *Boston Globe,* Dec. 14, 1977, 1.

21. Valerie Basheda, "Standing Short," *Los Angeles Times,* Aug. 24, 1989, 3, 33.

22. Isabel Wilkerson, "Revived Cleveland Finds Old Jokes Hard to Shake," *New York Times,* Dec. 8, 1986, A20.

23. Eric Lichtblau, "Latino Wins $30,000 Award over Cartoon," *Los Angeles Times,* Oct. 4, 1990, B3.

24. Isabel Wilkerson, "Ethnic Jokes in Campus Computer Prompt Debate," *New York Times,* Apr. 18, 1987, 6, and "U. of Michigan Fights Its Legacy of Racial Trouble," *New York Times,* Jan. 15, 1990, A12; Richard Bernstein, "On Campus, How Free Should Free Speech Be?" *New York Times,* Sept. 10, 1989, E5; "Taking Offense: Is This the New Enlightenment on Campus or the New McCarthyism?" *Newsweek,* Dec. 24, 1990, 48; Lena Williams, "It's Not Funny and I'm Sorry: Tacky Jokes of the Past, R.I.P." *New York Times,* Jan. 2, 1991, C1, C8; "City Plans a Ban on Ethnic Jokes at Work," *Boston Globe,* Mar. 5, 1987, 7.

25. Jennifer Senior, "Language of the Deaf Evolves to Reflect New Sensibilities," *New York Times,* Jan. 3, 1994, A1, A12.

26. Author's notes. Nov. 1988. The organization's emphasis.

27. George Meredith, *Comedy* (New York: Doubleday, 1956), 245. Meredith's emphasis.

28. Richard Bernstein, "'Just Kidding,'" H1, H34.

29. Fox Butterfield, "Parody Puts Harvard Law Faculty in Sexism Battle," *New York Times,* Apr. 27, 1992, A10.

30. Joseph P. Kahn, "Can't We Take a Joke Anymore?" *Boston Globe,* Oct. 24, 1993, 1, 26.

31. William Murray, "Unto the Sons," *New York Times Book Review,* Feb. 9, 1992, 3.

11. Tribal Reprisals

1. David Lilienthal and H. Allen Smith, *Buskin' with H. Allen Smith* (New York: Trident Press, 1968), 211-12; Alvin Schwartz, *Witcracks: Jokes and Jests from American Folklore* (Philadelphia: Lippincott, 1973), 80; and author's notes. Another ending of the Lone Ranger joke is "What do you mean *we, Keemosabe?*"

2. *Los Angeles Times Calender Section*, Mar. 13, 1966.

3. Robert Penn Warren and Ralph Ellison, "A Dialogue," *Reporter*, Mar. 25, 1965, 43.

4. Dick Gregory with Robert Lipsyte, *Nigger: An Autobiography* (New York: Pocket Books, 1970), 132; Mel Gussow, "Laugh at This Negro but Darkly," *Esquire*, Nov. 1964, 94–95; Redd Foxx and Norma Miller, *The Redd Foxx Encyclopedia of Black Humor* (Pasadena, Calif.: Ward Ritchie Press, 1977), 234–56.

5. Author's notes. From a black student, Boston, Oct. 1972.

6. Author's notes. From a white lawyer, Boston, Sept. 1983. Dundes observes that the joke is a standard rejoinder but "rarely told with a black participant in my experience. Usually, it's a yokel from the country or from a 'lesser' institution than Harvard!!!" Letter from Professor Alan Dundes to Dr. Robert Mandel, July 5, 1996, 6.

7. John A. Williams and Dennis A. Williams, *If I Stop I'll Die: The Comedy and Tragedy of Richard Pryor* (New York: Thunder's Mouth Press, 1991), 161.

8. *The Best of Chevy Chase*. Warner Home Video, 1990.

9. Joseph Boskin, "Good-by, Mr. Bones," *New York Times Magazine*, May 1, 1966, 90.

10. Williams and Williams, *If I Stop I'll Die*, vi.

11. Patrick Cole, "Comics Cope with the L.A. Riots," *Los Angeles Times*, May 11, 1992, F1, F4; David J. Jefferson, "Amid L.A.'s Sorrows, Black Comedians See Shards of Laughter," *Wall Street Journal*, May 11, 1992, A1, A4.

12. Steve Morse, "Comics Fight Violence with Laughter," *Boston Globe*, Jan. 8, 1991, 52. A second event was held the following year. See Jim Sullivan, "Yukking It Up to Stop Gang Violence," *Boston Globe*, Feb. 8, 1992, 13.

13. Rita Reif, "Black Stereotypes Featured in Dartmouth Exhibit," *New York Times*, Mar. 3, 1981, A11. For a fuller analysis of racial artifacts, see Joseph Boskin, *Sambo: The Rise & Demise of an American Jester* (New York: Oxford Univ. Press, 1986); Jessie Carney Smith, ed., *Images of Blacks in American Culture* (Westport, Conn.: Greenwood Press, 1988); and Patricia A. Turner, *Ceramic Uncles and Celluloid Mammies: Black Images and Their Influence on Culture* (New York: Anchor Books, 1994).

14. Anthony Tommasini, "An Honest, Funny Look at Gay Black Men," *Boston Globe*, July 5, 1992, 27.

15. Emily Toth, "Female Wits," *Massachusetts Review* 22 (Winter 1981): 785.

16. Naomi Weisstein, *Laugh? I Nearly Died!* (Pittsburgh: Know, Inc., n.d.), quoted in Charlotte Templin, "Self-Assertive Humor in Recent Women's Comedy," unpublished paper, WHIM Conference, 1987, 2.

17. Nancy A. Walker, *A Very Serious Thing: Women's Humor and American Culture* (Minneapolis: Univ. of Minnesota Press, 1988), 12.

18. Suzanne L. Bunkers, "Why Are These Women Laughing? The Power and Politics of Women's Humor," *Studies in American Humor* 4 (Spring/Summer 1985): 87.

19. Recounted by William Zehv, psychologist, Boston, 1983, from female students and others.

20. Bruce Lambert, "Millicent Fenwick, 82, Dies; Gave Character to Congress," *New York Times*, Sept. 17, 1992, D25.

21. Purvi Shah, "I'm Not a Feminist, But . . . ," *National College Magazine*, Nov. 1992, 12; "Beauty Contestant Denounces the 'Indignities,'" *New York Times*, June 16, 1988, A18; Katherine Bishop, "With a Résumé in Hand and a Ring in the Nose," *New York Times*, Feb. 13, 1992, A18.

22. Quoted in Dexter Brine, "In This Corner," *Boston Globe*, Aug. 10, 1978, 33.

23. Author's notes. From a jewelry designer, Boston, Feb. 1988.

24. Ann Landers, "Letters" *Boston Globe*, Sept. 10, 1988, 10.

25. Author's notes. Oct. 1992. Alan Dundes and Carl R. Pagter noted the appearance of the early version in *Work Hard and You Shall Be Rewarded*, 7–8.

26. Author's notes. From Mark Friedman, physician, and New York sources, Mar. 1988.

27. Author's notes. From a female anthropologist, Los Angeles, Oct. 1988, and a male ophthalmologist, Boston, Apr. 1990.

28. Mary Jo Neitz, "Humor, Hierarchy, and the Changing Status of Women," *Psychiatry* 43 (Aug. 1980): 220–21.

29. Author's notes. From a paralegal, Boston, Oct. 1992.

30. Phil Berger, "The New Comediennes," *New York Times Magazine*, July 29, 1984, 27.

31. Jannette Tucker, "Beyond the Neon: Spotlight on Women Comics," *MUSE*, Oct. 26, 1989, 6.

32. Janet Maslin, "Is Women's Anger a Laughing Matter?" *New York Times*, June 4, 1992, C13.

33. Ellen Hopkins, "Who's Laughing Now? Women," *New York Times*, Sept. 16, 1990, H1. Hopkins's emphasis.

34. Naomi Weisstein, "Why We're Not Laughing . . . Anymore," *Ms.*, Nov. 1973, 90.

35. Jim Sullivan, "Humor with a Feminine Slant," *Boston Globe*, Jan. 18, 1987, 72.

36. Phil Berger, "The New Comediennes," 38.

37. Hopkins, "Who's Laughing Now? Women," H37.

38. Bette Midler, *Mud Will Be Flung Tonight*, Atlantic 1985.

39. Roseanne Barr, *I Enjoy Being a Girl*, Hollywood Records, 1990 HR-61000, *The Best of Comic Relief 2*, Rhino, H0707; R2 1988.

40. "Tomlin, Flynn Honored by 9 to 5," *Boston Globe*, Apr. 27, 1989, 24.

41. Neitz, "Humor, Hierarchy, and the Changing Status of Women," 222.

42. Author's notes. San Francisco, Oct. 1978 and July 1981.

43. Paul Rudnick, "Laughing at AIDS," *New York Times*, Jan. 23, 1993, 21.

44. Patrick Pacheco, "Lightening Up: Humor as a Weapon Against AIDS," *New York Times*, Aug. 21, 1993, F12.

45. Max Benavidez, "Latino Comic Is a Barrio of Laughs," *Los Angeles Times Calendar*, Feb. 20, 1983, 1,3.

46. John Koch, "Comic Stands Up for Native Americans," *Boston Globe*, Nov. 11, 1990, 39.

12. The Tattered Dream

1. Reuters, Oct. 28, 1980.

2. "Settle Down—and Toughen Up," *New York Times*, June 8, 1993, A24.

3. Author's notes. Boston, Los Angeles, Denver, Nov. 1983, June 1987.

4. Author's notes. From many sources around the country, including Venice, Florida, Washington, D.C., New York, Boston, June 1987. For an explication of the Gary Hart jokes, see Alan Dundes, "Six Inches from the Presidency: The Gary Hart Jokes as Public Opinion," *Western Folklore* 48 (Jan. 1989): 43–51.

5. Author's notes. From many quarters, including Washington, D.C., Boston, Los Angeles, Kansas City, Aug. 1988, Mar. 1990.

6. William F. Honan, "Pearl Harbor All Over Again," *New York Times Book Review,* Aug. 12, 1990, 9.

7. William F. Fry, Jr., "Making Humor Acceptable to a Disaster-Oriented World," Abstract, *Fourth International Conference on Humor,* International Society of Humor, Tel Aviv Univ., June 1984, 1.

8. William F. Fry, Jr., "Humor and Chaos," *Humor: International Journal of Humor Research* 5 (1992): 231.

9. The phrase comes from Richard Christopher, "Ethiopian Jokes," *Maledicta* 8 (1984–85): 37.

10. Reinhold Aman, "Kakologia," *Maledicta* 8 (1984–85): 221.

11. Author's notes. New York, Boston, Venice, Florida, from many sources: teachers, computer analysts, physicians, students, and a real estate developer, Mar.–Dec. 1985. See also Richard Christopher, "Ethiopian Jokes," 36–42; Bennetta Jules-Rosette, "'You Must be Joking': A Sociosemiotic Analysis of 'Ethopian' Jokes," *American Journal of Semiotics* 4 (1986): 17–42; and Willie Smyth, "*Challenger* Jokes and the Humor of Disaster," *Western Folklore* 45 (Oct. 1986): 246.

12. Authors notes. From a variety of sources, New York, Boston, Chicago, Miami, San Francisco, San Diego, Los Angeles.

13. Ibid.

14. Author's notes. University students, Boston, Apr. 1989.

15. Author's notes. Recounted by David Mars, School of Public Administration, Univ. of Southern California, Oct. 1986.

16. Author's notes. Medical secretary, Boston, Aug. 1988.

17. Russell Baker, "So Far to Ithaca," *New York Times,* Apr. 28, 1987, A31.

18. Timothy Ferris, *The Mind's Sky* (New York: Bantam Books, 1992); Elliott Oring, "Jokes and the Discourse on Disaster," *Journal of American Folklore* 100 (July–Sept. 1987): 284.

19. Elizabeth Radin Simons, "The NASA Joke Cycle: The Astronauts and the Teacher," *Western Folklore* 45 (Oct. 1986): 261–77.

20. See Steve Emmons, "'Sick' Jokes: Coping with the Horror," *Los Angeles Times,* May 30, 1986, 1, 26; Nicholas von Hoffman, "Shuttle Jokes," *New Republic,* Mar. 24, 1986, 14; Patrick D. Morrow, "Those Sick *Challenger* Jokes," *Journal of Popular Culture* 20 (Spring 1987): 175–84; Elliott Oring, "Jokes and the Discourse on Disaster," 276–86; Simons, "The NASA Joke Cycle"; Smyth, "*Challenger* Jokes," 241–60. All jokes relating to the disaster derive from the above articles as well as from my own research.

21. Bob Marcotte, "Shuttle Should Be Off-limits to Sick Jokes," *Rochester Times-Union,* Mar. 20, 1986; Von Hoffman, "Shuttle Jokes," 14; and Simons, "The NASA Joke Cycle," 263, nn. 6, 7.

22. Walter Goodman, "Critic's Notebook," *New York Times,* May 15, 1986, C22.

23. Author's notes. Dr. Trevor Kaye, Boston, June 1988; students, Boston, Aug. 1988; Dr. Sheldon Benjamin, Los Angeles, Oct. 1988.

24. Paul Fussell, "My War," in Maureen Howard, ed., *The Penguin Book of Contemporary American Essays* (New York: Viking, 1984), 241.

25. John Powers, "Great Expectations," *Boston Globe Magazine,* Mar. 12, 1995, 32.

26. Cited in *Boston Globe,* May 5, 1992, 32.

27. Author's notes, 1982–95. From signs and graffiti in Boston, New York, Chicago, Phoenix, and San Francisco. See also *Boston Globe,* Mar. 20, 1993, 11.

28. "Eighties Is Hard-edged." Bruce McCabe, "The 80's: An American Attitude," *Boston Globe,* May 21, 1985, 75.

29. Recounted in "The Best and Worst of Everything," *Boston Globe Sunday Magazine,* Jan. 5, 1986, 12.

30. Don and Alleen Nilsen, "The Art of Darkness—Satire and Black Humor in the '90s," *Satire* 1 (Autumn 1994): 79.

31. Author's notes. From Matt Boskin, investment broker, New York, and a variety of other sources, 1985–87. For a fuller compilation and explanation of the cycle, see Alan Dundes, "The Name of the Game: A Quadriplegic Sick Joke Cycle," *Names* 3 (1985): 289–92, reprinted in his *Cracking Jokes: Studies of Sick Humor Cycles and Stereotypes* (Berkeley, Calif.: Ten Speed Press, 1987), 15–18.

32. Author's notes. From Boston Univ. students, Feb. 1982.

33. Ferris, *The Mind's Sky,* 12. Ferris's emphasis.

34. Author's notes. From Mitch Geffen, lawyer, Los Angeles, Feb. 1994.

35. Joan Wechsler, "Take My Doctor . . . Please," *Boston Globe,* Mar. 10, 1983, 1, 12; authors notes. From Larry Roth, ophthalmologist, Aug. 1987. Also see Jim Pietsch, *The New York City Cab Driver's Joke Book* (New York: Warner Books, 1986), 28–29.

36. Author's notes. From several sources, Boston, Los Angeles, and San Francisco, June 1983 and Mar. 1985.

37. Author's notes. From Larry Roth, ophthalmologist, May 1987, and other sources shortly thereafter.

38. The text can also be found in Alan Dundes and Carl R. Pagter, *Never Try to Teach a Pig to Sing* (Detroit: Wayne State Univ. Press, 1991), 47–49.

39. See also Alan Dundes and Carl R. Pagter, *When You're Up to Your Ass in Alligators . . .* (Detroit: Wayne State Univ. Press, 1987), 171–74.

40. Glenn Kramon, "Like Stocks, Jokes Are Cheap," *New York Times,* Oct. 31, 1987, 36, 38; Gerald Parshall, "Wall Street's New Bull Market: Jokes," *U.S. News and World Report,* Nov. 9, 1987, 16; Matthew Boskin, investment broker, Nov. 1987, and Al Sargent, administrative assistant, Boston Univ., Dec. 1987; and other sources in New York.

41. "Gallows Humor Gets a Workout," *Wall Street Journal,* Dec. 27, 1984, 15.

42. Cited in Peter Applebome, "So the Texan Who's Broke Says to the . . . ," *New York Times,* Jan. 25, 1987, 16.

43. David Maranis, "With Oil Money Drying, the Jokes Are Flowing Freely," *Miami Herald,* July 30, 1986, 2A.

44. Author's notes. Homeless: from a Boston Univ. student and Allan Jay Friedman, musical composer, and Dr. Sheldon Benjamin, Los Angeles, and others, Aug. 1989–Feb. 1990; Rhode Island: from Robert Erwin, Mar. 1991.

45. Author's notes. Students and friends, Boston and Los Angeles, Feb. 1982.

46. Author's notes. Students, Boston Univ., and friends in Los Angeles, Feb. 1982.

47. Author's notes. David Broome, student, Univ. of Arizona, Aug. 1986; Boston Univ. medical student from Univ. of Virginia, July 1986; and other sources.

48. Author's notes. Phil Gagen, stockbroker, Washington, D.C., June 1990.

49. Author's notes. Matt Boskin, stockbroker, New York, Oct. 1985; Alan Dundes; and other sources.

50. Author's notes. From a chemical engineer, New York City, and various sources, Los Angeles and Boston, Aug.–Oct. 84.

51. Author's notes. From a variety of sources, Boston, New York, and Los Angeles, Apr.–Aug. 1989.

52. Author's notes. From Neal Roberts, Boston disc jockey, Station WFYD, and many other sources, Nov. 1990.

53. Author's notes. From Eron Cohen, Boston Univ., and other students and friends, May 1990.

54. Author's notes. Submitted by Eron Cohen, student, Boston Univ.; Richard Landes, historian, Boston Univ.; a variety of students and friends, Boston, Ann Arbor, New York, and Los Angeles, Nov. 1991–Feb. 1992.

55. Author's notes. Selections of a variety of jokes offered by students, colleagues, and friends, Boston, Philadelphia, Washington, D.C., and Los Angeles, Nov.–Dec. 1991.

56. Author's notes. Many sources across the country, Apr.–Dec. 1993. See also Nilsen and Nilsen, "The Art of Darkness," 89.

57. Author's notes. From Sheldon Benjamin, Los Angeles, Feb. 1994.

58. David Broome, "Collections Inc. . . . Tasteless O. J. Simpson Jokes," *Fast Lane*, Mar. 2, 1995, 6; Alan Dundes, "From Jock to Joke: The *Sic Transit* of O. J. Simpson," *Zyzzyva* 10 (1994): 33–49.

59. Quoted by Norman Mailer. Walter Goodman, "Norman Mailer Offers a PEN Post-mortem," *New York Times*, Jan. 27, 1986, C24.

60. Paul Lewis, "Have You Heard the One About the Shuttle: The Challenges of Disaster Humor," unpublished paper.

61. Author's notes. From several sources, Los Angeles and Chicago, Mar. 1994. Also listed in Dundes and Pagter, *Never Try to Teach a Pig to Sing*, 118.

62. Author's notes. From students and friends, Boston and Los Angeles, mid-1980s. Also printed in Pietsch, *The New York City Cab Driver's Joke Book*, 19.

13. Postlude: How Many Jokes Does It Take to Change a Zeitgeist?

1. Alan Dundes, *Cracking Jokes: Studies of Sick Humor Cycles and Stereotypes* (Berkeley, Calif.: Ten Speed Press, 1987), 168.

2. Edward T. Hall, *The Silent Language* (New York: Doubleday Anchor, 1959), 75.

3. Quoted in Joseph Epstein, *Familiar Territory: Observations on American Life* (New York: Oxford Univ. Press, 1979), 62–63.

4. Arthur Asa Berger, "What Makes People Laugh? Cracking the Culture Code," *ETC: A Review of General Semantics* 32 (Dec. 1974): 427–28.

5. Peter Farb, "Speaking Seriously About Humor," *Massachusetts Review* 27 (Winter 1981): 763.

6. Henri Bergson, "Laughter," in Wylie Sypher, ed., *Comedy* (New York: Doubleday, 1956), 64–65.

7. Sigmund Freud, *Wit and Its Relation to the Unconscious* (London: Routledge and Kegan Paul, 1922); Henri Bergson, "Laughter," 64; Konrad Lorenz, *On Aggression* (New

York: Bantam Books, 1963), 284; Max Beerbohm, *And Even Now* (New York: E. P. Dutton, 1921), 309.

8. Karl Mannheim, *Essays on the Sociology of Knowledge* (London: Routledge and Kegan Paul, 1952), 291.

9. Carl Becker, *Freedom and Responsibility in the American Way of Life* (New York: Vintage Press, 1945), xv.

10. Mary Lee Townsend, *Forbidden Laughter: Popular Humor and the Limits of Repression in Nineteenth-Century Prussia* (Ann Arbor: Univ. of Michigan Press, 1992), ix.

11. Ibid., 197.

12. Garry Wills, "Hanging Out with the Greeks," *New York Review of Books,* May 13, 1993, 38.

13. C. Fred Blake, "Graffiti and Racial Insults: The Archaeology of Ethnic Relations in Hawaii," in Richard A. Gould and Michael B. Schiffer, eds., *Modern Material Culture: The Archaeology of Us* (New York: Academic Press, 1981), 88.

14. John Ciardi, "Manner of Speaking," *Saturday Review of Literature,* May 16, 1970, 10.

15. The works of Gershon Legman contain a massive amount of data pertaining to complexity and depth of people's humor: *Rationale of the Dirty Joke* (New York: Grove Press, 1968) and *No Laughing Matter* (Wharton, N.J.: Breaking Point Press, 1975).

16. Dundes, *Cracking Jokes,* vii.

17. Constance Rourke, *American Humor: A Study of the National Character* (New York: Harcourt, Brace, 1931), 297.

18. Elliott Oring, *Jokes and Their Relations* (Lexington: Univ. Press of Kentucky, 1992), 2.

19. Louis D. Rubin, Jr., "The Great American Joke," *South Atlantic Quarterly* 72 (Winter 1973): 84.

20. Arlen J. Hansen, "Entropy and Transformation: Two Types of American Humor," *American Scholar* 43 (Summer 1974): 406.

21. Naomi Bliven, "Crash," *The New Yorker,* June 23, 1986, 97.

22. Wylie Sypher, ed., *Comedy* (New York: Doubleday, 1956), 193.

Index

229